I0118106

# SEVEN SUMMERS WITH PEREGRINES

## Finding Midlife Adventures

Jean C. Beyer Ruhser
Gary G. Ruhser

Copyright 2016 by Jean C. Beyer Ruhser, Gary G. Ruhser

All rights reserved. This book or any portion thereof may not be reproduced or used in any manner whatsoever without the express written permission of the publisher except for the use of brief quotations in a book review.

This book is entirely the creation of the authors and the authors are solely responsible for the contents. We have tried to be accurate with respect to any facts applicable to The Peregrine Fund, but this is a work independent of and without the specific authorship of The Peregrine Fund. Any mistakes or errors are our own.

Any reference to any product is intended to be positive and to respect any trademarks thereof.

All photography is by the authors.
Front cover: Jean climbing CSKT Tower, Montana, 1992.
Back cover: Gary at World Center for Birds of Prey, Boise, Idaho, 1991.

This book is dedicated to our daughters,
Gayle and Janis,
with heartfelt thanks for their constant love
and support.

And to our granddaughter, Jayne,
who was born after these adventures,
and thus missed out on hearing about them at
the time.

Table of Contents

## C. PERSONAL STORIES

## PHASE FOUR – INTENSE OBSERVATION PERIOD:
Weeks two, three, and four

## A. INTRODUCTION TO DUTIES DURING INTENSE OBSERVATION PERIOD

## B. STORIES FROM INTENSE AND SEMI-INTENSE OBSERVATION PERIODS

## C. PERSONAL STORIES

*Preface: Figures 1 and 2*

*Figure 1: Gary at World Center for Birds of Prey, Boise*

*Figure 2: Gary in kitchen area of Grave Point camp*

## PREFACE – our background, re-assessing our lives, The Peregrine Fund history

In June 1990 we graduated our younger child from high school and celebrated our 25th wedding anniversary with a combined party for family and friends, packed said child off to the summer school dorm to start college where her older sister would also be attending classes, sold the beef cattle, gave away the chickens, planted a very limited garden, "supered" the bee hives, "burned" our mortgage, and split up for the summer. Gary left first, heading to the Boundary Waters Canoe Area Wilderness (BWCAW) in northern Minnesota where he would be working that summer on a campsite and portage rehabilitation crew. Jean packed dehydrated foods and camping gear into the back of her small-sized pickup and drove west 1200 miles further than her longest-to-date solo road trip, ending in western Idaho where she would be working on the Rocky Mountain/Northwest Peregrine Falcon Reintroduction Project for the summer.

We had started out laying down the pattern for our married life by following the form we saw among adults around us while we were growing up in small rural communities in Iowa during the 1940s and 1950s. We graduated from high school, went off to college, and married in 1965. Though the lifelong occupation of both sets of parents was farming, after obtaining our degrees, we chose to seek jobs in engineering and teaching for which college had prepared us. Gary's first engineering job was in West Allis, a suburb of Milwaukee. Jean's first teaching job, while Gary finished his last year of college, could not be repeated during that year in the big city, so she took a job as a typist. City life did not suit us, and when Gary transferred after a year to an engineering job in a much smaller city, we found an apartment outside of town. Jean took another typing job and also began working part time toward a master's degree.

We started deviating a little more from a regular young couple's pattern when, after a year in that rural apartment, we purchased a small farm as a place to live instead of buying a house in town or in a suburban or rural development. We lived on that farm at first in a mobile home, and four years later built a house there.

Then for a couple decades we conformed more or less to those patterns set by adults we knew, raising a family of two daughters and working at our engineering and teaching careers, with Jean completing her master's degree and teaching only part time while our daughters were small. Along with those "city" jobs, a few years after we moved to the farm we took up farming for ourselves, thus returning to our rural roots and making farming our lifestyle if not our primary occupation. Gary raised beef cattle and the pastures, corn and hay crops to feed them. Jean helped with the farming, baked bread, kept bees and maintained a large garden, a small orchard, chickens, even ducks, geese and dairy goats, to provide much of our food.

As our older daughter, Gayle, progressed into college and the younger one, Janis, neared the end of high school, a certain amount of re-evaluation and restlessness set in, not too unusual at this life stage when adults ask themselves whether their careers are adequately fulfilling, or whether there are any unmet goals or dreams that deserve to be attended to in the post-childrearing stage of adulthood, when retirement is still "way out there" in the future. Gary was finding engineering challenging, interesting and a good way to make a living, but what about his boyhood dream of becoming a wildlife ranger? Jean believed teaching was the right career for her, and biology was the subject she still loved teaching, but what about her feeling that she ought to be <u>doing</u> biology, as well as teaching it? Should we perhaps be living more varied lives NOW instead of waiting for retirement, NOW while we were still active and healthy, NOW when we could have some new adventures? Was it possible for us to find some kind of outdoor, environmental work that we yearned for, that would benefit the natural world? Our summer plans for 1990 would begin to provide some answers to these issues. Hacking Peregrine Falcons for, what developed into, seven summers in the 1990's for The Peregrine Fund would be the means.

Peregrine Falcons are raptors, birds of prey with hooked beaks and sharp talons. Specifically, the Peregrine is a falcon, with a falcon's characteristic large head, long toes, and long, pointed wings. Falcons catch their prey on the wing, in chases or with high-speed dives from above, called stoops. Peregrines are famous for these dives, having been clocked at speeds in excess of 200 miles per hour, and they literally knock their prey out of the sky with a closed "fist" or overtake it and swoop up from below to grab it with those long toes and sharp talons.

Peregrines were extirpated east of the Mississippi River by 1968, reduced by 80-90% in the west by the mid-1970s, and their numbers had also fallen in several other large parts of their nearly world-wide distribution. This precipitous decline was caused by reproductive failure, and many believed extinction was inevitable. Early research and an historic conference held in 1965 in Madison, Wisconsin, began to place the blame on organophosphate pesticides accumulating in prey species and subsequently in the tissues of Peregrines and other raptors, interfering with eggshell production and other aspects of their reproduction. By 1972 use of these chemicals had been restricted in the United States and some other countries, making recovery a possibility for the species.

The Peregrine Fund was incorporated early in the 1970's, when Tom Cade and a small group of graduate students began research on how to breed Peregrines in captivity at Cornell University's Laboratory of Ornithology in Ithaca, New York. Falconers, a diverse group of individuals, were united by intense concern about the decline of Peregrines, and by their interest and willingness in helping to save the species. They contributed their knowledge of handling the birds; a number of them became actively involved in the reintroduction effort, and in some cases even allowed their falconry birds to be used in the breeding program. Many people believed it would be impossible to breed Peregrines in captivity, but by 1973, the first 20 young had been produced and in 1974, the first releases occurred—two young falcons were fostered into a failed nest in Colorado for the wild parents to finish rearing, and two more were released from a rooftop in New York. The name of the organization came from the fact that interested and concerned members of the public had begun sending money to support the efforts to re-establish Peregrines. In 1974 The Peregrine Fund began collaboration with the Colorado Division of Wildlife on western operations, and in 1984 moved their headquarters to Boise, Idaho. Many agencies, organizations and individuals partnered with The Peregrine Fund; working together, all these different entities and individuals consistently built success out of propagation and reintroduction efforts exerted over several decades. In 1999 a celebration was held in Boise and attended by more than a thousand people to mark the de-listing of the Peregrine Falcon from the Endangered Species List in the United States. The species, by this time, was no longer considered endangered or threatened. During the years 1974-1999 a total of 6769 Peregrines were released in the United States and Canada, 2109 of those in eight western states. It was our privilege to work with The Peregrine Fund in the release of

66 Peregrines at eight different hack sites in the states of Idaho, Wyoming and Montana during the years 1990-1996.

*Preview: Figures 3 and 4*

*Figure 3: Jean with our gear and supplies at Holter Lake*

*Figure 4: Gear tent, kitchen, sleeping tent at Holter Lake*

## PREVIEW – One of the Adventures

*From the Journals: Holter Lake – Jean*
*9 June 1992 – I sit by our pile of equipment and supplies, a pile*
*three feet high and eight feet across, on the bank of Holter Lake*
*while Gary takes a picture. We and all our gear have just been*
*carried by boat the length of this impoundment of the Missouri*
*River and landed half a mile from where we will camp for seven*
*weeks while helping reintroduce endangered Peregrine Falcons*
*to the wilds of Montana. The high banks along much of the*
*lakeshore make this the closest spot for the boat to land us. We*
*have five hours to move all this gear half a mile uphill and at*
*least put up a tent to sleep in tonight, before the boat returns to*
*take us to our truck. We must then move our truck to its summer*
*parking place, hike three miles back in to camp, and secure our*
*gear before dark. The scenery is dramatic with the hack cliff*
*rising high above the lake behind me, a mile's hike from camp. I*
*am daunted by the work ahead, thrilled and proud to be here,*
*eager to begin work.*

Nearly all of the gear and much of the food we would need for
the next seven weeks was piled in an ungainly mound, on,
around, and near the concrete picnic table and bench of the
Holter Lake Bureau of Land Management (BLM) Campground:
waterproof ponchos, three tents, several tarps, clothing, two
camp stoves, our specially-made, rodent-proof camp kitchen,
five- and six-gallon water jugs, insulated drinking mugs,
containers of food, two binoculars, two spotting scopes with
tripods, three cameras, books to read, journals and pencils and
pens to record our experiences, sleeping bags, self-inflating air
mattresses, shovel, pick axe—everything we could think of to
sustain our living and working needs for the next two months
while not burdening ourselves with anything that could be
considered excess. All these possessions had been disgorged
from our Ford pickup truck after we had driven 1300 miles from

our farm in Wisconsin. As we waited for the BLM campground manager who would be our boat captain and guide to pull the boat into loading position at the nearby dock, we could not prevent ourselves from running through a mental check list to consider what we might have forgotten.

Soon the 16-foot power boat was securely docked and we carried load after load to the boat; our guide placed our gear and supplies into the watercraft, organizing all of it carefully to balance the boat fore and aft, port and starboard. This was a challenging process because the boat was built for speed and carrying several passengers, not to serve as a barge. After we all donned life jackets and left the dock, the campground manager slowly and carefully brought the boat up to a speed he deemed safe given that we were still top heavy and front heavy. He slowly took us toward what we had nicknamed Gull Landing from our early exploration the day before, a point on the far shore of Holter Lake, southward and three miles from the dock. The lake waves and wind were modest but rocking and pitching of the craft as we encountered other boat wakes gave us some apprehension as we each looked to the driver for assurance this unusual load would not tip over. Part way across the lake a storage tub lid blew off and our boat captain circled back to retrieve it while Jean added some extra lashing over our precarious load in order to keep everything in place.

We relaxed somewhat as the boat was steered into shallow water near shore and brought to a halt, its driver determining how close he could get to shore without injuring the bottom of his boat, and still protect the prop of the outboard engine. Jean leapt to shore without getting too wet but our guide gamely stepped out into water over his boot tops to begin handing her all our equipment and supplies as Gary handed those goods to him from the boat. As Jean continued to organize parcels, jugs, bags, packs and assure everything was on dry ground, Gary began to carry the items up a dry drainage channel, then up a steep rocky bank, onto and over the mixed prairie grasses of the peninsula, continuing in a gradual slope several hundred yards uphill and then to the site we had selected the previous day as the best locale for our camp site for the next seven weeks. Here, approximately one-half mile from Gull Landing, we would reside while attending to the needs of five young Peregrine Falcons that would be brought to us the next day to be reintroduced into this area of the Rocky Mountain West.

After our BLM captain-and-guide had quickly finished discharging our equipment from his boat and promised to return at 5:00 PM to pick us up and deliver us back to our truck, he motored across the lake to the campground, leaving us behind to attend to our goal of setting up camp. This left us with a lot of work on a full-sun day in 80 degree temperatures and no time to take a break as we carried load after load after load up-slope to our campsite. Dehydration set in as we worked up the sweat of near exhaustion and we finally sat down to drink some water to replenish our waning strength. As Gary set up one tent for the night, Jean prepared a quick sandwich meal to make up for the lunch we purposely had skipped as we raced the clock to have a dry and secure habitat for the coming nightfall.

We arrived back at Gull Landing just as the boat was pulling in and were taken, via the water route back to our truck at the campground. Now a series of other obligations awaited us, all needing completion before day turned to night as the first shadows from the mountains to the west were beginning their march downslope toward what we already thought of as our peninsula, our camp, our new summer home.

We hopped into our truck, which still held a variety of supplies to be accessed periodically throughout the summer: additional books to read, more canned and dried foodstuffs, spare clothes to accommodate weather patterns we had not yet had the opportunity to ascertain. Then we drove our truck eight miles back around the north end of Holter Lake and met the young manager of the Ox-Bow Ranch, where our truck would be parked for the summer and where a small freezer would be installed to hold the bodies of several hundred small Coturnix Quail, food for our falcons until the falcons learned to catch their own. After we parked at the end of the two-track access trail, as close as any vehicle other than a boat could get to our campsite, we strapped into our big external-frame backpacks and hiked back to camp, a distance of three miles on an old hiking trail, originally a cattle trail.

Darkness was nearly upon us as we crawled into the tent, gray-black clouds were building and the wind gradually rising. Our minds and bodies were filled with the competing emotions and feelings of nearly total exhaustion from a long day of constant activity versus the comfortable excitement of being in our remote wilderness setting wondering what tomorrow would bring. As the wan light from our flashlights bounced off the tent walls and guided us to our sleeping bags, we were totally content with being where we were, ready to engage in our assignment and the outdoor living necessary to help young falcons reclaim their place in this rugged mountain river valley.

So began Gary's second summer/Jean's third of working for The Peregrine Fund as grantees of their research program, "Caring for and Making Observations of Captive-produced Peregrine Falcons at a Hack Site." Our responsibilities as Hack Site Attendants included watching over the release site, providing food for young Peregrines daily and recording details of both the falcons and our own activities each day. At this site we would live with rattlesnakes as neighbors, cope with tent poles bent by high winds, routinely hike up to six or eight miles in a day during our "town trip" days, recognize individual meadowlarks by their songs, and watch mule deer pass by within 15 yards of us, sometimes as near as five yards, as we ate evening meals outside our tent.

At the Grave Point site the previous summer, 1991, we had a four-engine Forest Service plane roar low over our camp as it prepared to align itself in a steep canyon to drop smoke jumpers onto a fire on the Oregon side of Hells Canyon, the smoke, flames, and parachutists plainly visible from our hack site area. There we lived in a veritable garden of bright and beautiful wild flowers, feeling a pang of guilt for needing to step on some of them as we traveled from camp to tower and elsewhere around the area each day. Other sites, other summers took us to the banks of the Green River in Wyoming, to the middle of a private ranch owned by a philanthropist, astride the Benchmark Road at Wood Lake west of Augusta, Montana, and to work with a Native American Tribal organization. We lived with Short-eared Owls fluttering past our observation site, had a bear break into our camping trailer and pull Gary's briefcase and his summer's money supply out through the broken screen, were cautious with the bull moose while we walked the last distance to one hack tower, and were even more cautious when the skunk would not let us near the tower to retrieve remnants of the day's feeding of quail. We shared our sites with badgers, Columbia ground squirrels and other squirrel species, with Rocky Mountain sheep, white-tailed and mule deer, pronghorns, elk, mountain goats, bears, pocket gophers, mink, otter, beaver, red fox, muskrat, jack rabbit, snowshoe hare, mountain cottontail, porcupine, marmot, weasels, coyotes, toads, assorted snakes, various other small critters, and birds in abundance.

This book, then, is filled with stories of what we did during those summers we spent with Peregrines, why we did it, and how we did it.

*Figure 5: Peregrine at Green River*

*Figure 6: Young Peregrines in early flight practice*

# INTRODUCTION TO THE BOOK

Outline – Reintroduction Phases, parts A, B and C

Reintroduction of Peregrine Falcons after their population crash, involved a great many people, agencies and tasks in which we were not involved. Some of these topics will be covered in brief in this book to give the reader necessary background information; these topics include the discovery of the problem, research and early efforts, the formation of The Peregrine Fund, funding, captive breeding, and location of release sites, otherwise known as hack sites.

Our participation in Peregrine Falcon Reintroduction as Hack Site Attendants (grantees working with The Peregrine Fund) had several stages, which comprise the main portion of the book and these are illustrated by tales of our adventures during those wonderful summers. After a description of each hack site where we worked in the summers 1990-1996, the stages of the reintroduction process as we knew it are presented as the following main parts or phases: Installation, Post-installation while we monitored the falcons in the hack box, Release, Intense Observation Period, Relaxed Observation Period, Final Week on Site and Closing, and Preparing the Final Reports. Within each of these main sections or phases of the book, are three sub-sections labeled A, B and C. In each case part A provides information about what happens during that phase of the reintroduction process, our duties during that phase, and the development of the young Peregrines. In each phase, part B contains stories about the activities and events of that phase, and part C provides stories about the effects of these summers of field work on us personally.

The main part of the book closes with a Concluding Comments section in which we explore how these experiences enriched our lives. There is also an Acknowledgments section, a list of References, and additional information within the Appendix section of this book.

*Description of Hack Sites: Figures 7 and 8*

*Figure 7: Cliff hack site at Holter Lake*

*Figure 8: Installing Peregrines at CSKT Tower*

# DESCRIPTION OF OUR EIGHT HACK SITES

Release sites, otherwise known as hack sites, were chosen by Peregrine experts with consideration for conditions that would make successful reintroduction most likely. It was important that the locations be suitable for the falcons to return in future years and breed at the site or somewhere nearby. Thus, release sites were chosen that included suitable nest sites: cliff ledges, a hacking tower, or in some cases, other existing structures such as bridges or tall buildings. It was also vitally important that each release site include a good prey base to serve as ample food not only for the young released birds that would be learning to hunt, but later for adult falcons, and eventually for breeding adults to capture and use to feed their offspring. For Peregrines this means birds, lots of birds. Other qualities considered for a release site were isolation from too much human disturbance during release, but also during future nesting seasons, reasonable safety from a variety of mammalian and avian predators, and avoidance of sites where other raptors were already nesting. Additionally, attitudes of residents of the areas were investigated, and funding sponsors for the sites were sought.

At each release site, The Peregrine Fund's Reintroduction Specialists, also known as Release Specialists, installed a large plywood box, called a hack box, five feet wide by four feet deep by three feet tall, which would be utilized to keep the young falcons safe while they were confined and acclimating to the release site. The hack box thereafter served as the Peregrines' "home base" after their release and prior to their eventual migration. The box had a small access door on one side for insertion and care and checking of the Peregrines. The front of the box consisted of a large removable door covered with bars on the inside and wire mesh on the outside to keep the falcons in until release and to keep predators out while the Peregrines were confined for the five to seven days prior to their release. The floor of the box extended out on the front side to form a deck or porch on the box, where an incoming falcon might land after release. In the back corner of the box opposite the access door, a narrow piece of plywood was mounted from floor to ceiling to provide a small place for the Peregrines to shelter behind. This area was called the "hide" and made a convenient place to briefly confine all the falcons preceding their release by temporarily taping a piece of cardboard over the hide opening. A long string was attached to the cardboard as a means to pull the cardboard away when the falcons were released. On top of the box was a plastic pipe feeding tube with baffle beneath it through which food (quail) was dropped. The tube and baffle prevented the Peregrines from knowing the source of their daily food ration while in the box. A few small holes were drilled in three sides of the box in order to allow observation of the Peregrines by the Hack Site Attendants. An inch or two of gravel covered the interior base of the hack box. A couple of large rocks were positioned on the gravel to provide a place for the falcons to perch instead of always resting directly on the gravel.

The hack sites where we worked during our years with the Rocky Mountain/Northwest Peregrine Recovery Program were of two types; at some of the sites the hack box was placed on a cliff while at other sites the hack box was located on a tower, usually a tower that was specifically constructed for the purpose. We worked as Hack Site Attendants for Peregrines for seven summers, 1990-1996, in three Rocky Mountain States, at eight different sites, for 11 releases. These numbers include two years at one site, one summer at two sites one after the other, one site where two hack boxes were placed on the same tower and two groups of Peregrines were released at the same time, and one site where one box was present but two groups of Peregrines were released one after the other a few weeks apart.

## Grave Point, Idaho – June, July, August 1990 and 1991

The Grave Point hack site was located southwest of White Bird, Idaho, at the top of a ridge midway between the Salmon River valley to the east and the Snake River valley to the west. The site is within the Nez Perce National Forest; that agency sponsored the release in 1990, and helped provide funding for the effort to re-establish Peregrine Falcons in this area, along with Idaho Department of Fish and Game in 1991. Although Douglas fir and Ponderosa pine grow in abundance in the surrounding area and along the road leading up to it, the most notable features of the Grave Point prominence were its mostly grassy, treeless summit and the 50-foot tall, old wooden fire-lookout tower built on the highest elevation. The hack box was located on the south side of the cabin at the top of the tower. At 5630 feet elevation Grave Point is 4470 feet above the Snake River Valley of Hells Canyon and 4070 feet above the Salmon River near White Bird. This hack site offered stupendous long-distance views of the surrounding mountainous scenery and dramatic river valleys. Ample spring rainfall provided an impressive display and diversity of wildflowers in 1991.

## Holter Lake, Montana – June, July 1992

Holter Lake is a Bureau of Land Management (BLM) impoundment of the Missouri River near Wolf Creek, Montana, just six miles downstream (north) of the famous Gates of the Mountains as named by Lewis and Clark in 1805 during their western expedition. The hack box, at 4400 feet elevation, was located at the top of a cliff on the western side of the lake 800 feet above the lake surface on lands adjoining Holter Lake and administered by the BLM. The Butte District of the BLM was the sponsor of the Holter Lake site. Douglas fir, Ponderosa pine, and occasional Rocky Mountain juniper dominated the box area but mixed prairie grasses and prickly pear cactus occurred on dry bench land nearer the lake and these lower grounds were cut with ravines containing chokecherry, serviceberry, and wild currant bushes. The Holter Lake hack site was our most rugged location as it was located over three miles across the lake from the BLM facilities and our remote camp site was three miles from where our truck was parked on a private ranch.

## CSKT Tower, Montana – July, August, September 1992

The CSKT Tower hack site was funded by the Confederated Salish and Kootenai Tribes (CSKT) of the Flathead Reservation and was located near Ronan, Montana, in the midst of private farming and ranching lands and tribal lands administered by this progressive Native American organization. Two hack boxes at an approximate elevation of 3060 feet faced east on top of a 30-foot tall tower constructed for this purpose in the midst of mixed-grass fallow fields dedicated to aiding the production of waterfowl. The Mission Mountains twelve miles east could provide valuable cliff nesting sites to successful adult Peregrines and gave us dramatic skyline vistas of this very picturesque mountain range. At CSKT Tower we could drive right up to and park at our campsite. There we experienced the widest range of temperatures, from a high of 102 degrees down to lows in the low 30s and woke on 23 August to a bit of snow on the ground by our trailer and more on the Mission Mountains. Because of its visibility within the neighboring community, we had the most visits by members of the public here, and thus were involved in considerable public outreach and wildlife education at this site.

## Green River, Wyoming – July, August 1993

The aptly named Green River site was situated next to the Green River north of Cora, Wyoming, in a broad ranching valley surrounded on three sides by mountain ranges: the Wyoming Mountains to the west, the Gros Ventre to the north, and the Wind River Range to the east. The hack box was mounted atop a 28-foot tower built on the west side of the river and our daily access to the tower from our campsite on the opposite side of the river was routinely via canoe. The tower site was funded by the Rock Springs District of the Bureau of Land Management (BLM) and located on lands administered by the BLM, but our drive-in access to the site was across private ranchland. Willows grew thickly along the river banks and adjoined hay fields and wetland meadows harboring abundant wildflowers. Sagebrush covered the higher, drier base of the valley until it transitioned to the lower mountain slopes of Aspen and Douglas fir. The 7600 foot elevation of Green River made it our highest and coolest campsite. There were only a few weeks at the peak of summer when the temperature at some time during the week did not dip below freezing.

## Bar None Ranch, Montana – July, August, September 1994

The Bar None Ranch hack site was located in a small mountain valley, rimmed on the west side with cliffs, on the Bar None Ranch near Toston, Montana. The hack box faced northeast at an elevation of 5080 feet on top of the cliff and we observed the box from near our campsite on the valley floor. Access to the hack site and our camp was only possible with a four-wheel drive vehicle via a difficult six-mile drive along a creek, through tunnels, up a gully, and over and down a steep ridge while we traversed the area's sage, mixed mountain grasses, and sweet clover amongst scattered clumps of Douglas fir and Rocky Mountain juniper. The site was funded by the Turner Foundation. Numerous western wild fires broke out in the summer of 1994, including several small fires nearby, and we often experienced vivid reddish sunsets and sky glow.

## Wood Lake, Montana – June, July 1995

Named for the adjacent mountain valley lake along the Benchmark Road west of Augusta, Montana, the Wood Lake hack site was funded by the Lewis and Clark National Forest, the Boone and Crockett Club, and the Great Falls District of the Bureau of Land Management. The hack box faced east at an elevation of 6120 feet on top of a cliff overlooking the public campground below. Painted in camouflage colors by Release Specialists, the hack box was noticed by relatively few campers. Mixed grasses and shrubby cinquefoil with occasional aspen groves were on the flat, narrow valley floor while the steep and high areas were characterized by grassy meadows, rock slides, cliffs and the surrounding coniferous forest of Douglas fir, Lodgepole pine, and Engelmann spruce. Installation of the Peregrines took place on 8 June during a vigorous and accumulating snowfall. On several days wild Bighorn sheep were observed at the hack box area.

## CSKT Cliff, Montana – July 1996

CSKT Cliff, west of Dixon, Montana, was a unique and separate site from CSKT Tower site described above but was likewise funded by the Confederated Salish and Kootenai Tribes (CSKT) of the Flathead Reservation. The hack box faced east at 4700 feet elevation on top of a large, dominant cliff and was 1200 feet above the Flathead River coursing through the valley below. Although large grassy hills were north and east of the site, the immediate area was rather rocky and covered with

Ponderosa pine, Douglas fir, serviceberry and wild currant bushes, and sparse grass as the vegetation, and the mountain rose gradually higher to the west offering good habitat for numerous bears. Although a beautiful location offering expansive views east to the river valley below, this site was our most frustrating as all the young Peregrines were killed by avian predators within a week of being released. After we were certain that none of our Peregrines had survived their initial encounters with life in the wild, we were reassigned for the remainder of that season to the Willow Creek Reservoir site by our supervisor at The Peregrine Fund.

### Willow Creek Reservoir, Montana – July, August 1996

The Willow Creek hack site, near Augusta, Montana, was named for the reservoir formed by the damming of Willow Creek. The reservoir and immediate surrounding area lie in the midst of a broad, flat to gently rolling dry, short-grass prairie area, with interspersed grazed ranchland and irrigated farmland. The Continental Divide and Front Range of the Rocky Mountains form a dramatic vista about 25 miles west. The east-facing hack box was at an elevation of approximately 4200 feet and sat on top of a 28-foot tall tower. Cattle and sheep occasionally grazed the areas near the tower. This site was funded by the Bureau of Reclamation. Early hack site duties of feeding and observing the young Peregrines had been performed by another team of attendants, and we assumed site responsibility for the final three weeks.

*Phase One, Installation: Figures 9 and 10*

*Figure 9: Jean and Specialist carrying Peregrines*

*Figure 10: Peregrines arrive at Wood Lake in snowstorm*

# PHASE ONE – INSTALLATION: beginning of week one

## A. INTRODUCTION TO INSTALLATION

Young Peregrine Falcons released by the hacking process at the hack sites where we worked in the Rockies were raised in captivity by The Peregrine Fund at the World Center for Birds of Prey facility in Boise, Idaho. Adult pairs, each kept in their own chamber in the breeding barn, generally copulated and produced eggs in the normal way despite being in captivity. The eggs were promptly removed to be hatched in artificial incubators under very controlled conditions, because in some cases eggshells were still abnormally thin, and because the hatching rate was higher by this method. Meanwhile, the adult pair was kept in reproductive condition and behavior by replacement of their eggs with artificial "dummy" eggs, which the adults continued to faithfully incubate. After hatching, the young falcons were fed by hand for about 10-14 days to ensure they were given a good start. At this young age, the chance that they will imprint on humans is low. The young were then given to an adult pair in a breeding chamber, the dummy eggs being removed at this time. It must have been something of a shock to have rather large young appear suddenly in place of eggs, but the young were given to the adults in a hungry state and their food-begging calls stimulated the appropriate feeding response from the adults.

By about 36 days old (usual range 34-38 days), young Peregrines are full size, well-feathered (with perhaps some nestling down still present), and nearly ready to fly. At this time they were taken from the adult birds in the breeding barn and made up into groups of about 4-6 of similar ages, but usually with both sexes represented in each group. The falcons were placed in large, cube-shaped, strongly-constructed cardboard boxes measuring about two feet on each side, with holes cut in the sides for ventilation, to be transported to the various hack sites where they were to be released. The breeding period in spring and early summer produced young ready to be placed in hack boxes over a several-month period during the summer. Release Specialists then transported the Peregrines to the hack sites, usually by double-cab pickup truck in which the boxes of Peregrines could be placed on the seat behind the driver so that any distress calls from the birds would be heard during the long drives.

Upon arrival at the hack site, the falcons often had to be carried in the traveling boxes some distance to the hack box, where the Release Specialist carefully picked up the young falcons one at a time and installed them in the hack box. Usually, one attendant assisted by opening the hack box door when the Specialist was ready to place a falcon into the box, and then closing the door quickly to contain the young falcons.

The job of Hack Site Attendants after installation was to feed the young falcons daily and to take detailed notes about them and conditions at the hack site. Generally, we arrived at each site either at the same time as the falcons or, when possible, the day before. Each site presented different camping challenges. The literature sent to us before each job included a list of recommended items to bring with us, but this was a very general list and invariably there would be something important missing from that list that we would need at a specific site.

We were required to call The Peregrine Fund twice each week to report on the falcons, the site, and ourselves. These calls provided us opportunities to ask questions, report problems, or other news from our sites. During our first week at each site, we used either the day of arrival or our first "town trip" to locate a pay phone for calls home and to Boise, a place to do weekly laundry, a post office where we could arrange to receive our mail "General Delivery," a gas station, perhaps a store of some kind, somewhere to fill our water jugs, the location of the quail freezer, and possibly a facility where we could take showers. We also needed to find somewhere we could properly dispose of camp refuse.

The location for the quail freezer containing the food supply for the Peregrines was arranged by The Peregrine Fund and the sponsoring agency in advance for each hack site; arrangements were also made for a source of potable water for attendants. Often the sponsoring agency also provided other amenities such as shower facilities, a phone we could use, perhaps a mail drop, and certainly a way to contact someone in the agency if we had questions or problems.

## B. INSTALLATION STORIES

Installation at Grave Point, 1990 and 1991

Since Jean already knew the location of the Grave Point tower and the specific spot where attendants were to place their camp, we were able to arrive at Grave Point the day before the falcons in 1991. Jean had driven out on her own from Wisconsin again, taking time to visit her cousins in Boise. Having decided to quit his engineering job in order to help reintroduce falcons, Gary worked as an engineer to the last possible day and then used leftover frequent-flier miles to fly to Boise. Jean met Gary at the airport and took him to the World Center for Birds of Prey, so he too could tour the facility before we made the long drive north to White Bird and Grave Point. Before driving up the mountain, we checked in at the Nez Perce National Forest's Slate Creek Ranger Station, were shown the garage wherein the quail freezer would be kept, and the spigot we could use to fill our water jugs. Knowing the winding, gravel mountain roads from the summer before, Jean drove and Gary held on, while taking in the incredible vistas and beginning to learn the route.

We used this early arrival to get a head start on moving our gear from our truck two-thirds mile uphill to the camp location. We had to park outside a locked gate, even though there was a drive-able road past camp and all the way to the tower. We were told that local people would have been deeply resentful if we could drive in where they could not, so only the truck delivering Peregrines the next day would be allowed past the gate. We knew this limitation from 1990 when Jean and CJ had not been warned to bring good quality, large backpacks and thus had to borrow one from the U. S. Forest Service to help carry regular supplies of quail, ice, water and everything else needed up to camp. Jean and CJ therefore had greatly appreciated the Specialist's concern in 1990 and his offer to let us load a few of our heaviest items into the back of his truck for the trip from the gate uphill two-thirds mile to the spot where we were to set up camp. Reaching this point, the Specialist stopped his truck and we unloaded our 5-gallon jug of water, CJ's chuck box (camp kitchen), and one other heavy item, and were each issued a 2-person tent, a single-burner camp stove, and a camp lantern. We also unloaded the large cooler, spotting scope and tripod on loan from The Peregrine Fund before continuing up the hill to the tower to install the falcons. Aware of this locked-gate/two-thirds mile uphill road situation, in 1991 we brought our big, external-frame backpacks from home. In addition, Gary had constructed a hand-cart with two wheels that could be conveniently removed allowing the cart to be folded flat for packing in our truck. We named this cart our "mule" and we used it to tow large items such as the plastic storage tubs of clothing and large water jugs (five- and six-gallon sizes) that two-thirds mile uphill distance from our truck to camp. By that evening we had our 4-person tent set up and outfitted with mattress pads, sleeping bags, pillows, flashlights and a plastic tub of clothing for each of us as we began organizing our camp. We continued to bring up loads of gear and supplies the next morning while awaiting delivery of the Peregrines.

When the Release Specialist arrived in the afternoon in a Peregrine Fund pickup with five young falcons in their transport boxes, he was followed up past the gate by a forest service pickup containing two Forest Service biologists plus the wife of one as observers. One of the biologists photographed the installation process for the Forest Service.

Both of us climbed the 50-foot tower's stairs, each carefully holding a box of falcons, while the Specialist carried the third box—no more than two falcons were transported per box. This batch included three females and two males. Our Specialist carefully placed the falcons one by one into the hack box with Jean operating the door for him. Only one falcon, a female we subsequently named Black for the color of her identifying leg band, proved difficult and gripped the Specialist's hand tightly with one foot, and partially with the other foot. She also bit him hard in the hand several times, drawing blood.

*From the Journals: Grave Point – Jean*
*22 June 1991 – The last falcon to be installed, a female we called Black, was quite feisty when the Specialist picked her up with both hands to move her from the transport box to the hack box. She bit him several times in his hands, bit him hard drawing blood. She also clutched his hands with her talons, one foot pressing lightly but the other seating its talons more deeply. Here was an illustration of the skill and concentration, the complete dedication of these Release Specialists—an*

*ordinary person, if set such a task, might attempt to shake the*
*offending falcon off, even drop it because of the sudden shock of*
*pain. Our Specialist held on calmly, but with both hands needed*
*to hold the falcon and indeed, trapped by the talons of the bird,*
*he could only ask for help. I tried quite gingerly to pull the*
*talons one by one out of the Specialist's hand, afterward*
*placing each talon curled harmlessly against the flesh. One rear*
*talon had deeply punctured the webbing between thumb and*
*index finger of one hand; having left this one until last, I*
*attempted to pull the talon straight out and was quickly told to*
*stop, that I must pull with the curve of the talon. Finally, Black*
*could be placed in the hack box, and the door closed to secure*
*the young falcons in their new, temporary home. Before we*
*climbed down from the tower, the Specialist turned to me and*
*asked, "Did I flinch?" No. He did not.*

For all of the falcons we attended in those adventurous years,
we resisted choosing human-type names, believing that since
they were to be wild and free, they should not be so burdened.
Some falconers and other reintroduction personnel we met
seemed disappointed with us in this regard; certainly the
falconers' birds were personal to them and were given names.
Regardless, we needed to be able to identify the individual
falcons at our hack sites, to call them something in our
observation notebooks and eventually in our official reports.
Before being delivered to a hack site, each falcon was given an
official metal band on one leg from the United States
Geological Survey (USGS) Bird Banding Lab, with a unique
identification number, too small for us to read even with a
spotting scope, and the phone number of the Bird Banding Lab
at Patuxent Wildlife Research Center in Laurel, Maryland. All
official bird bands have unique identification numbers and the
phone number to enable anyone who finds a dead banded bird
to call in a report of the date, location and finder. The other leg

had a Peregrine Fund band with larger numbering that could be read with a good spotting scope from concealment at about 70 yards. The USGS band is normally silver metal, but could be painted over in the case of these falcons to make them individually identifiable by the Hack Site Attendants using scopes from their Observation Point (O.P.), a dedicated location from which the hack box and surrounding area could be observed without being so close as to disrupt normal falcon behavior. We therefore used these colors to "name" and identify the individual falcons. Hence at Grave Point in 1991, we called "our" falcons of that year Green, White, Black, Yellow and Red.

In 1990, spray paint had been applied in a 1-2 inch circle on the feathers on one side of the falcons. This made identification of individuals very easy for Jean and CJ until the paint began to flake off. When this was noticed, the attendants made sketches of the facial markings of each falcon; these sketches and familiarity with the falcons' behaviors and habits made them recognizable even after all the paint was gone. The designations given by Jean and CJ to the falcons they cared for in 1990 were based on these paint blotches: Left Green, Right Green, Right Orange, Left Orange and None (no paint blotch). Having heard about these paint blotches, it was worrisome to Gary to find they had not been applied to the 1991 batch of young falcons, and instead the USGS bands had been painted different identification colors. However, he too soon became proficient at recognizing the five individual falcons at the Grave Point hack box in 1991.

Another characteristic of falcons, and indeed of most raptors, which aids in identification of individuals, is that the males are notably smaller than females, while in most bird species the male is the same size or larger than the female. A number of hypotheses have been proposed as to why this reverse sexual size dimorphism evolved in some bird groups and especially raptors. One hypothesis is that the female, being larger, can more easily still hunt successfully when eggs are developing within her body during the early part of the breeding season and can accumulate more resources for egg production. Her larger size and stored reserves would also help during the part of the breeding season when she hunts less and the male must provide both for himself and partially for her as well as for the young during both the incubation period and the early days after hatching. Another hypothesis holds that possible aggression of the male toward female and young is thwarted by the female being larger. Or, perhaps his smaller size facilitates the male's dramatic aerial courtship displays. Still another possible explanation is that by being of different sizes, the male and female compete less directly for food, since the male is adapted to hunt smaller, swifter, more numerous prey, and the female is adapted to hunt larger, more sluggish, less numerous prey species. She returns to serious hunting once the young have grown enough to be left alone at the nest for periods of time; this is when the need for food to feed a batch of growing young is greatest and both adults must hunt.

Both Jean and CJ took print and slide photos during their hack site job in 1990. Jean prepared a program about her experiences at Grave Point in 1990 using her photos and a few from CJ; she presented this 35mm slide program several times to share those her 1990 experiences with Gary, as well as other family members and friends, and with her colleagues at the University of Wisconsin-La Crosse. Gary strongly wanted to add to that collection of photos, especially in 35mm slide format. Each summer, at each different hack site, it was important to us to document our experiences with journal entries as well as photos. Over the years Jean showed 35mm slides to many,

many of her students, especially students in her Ornithology classes, to introduce them to the concept of doing fieldwork. Although Peregrine hack site jobs were scarce by the mid-1990s, a number of her Ornithology students were inspired enough to find fieldwork jobs for themselves, even in distant places such as Chile and Australia, and to go on to earn advanced degrees. We have also given programs together to various other interested groups.

The first year, Jean brought all her print and slide films home to be developed; they were generally satisfactory, but the problem with this was her inability to find out while still on site that she had missed photographing certain aspects she later wished to include in her slide presentations, nor could she re-take any photos that had not turned out well. To deal with these issues in later years, we sent some films taken early at each site by mail to a developer in Seattle. When we received the developed films back through the mail, we reviewed the prints and slides, using a small hand-held, battery-powered viewer for the latter. In this way we could take more photos while still at a hack site. At least one year, Gary called our local photo shop back home in Wisconsin and had more films mailed to us. After seven summers, we had accumulated several thousand photos, predominantly slides—of course not all of them useable. Imagine how much better it would have been if we could have recorded our experiences with digital photography and evaluated our photos frequently with a laptop on site!

*From the Journals: Wood Lake – Gary*
*9 July, 1995 – One reason I like this Peregrine hacking job is that it is very similar to hunting. I have always enjoyed the hunting I have done since coming into it as a result of my youth on an Iowa farm in the mid 1950's and I have always strived to be an expert and ethical hunter. In Peregrine hacking, just as in*

*hunting, you spend lots of time outdoors, get to know the animal or bird you are dealing with, see their habits, learn to predict them, try to outsmart them, be wary enough and good enough to be able to see, hear, sense them and also get to see all the other accompanying wonders of being out-of-doors in their environment, be it a hunter's quarry or a hack site Peregrine.*

*Like this past Saturday morning. When I exited our camper for the first time I glanced up to the cliff top, as I always do, and saw this big full-curl Bighorn ram looking over the edge of the cliff with our falcon, Black, perched in a nearby dead tree cacking loudly at the ram. Biggest ram we have ever seen here. I went back in to the camper, retrieved and set up the camera and tripod and got several good pictures. I waited a while for any further developments but there were none. Jean and I were going up to the hack box together to feed and we wanted to travel light so we left both the binoculars and our cameras in the trailer. We were walking down the Benchmark Road and about to turn toward our trail going up to the top of the cliff when the ram was joined by six other nearly full-curl large Bighorn rams and all seven came vertically hurtling down the front of the cliff, angling this way and that, clattering rocks like fury, but never slipping and always being sure-footed in their descent until they headed off east out of our view and into the trees. Partway into this scene Jean asked if I wanted to return to the trailer and fetch my camera, but I just said, "No, then I'll miss seeing all of this." That which we were witnessing.*

*And timing the episode mentally in my head that is about what would have happened. I would just be getting to the camper trailer and the whole scene would have been over. As our friend John, an excellent photographer, would say, "It was something!" Quite an imposing sight. One for the memory. And as John also says, "Some of my best pictures are the ones where*

*I did not have a camera." Captured images of those fine magnificent sheep would have made for wonderful photo slides but instead they will remain pictures in our minds, for our eyes only, for no one else will see what we saw in those precious few moments, and which remain visible only in our memories.*

The Grave Point site provided us with one of the longest "town trip" distances of any of our hack sites. Twice a week we drove a 52-mile round trip, most of the distance on dusty mountain roads, to make a routine "circuit." After reaching the highway, the circuit included the laundromat, pay phone, post office, gas station, ranger station, water spigot, public dumpster and quail freezer locations. Typically, we also stopped at a fruit stand along the highway portion of the trip, where in 1990 Jean found bread only once in seven weeks, but she and CJ could often get fresh fruits and vegetables. Spring in 1991 was wet and cool, so that the fruit stand was not open for the first few weeks we were on site, and this dearth of fresh foods was deeply disappointing. White Bird had no store, just a gas station with a very small assortment of canned food. Twice in 1990, it was necessary to drive the extra distance north to Grangeville, Idaho, to purchase supplies not available in White Bird, such as one-pound propane cylinders to power our one-burner camp stove, and plastic containers in which to store books and clothing to keep them dry in the tent if water ran in underneath during a rainstorm—the cardboard boxes we brought these items in the first year having proved a poor choice. Fortunately, in both years we had prepared well and brought a great deal of canned and dehydrated food from Wisconsin. In 1991 it rained much more than the year before, so Gary drove to Grangeville (an 86-mile round trip one day instead of the usual 52 miles) to get extra tarps and rope in order to make a more complete "roof" over our tent and camp kitchen area. We were even able to catch some extra water off that tarp system for washing.

Unique to the Grave Point site was the need to keep track of time in three time zones. The hack site was just over the line into the Pacific Time Zone, so both summers we set our watches to Pacific Time and made entries in our observation notebooks according to that time. When we went to town to make the required calls to The Peregrine Fund, it was necessary to think in Mountain Time because Boise was in that time zone and we had to make our calls when the office at the World Center for Birds of Prey was open; to this end we set our truck clock to Mountain Time. On these twice-weekly town trips, we also made calls home to family members and others, and this meant mentally adjusting to the time back home in Wisconsin in the Central Time Zone. In some cases, we might try calling three different family members and still not connect to anyone, instead leaving scattered answering-machine messages to say we were okay. Jean also sometimes made calls to her Biology Department chairman at UW-La Crosse after receiving a letter asking her to check in about a job opening for the coming fall. Gary also made calls relating to his recently relinquished engineering job and possibilities for the engineering consulting jobs he was seeking.

Installation at Wood Lake, 1995

On 7 June we pulled our camper trailer into the Wood Lake campground on a wet, but well graveled roadway, late on a rainy and foggy afternoon. As the elevation rose on the drive into the mountains, light snow had begun falling and we became apprehensive about finding firm ground on which to position our camper for the summer and whether the scheduled Peregrine release for the next day could still occur if conditions worsened. The dark low skies lent a sense of pessimism as evening enfolded us without our being able to see the tops of the valley walls and get a clear sense of where we would be spending the next seven weeks. But we were committed and felt measurably better once our camper was parked, leveled, and the camper's small propane furnace had taken the chill away. Having made a rare grocery stop as we passed through town on our way into the mountains, we feasted on fresh salad and fried chicken breast and recognized again, as we had each summer, how fortunate we were to be engaged in such a life of outdoor living in a wilderness setting and to be doing environmental work. Our mutual hug of joy after supper went beyond one another and encircled our new life setting as well. With grins on our faces we fell asleep with the snow and sleet gently ticking on the metal roof and furnace vent of our camper at its summer location in the mountains. That night we were eight miles from the nearest human, a rancher on the edge of the plains, and we were 24 miles from the nearest town, Augusta, Montana—population, less than 300.

The following morning we awoke to totally overcast skies, the clouds scudding by rapidly overhead, careening down our mountain valley, swirling through the mountain tops. The ground was totally white, snow still falling in intermittent showers, driven into our faces and clothing by the wind. At home on our farm in Wisconsin, temperatures were in the mid 60's that day. Late in the afternoon our solitary vigil was brought to a resounding halt by the arrival of what appeared to us as a Peregrine Installation Convoy—three vehicles carrying 11 people and six young falcons were parked off the road near the base of the cliff which all 13 of us would soon ascend. As we joined them with quick introductions all around, everyone was donning winter clothing, keeping their backs to the biting wind and snowflakes, organizing their equipment, grabbing cameras, and trying to peek at the Peregrines in their boxes. There were Fish and Game people, bear experts, Peregrine Fund

Release Specialists, Forest Service personnel, a newspaper reporter, and the two of us.

Bears were known to be in the area so the bear experts were the first ones up the mountain to the cliff edge carrying their wire, poles, insulators, battery-powered electric fencer, and installation equipment. They installed a small three-foot high, electrified fence around the hack box to prevent the possibility of a wandering bear, upon smelling the young Peregrines (or their food) enclosed in the hack box, from then powerfully ripping into the box and destroying these precious birds. The rest of us personnel gave the bear experts a head start to perform their assignment, but we soon grew tired of standing around trying to stay warm in the inclement conditions and zig-zagged our way up to the cliff to join them as they completed their task. In spite of even gustier winds, our exposed position at the cliff edge, and six inches of snow at the box, the Peregrine expert calmly caught each falcon and installed it in its new clifftop home, the birds fluttering their wings when released into the box now that they could feel the rush of fresh and moist air. We got a quick lesson on energizing and de-energizing the fence from the bear experts so that we could safely access the box and feed our birds without hazard of electric shock, before we all carefully made our way back down the steep slopes, slippery with their coating of snow, from the cliff to the vehicles far below. At the clifftop we had caught glimpses of our camper, snug below us in the valley surrounded by mountainous terrain, whenever the skies briefly lifted before dropping yet another flurry of snow upon the anxious participants in this venture.

Back on the valley floor most of the crowd quickly dispersed; now the birds were totally our responsibility. We invited the two Release Specialists into our camper to warm up, have some hot chocolate, and share a traditional 1-2 hour visit exchanging familiarization stories of their lives and ours. What we held in common was our devotion to Peregrines and living our lives in relation to the outdoors. What brought each of us here and how we lived outside of this mission, were rich fodder for mutual discussion.

When the Specialists also departed just at nightfall, the silence and the solitude left us feeling as though we were alone in the world.

*From the Journals: Wood Lake – Gary*
*9 June 1995 – We had been under clouds for four days, under snow for three days. It was dark and quiet, the wet snow-covered forest and hills absorbing all sound, and it seemed as though it would be dark and cloudy and snowing forever as the days marched to the Millennium. Yet the calendar says 9 June and surely the sun will shine again and reveal to us the mountain scenery we are truly amidst. Now we have only slight hints and our view-scape is limited to hundreds of yards. We need not go to town for several more days and armed with food, shelter, and warmth we revel in the contentment of our satisfaction and adventure—the joy to be in such a place at such a time. It is all quite lovely, satisfying, quiet. Only the trepidation over the future welfare of the falcons and our own comfort at the outdoor remote observation sites after the 14 June release gives us some alarm. But that is the future, now we are content. Light snow continues to fall gently. Inside the trailer we hear only a symphony. A symphony of the sounds of snow and heat intermixing. Drips melt off the roof striking a tinny projection of the furnace flue, or other drips hit our small wooden front deck, now fast, now slow, now rapid, now a burst of drops, then slowing again—drummers in the symphony, the cracking of the furnace as it heats and cools adds to the*

*staccato. Within the orchestra the violins of the furnace, now pilot flame only, now full-flame, feed a constant harmony. And the beat and the tones go on and on, the only sounds in this world of silence. Too much snow is already on the roof to hear the flakes themselves impacting. Now they land silently, there to remain until heat brings them into our symphony.*

The day after installation, the big, bright, beautiful sun burst forth revealing our bigger world of mountains and valleys and cliff and forest, yet all white with snow. Alerted by a nearby deep buzzing Gary observed a male Rufous Hummingbird about two inches from our window as he hovered and caught water drops from the melting snow on the roof before he landed and rested on our truck's rear view mirror. The hummingbird was a lovely sprite of colorful life in our world of white, along with some green patches of ground cover gradually reappearing as the sun exerted its power.

Climbing the Tower Alone, CSKT Tower, 1992

After spending nearly seven weeks on site at Holter Lake, on 24 July we back-packed our final three-mile hike to our waiting truck parked on the Ox-Bow Ranch. As we walked along the shore line a coyote pack across the lake sang out to us as though they might be saying, "Goodbye, friends," just as one of theirs had welcomed us to our campsite that first night seven weeks earlier with his barking and appearance on the ridge-top skyline. Twenty-four hours later, on 25 July, we were at our next assigned location and for the coming seven weeks would be camped at CSKT Tower. In the intervening 24 hours we had driven 200 miles, visited two good friends overnight in Missoula, had long and wonderful showers in their home, and replenished our camping supplies with the expenditure of nearly 200 dollars at the large grocery store recommended by our friends. In addition, our friend Richard helped Gary locate two conduits and two wooden 2x2s at the local lumber store, then to cut the conduit and 2x2s to length and drill holes in each of these four pieces. We wanted to be prepared for any eventuality at the CSKT Tower site and roughhewed these structural supports to mate with a lean-to tent, which we had ordered while at Holter Lake, to be delivered to our friends' house.

In a coincidence of fortuitous timing we met our next Release Specialist at a gas station in Missoula while we were fueling our truck and were invited to follow him to the CSKT Tower. We drove directly to the release site where we gazed upon a recently-erected tower of four telephone poles with a platform on top, about ten feet square, and 30 feet above the ground. One ascended to the platform by grasping and stepping on five-inch, L-shaped metal rods, known as "deer steps" screwed perpendicularly into one of the vertical poles and spaced about 20 inches apart. On top of the platform two hack boxes were positioned for a double simultaneous release of ten falcons, five in each box, the falcons to be delivered and installed the next day. The tower was an imposing and slightly ominous structure. There were no guard rails and we stole furtive questioning glances at one another, while bravely proclaiming to our Specialist, "Looks good, we can handle this." We each seriously wondered if we could. We were after all, 48 years old that summer, and not as nimble or as young as many of the people erecting and attending these sites. It was the first hack tower either of us had seen which had been erected solely for the release of Peregrines. The tower at Grave Point was a different structure entirely, time proven through 50 years of fire-watch use and stoutly constructed of heavy timbers with flights of stairs and abundant guard rails for access to the tower balcony. The structure at CSKT struck us as decidedly unsafe and neither of us had any experience climbing up and mounting ourselves on top of such a structure. With vivid imaginations, we saw not necessarily ourselves, but instead our partner in a crumpled heap on the solid ground beneath the tower after helplessly witnessing the accident from our observation point. It was an unsettling image.

After informing us we would be provided a camping trailer for our use from the local sponsors, our Specialist next guided us to his family's "duck shack," an old hunting and recreational cabin on the north side of the nearby Ninepipe National Wildlife Refuge, where he invited us to sleep for the night since the trailer wasn't being delivered until the next day. After a pleasant evening of fellowship with several other conservation-minded people, the next morning we got up and drove first to the refuge to explore a bit what would likely become a favorite food resource area for our falcons, their hack boxes being within a few miles of this large and watery mecca of birdlife. But our primary goal for the morning was for each of us to climb and surmount "That Tower" while no one else was there. We each knew we had to dispel any sense of fear in order to successfully accomplish our assignment. One of us, taking turns, would be climbing up and down that tower, at least once each day, often twice, for the next seven weeks.

The tower legs each had a piece of sheet metal wrapped around them at a height of six feet to prevent mammalian predators from climbing the tower and getting at the precious falcons or their food quail. Therefore, the "steps" to the tower platform could not be reached without a ladder that was yet to be delivered. To deal with this, Gary backed our truck up to one tower leg while Jean guided him to bring the truck to where the back end was just a few inches from the tower pole holding the metal rods or rungs to be used as both handholds and steps as we climbed the tower. We each had to climb onto our truck tailgate, then onto the topper of the truck bed, whereupon we could easily reach the first of the tower rungs. In turn then, each of us climbed the tower, crawled over the edge onto the platform, walked around the boxes, looked over the tower floor edge, and became familiar with the tower and the sight of the ground so far below, while the other partner verbally guided, coached, and waited anxiously for a successful ascent and descent. Mission accomplished! We had each done out of the public eye what we had not been sure we could actually do. And, because of our concern for each other, we promised to always climb slowly and deliberately, to maintain three points of contact at all times, e.g. when moving one foot to a different rung, we would keep the other foot and both hands firmly on other rungs rather than moving one hand and the opposite foot at the same time. Our worry and concern resolved, we waited for the Specialist to bring our falcons on this installation day.

Around 12:30 PM, what seemed to be an army moving in, was instead a short convoy of four trucks containing the ten falcons in their traveling boxes, two Specialists, parents of one Specialist, his grandmother, his former high school teacher, two biologists for the tribe, one biologist's wife and two children, and three dogs. The formerly quiet rural setting became instead a mass of commotion as trucks were parked, Specialists readied the falcons for being lifted in their transport boxes by rope up to the tower platform, lawn chairs became occupied with visitors, cameras were uncased, and introductions made all around. Jean climbed to the top of the tower along with one Specialist and one biologist to assist in the insertion of the Peregrines into each hack box, while Gary took photos of the event from the ground and watched along with the remaining interested viewers, all gazing excitedly up to the minor acrobatics and maneuvering taking place up on the high tower platform. With installation complete, the three tower climbers all descended one at a time. As Jean alighted on the ground the three women among our visitors all spontaneously, simultaneously broke out in applause and cheering for one of their "own" being so brave as to nonchalantly climb what they apparently would not willfully choose to do. We were glad we had practiced the tower climb when no one was around to view our initial trepidation. As the summer progressed, in spite of rain or wind and vibration pushing the tower around a few inches we each became "cautiously comfortable" with going to the tower platform and hack boxes, except near the end of the job when there was frost or even snow on the rungs and tower platform— then we were fearful again. But the viewing partner always worried until the climbing partner was safely back on the ground. It was watching the other that was always more uncomfortable.

Preparing the Site for Walking, CSKT Tower, 1992

Considering how much sitting time would be necessary at each hack site to fulfill our observational duties, we always wanted to assure we could get in an adequate amount of exercise to keep our bodies in trim. At all of our release sites, except CSKT Tower, this was relatively easily accomplished due to their remote settings within natural, near wild, habitats. These remote settings offered back-country roads and trails seldom traveled by vehicle; or old hiking or cattle trails; or expansive natural forests, public or private rangeland and pastures; on all of which we could walk long distances unfettered by obstructions or lack of permission to be there. And walk we did, enjoying the opportunity to explore and learn more about the habitat in which we found ourselves living for weeks at a time, invigorated and strengthened by the elevation changes in the terrain.

Conditions at CSKT Tower were different. Although we could see mountains on all sides of us, we were not in them. We were within a rural farmland and ranching community, with public roads in the normal grid pattern of every one or two miles and numerous rural family farms and ranches set every one-half to one mile apart. These roads were publicly dedicated and maintained for all to use. The land on which our release tower was erected, and where our loaned camper trailer was placed, was in a conservation plan dedicated to waterfowl production. The land had been farmed in the past but was in 1992 lying fallow in anticipation of further conservation efforts. As such, much of the terrain on which we were located had been infested by cheatgrass (*Bromus tectorum*), an introduced, opportunistic, invasive annual grass that readily supplants preferred native species. Cheatgrass is awful stuff.

Cheatgrass produces abundant seeds, can grow in poor soils, out-competes native species, and is relatively unpalatable for grazing animals, even dangerous from the sores its sharp seeds can cause. It is also fire-prone, igniting easily after it has dried down. Aldo Leopold in 1949 was one of the first authors to point out the dangers of spreading cheatgrass in the American West. For walkers and hikers like us, the primary problem is the sharp-tipped seeds with their barbed awns. The seeds easily break off from the plant and attach themselves to socks and lower pants, and with their sharp points penetrate to your skin. Furthermore, their removal from your clothing is difficult and tedious. Generally you cannot pull the seeds out backward and must instead find the sharp point and extract the seed in the same direction as it entered your clothing. And once the skin is contacted with that sharp point, it just plain hurts to leave them there. They cannot be ignored.

The small camper trailer supplied for our use by a local sponsoring agency had been parked in the middle of an 80-acre field with a lot of cheatgrass growing in it. From fence line to fence line there was no way to avoid all of it. The "lane" to our trailer was been driven on by ourselves and visiting guests and the vehicle tires had flattened the cheatgrass. Therefore we had at least one place to walk with less concern for cheatgrass seeds catching in our socks. We could, and occasionally did, walk that short lane to access the nearest gravel road where we could also walk safe from cheatgrass. But on the road we were exposed to stones flung by passing cars and trucks and had to breathe incredible amounts of dust, left in the wake of each passing vehicle. Our "walk" solution was to drive three times around the inside perimeter of the field to crush the cheatgrass low and flat and thereby create a one and one-half mile loop trail that we could hike on without concern for the sharp seed heads.

This self-created walking trail worked well for us that summer in the Flathead Lake valley. Vehicles passing through the neighborhood did not have to slow down for us. We did not have to watch out for them. Our trail system allowed us to stretch our legs and was always available. The far-distant scenery was superb. The sharp pinnacles of the Mission Range were twelve miles east of us, the Moiese Hills of the National Bison Range were 15 miles south, and the lower mountaintops of the Lolo National Forest 30 miles away formed our western skyline. Many of the fields in the area had impressive rock piles spaced randomly around their perimeter, and our field was no exception. Early settlers and farmers picked these rocks out of their fields to enable tillage. Some piles were round or square in shape, 10-30 feet on a side and placed near some other natural obstruction such as a pothole or rock outcropping. Others were more linear along the field borders in the 10-foot wide range and up to 30 feet long. These rock piles often held perching

Short-eared Owls, which would come out near dusk or when we ventured too close to their reclusive day-time hiding spots. Short-eared Owls fly like large moths: short, quiet, intermittent, gliding flaps propelling them in erratic twists and turns as they seek out their evening meal of late-flying insects. Once we flushed 13 owls out of the same rock pile and stood briefly awed—they are not particularly frightened of humans, and we stood in their midst as they swirled around us.

On other walks we brought home several rock samples of what we thought might be chert or flint-like pieces that might have the characteristics of rocks used by Native Americans for making their tools, and we practiced at knapping the stones into shapes. Once we saw three weasels cavorting in the grass, acting and undulating very much with the grace of otters in the water but without the water. We often saw the long-winged Northern Harriers floating low over our field looking for a mouse or vole meal, gliding effortlessly from spot to spot. Once we were that spot as a Harrier circled twelve feet over our heads eechip-chipping, a vocalization of mild alarm at our occupation of his hunting grounds. It was a good hunting ground for hawks and owls as we also often saw voles moving through the grasses around us, following their little trails. One early, frosty morn late in our stay, we were pleasantly stunned to see 15 Hungarian Partridges moving past our camper busily engaged in pecking for small seeds and insects. How close they were while we were in our "blind!" How intent they were at meeting their survival goals!

Selected for our Sense of Responsibility, Bar None Ranch, 1994

Except for Grave Point in 1991, which Jean had already experienced the previous year with her friend, CJ, we never knew before arrival what the physical appearance of each hack site would be, exactly which accouterments might prove valuable, what the access would be like, or even where to meet the Release Specialists in order to be led to the hack site. For The Peregrine Fund, the challenge was to select a meeting point that someone who had never been to the area before could confidently locate, and then to specify the meeting time. For several sites the local forest service public outreach office was a logical selection and easy to find. In 1996 our first meeting was at the headquarters of the National Bison Range near Dixon, Montana. For the Bar None Ranch in 1994 we met our Specialists at the Bunk House Bar and Grill in Toston, Montana.

We parked our pickup in front of the bar and at the appointed time the blue pickup truck of The Peregrine Fund pulled in beside ours. "Follow me!" The ranch foreman had unlocked the sturdy metal gate barring casual access to the large private ranch and we continued to follow on the now narrower gravel road onto the ranch yard. There we got out and met the friendly ranch foreman and his charming wife. After being shown the ranch buildings, where the freezer holding our quail would be located, where we could take showers in a small guest house converted from its origin as a country school house, where the foreman's and the owner's houses were, we drove out of the yard and learned the trail to our hack site. Just getting to the normally locked ranch gate on a gravel road had been breath-taking; it provided a terrific over-view of the Missouri River valley as well as the ranches, valleys, contours on either side of a high divide; this struck us a dangerous, precarious, and frightening road. Yet new, narrow, rural roads wending hillsides up and down often strike an unaccustomed driver that way; through continued usage those impressions fade to familiarity and comfort, at least in good weather. Yet this scary gravel road from the highway to the ranch provided easy transit compared to the rugged six-mile trail from the ranch buildings to the clifftop hack site.

This hack site trail started off easy enough as a firm, gravel-covered two-track, but then we turned onto an old railroad bed, long abandoned and no longer containing rails, with a rocky road bed that wound next to a small stream. The railroad bed was level enough, but in three places one had to carefully position the truck tires on one-foot wide boards that replaced the rails across railroad ties on the bridges spanning the stream. The route also went through two old tunnels cut through rock by hand, blasting dynamite, and steam powered machines. The tunnels looked solid enough until one thought of them having been constructed about a century ago. After two miles on the old rail bed we turned left and entered a rugged, tight little wooded canyon, twisting and turning with four-wheel drive engaged, visibility forward sometimes down to ten yards before the next sharp bend. Trees, brush, and branches scraped the sides of the truck as we tried to guess where the trail would turn next as it rose gradually up the valley for another two miles. Eventually we met another, intersecting trail that took us the final mile up, over, and down a high, semi-open ridge, and finally down into the valley base below the hack site cliff on the far side. Wow. That drive was a spooker! We always tried to imagine the site and the access before actually seeing it, but reality never matched the imagination. The roads were pleasantly dry and firm as we came to our new assignment that first day, but later in the season we would be returning down this same final slope, going very slowly and cautiously after a rain storm, when the clay gumbo soil of the ruts in the trail turned into the expected greasy slide and the wheels of the truck slid 20, 40, 60 feet at a time downhill while not rotating. Any turning of the steering wheel or braking of the wheels was futile and, in fact, dangerous. Fortunately, we were by that time prepared for the possibility and gritted our teeth and rode out the steady slip, assuming and hoping we would stop before leaving the road bed and tipping over.

On this, our first trip, we parked at the base of the hill, hopped out and began to survey the area for our preferred camp site. As we discussed the site, the views, where the hack box was located, where the best spot to observe the Peregrines would be, The Peregrine Fund Specialist told us we had been purposely selected for this site in order to repair a negative impression which had developed earlier and caused some concern from the ranch foreman and the ranch owner, and which The Peregrine Fund wanted us to correct. By this time The Peregrine Fund had evaluated our performance and reliability through working with us at four previous sites, and knew we could be the best answer to keeping relations in good stead with the sponsor of this remote ranch hack site. We felt honored to be so selected and worked earnestly to meet our employer's and hosts' expectations throughout the summer. We left the Bar None Ranch ten weeks later and the following year we learned from our boss at The Peregrine Fund that the ranch foreman had inspected our site after we left and was unable to find our latrine or any scrap of refuse, Jean having picked up even items as small as a bit of red thread that had unraveled from our clothing and having scattered the blackened stones from someone else's old campfire lit without permission. The matted-down tent site was already returning to normal. The ranch owner and foreman were well-pleased and we took it as the fine compliment it was intended to be, from ranchers who loved their land, to visitors who believed in living respectfully outdoors.

The Peregrine Fund personnel were back on site the second day with our falcons and they, and we, and the ranch foreman and his wife all gingerly stepped over the last crevasse before the cliff edge, to watch the falcons being installed in short order in their new home at the edge of the cliff. Our visitors left after a short and pleasant tailgate visit at their trucks and we began our summer duties.

*From the Journals: Bar None Ranch – Gary*
*15 July 1994 (the day after Installation) – A dewy but calm and sunny morning greeted us as we arose at 7:00 AM (0700), having slept in while we yet can with the falcons enclosed in their hack box. In the night we both heard the dreaded Great Horned Owl, nocturnal nemesis of young falcons. It is a sound we do not want to hear on a Peregrine site, unlike the pleasantness the hooting provides at our home in Wisconsin or in our memories of growing up on farms in Iowa. We hiked up to the hack box after rising, hardly an easy walk, but rather strenuous especially for flat-landers not yet used to the mountain elevations. Exciting views, however. Why not? It is a precipice and a cliff and they always offer grandeur. What kind? The best kind: vistas, elevation, valleys, a bull elk, finches, miles of trees and mountains and hills. And no dwellings or human structures. Very quiet here this morn. Bagels on the cliff, cereal here at camp, dishes done, we are pleasantly bushed and relaxing a bit before more tasks vital to a seven-week stay nursing young falcons through their flight training.*

*16 July 1994 – Wish I could feel a bit more relaxed and calm. But we are early in the understanding and comprehension of this site. It's all new and it is getting dark and it is getting late. We are in rattlesnake, lion and bear country where we will sleep with only a nylon cloth between us and them. Fear of the known, fear of the imaginable, one hardly knows which is worst. On the way back from the hack box, stumbling, weaving, a bit unstable, I am giddy and drunk on the rush of excitement,*

*the maybes, the hike, the potential, the mystery. Back at camp I*
*arrive before Jean returns from her walk and sit by the lean-to,*
*fresh drinking water near at hand, making notes, darkness*
*coming in as the sun sinks farther behind the cliff and shadows*
*race from the west to envelope camp in a darkening fold of the*
*night and I must not worry, not yet, about the arrival of Jean.*
*This calls for trust, letting the other partner gambol about in the*
*wilderness, wanting them to enrich themselves. But love and*
*fear of loss, their safety makes it hard. Ravens caw from the*
*north hills, swifts chitter in their rapid flight over the cliff, and*
*the wind rushes in a loud whisper through pine, fir, and the*
*thick lush grass of this ranch, tumbling down canyons and hills,*
*now loud, now soft, washing up the slopes, there to mix and*
*whirl as it makes its way across Montana, teasing with me a*
*moment in its journey.*

## Installation at Holter Lake, 1992

As mentioned in the Preview section, our first day of work at
Holter was very long and strenuous as we loaded our gear in a
boat, were delivered the length of the lake, moved all our gear
half a mile uphill to our selected campsite, and began to set up
camp. The falcons were delivered, also by boat, the very next
day and had to be carried in their transport boxes up to the hack
box on a cliff above the lake. A long piece of strapping was
woven in and out of the ventilation openings around each
transport box and tied into a loop that could be placed over one
shoulder and the box steadied with both hands as it rested
against the opposite hip. Jean was allowed to carry one box of
falcons, while the Specialist led the way carrying the other two
boxes. First we carried the falcons the half mile from the boat
landing to our camp and set them in the shade, while we went
back down to the boat to bring up the cooler with ice and quail,
five gallons of water, the scope, tripod, notebooks and the

checks for the first half of each of our grants. As soon as this was done, we picked up the Peregrine boxes and began the next stage of the hike, a mile from camp uphill to the hack box on the edge of a cliff. Gary brought cameras and notebook to record the installation, and our water bottles. It was a hot, sunny day and Jean got overheated on the hike, despite walking slowly to avoid jostling the falcons, and stopping to rest at intervals. The installation went smoothly, with Gary stationed on top of the hack box to take photos and operate the door for placement of each falcon. Jean held each falcon transport box, helped pull out a talon inserted by one of the falcons into the Specialist's hand, and tried to distract the most aggressive female. Our Specialist told us that the aggressive bird was the daughter of a wild bird captured in Texas, "The real thing," in his words.

On installation day, we were both still somewhat exhausted from strenuous efforts made to reach and set up camp the day before. Another reason for Jean's exhaustion, however, was that she was still recovering from an infected, poisonous bite inflicted by a spider at the beginning of our trip out to Montana that summer. The rest of this spider bite story will appear a little later in the book.

As exhaustion from those first two days at Holter faded, as the effects of the infected spider bite lessened and the wound healed, we gradually became used to the hikes required by the terrain and locations of this site. Our camp was three miles by hiking trail from our truck, so it would have been very demanding to backpack all of our water. The general recommended minimum of water needed is one gallon per person per day for cooking and drinking. From this quantity you might also be able to wash your hands, face and feet plus minimal dishes daily if you are very, very sparing in your use of water and if the weather is not too hot so that you have to drink more. Twice a week we hiked out to our truck, drove to town for laundry, mail, and phone calls to The Peregrine Fund and to family members. We also went to the BLM campground to fill our large five- or six-gallon water jugs and leave them with the BLM campground manager. Those jugs were brought in full the day we and our camp gear and supplies were delivered down the length of the lake to our campsite by boat, and the campground manager delivered them to us refilled again on four subsequent Mondays to keep us supplied with potable water during our seven week stay.

The only other site where we had to backpack our water supplies was Grave Point. There we brought the big water jugs we had filled during a town trip by pickup as far as the locked gate where we had to leave our vehicle. Returning from town, the most urgent supplies to be backpacked uphill the two-thirds mile to camp were the frozen quail, new-made ice for the coolers, and any fresh foods we had purchased. In the first load, the attendant who had made the town trip also brought up the new mail, and the clean laundry. That attendant then grabbed field notebook, binoculars, mail, and anything else of immediate need and went up to the O.P. to relieve the other attendant who had been on observation duty alone four hours or more. This attendant was only too glad of a chance to get up and move, to go down to camp and hang up laundry, and maybe make a trip down to the truck to bring up some water. At the Grave Point site we developed the habit of one or both of us hiking down to the truck most evenings to bring up water, often in half gallon jugs filled from the big five- and six-gallon jugs left in the truck, a new book to read, cans of food needed for the next couple menus and so on.

Regarding the Holter site, after completing our tasks in town and at the BLM campground each time, we drove back into the

Ox-Bow Ranch and stopped to get a several-days supply of quail and ice from the freezer kept for us in a ranch out-building. To avoid paying for ice twice a week on our hack site jobs, we filled plastic jugs with water and froze them in the quail freezer, having brought with us enough jugs to switch them out in this way twice a week. As the ice thawed in the quail cooler and our food cooler over the next few days, we poured the water into a bucket to use for washing. We could not bring ourselves to drink the melted ice water from those containers that had been in the freezer with dead quail! We then drove the truck to its parking spot on the ranch, as close as the terrain permitted to our camp, shouldered our packs loaded with quail, ice, clean but wet laundry, some fresh foods, a few canned goods from the stocks in the truck, mail, at least enough water for the hike, a new book to read from the box in the truck—quite a heavy load for each of us every time—and hiked back toward camp. This involved very careful packing, because most of the way back, one person put down their heavy backpack load in the shade off the trail and hiked up to the O.P. (a mile away from camp) to check on the falcons. The other person continued on to camp to put away fresh foods, quail, ice, etc. and to hang up the laundry.

Why did not we dry the laundry in town to save weight for the hike back to camp, you wonder? All of this took time, time away from observing and protecting the falcons. In very few of our locations could town trips be accomplished in less than four hours. At most of our hack sites, the town trips twice a week were made solo, with the other attendant staying on duty with the falcons. However, at Holter we had seen several snakes in the first three days, two of them rattlers, so we decided it was unsafe to make the three-mile hike to the truck alone, be gone for hours, then hike the three miles back to camp all while the person on duty was alone, as was the one making the two long hikes and town trip. If either of us was bit by a rattler or got into some other trouble during these long periods alone, it would be a very long time before it was discovered and help could be obtained. Besides, it took both of us to carry everything out (refuse, dirty laundry, containers to refill for water supplies and other containers to fill and put into the freezer to make ice for the camp coolers, letters to mail, books we had finished reading, and so on), and likewise to carry everything we needed back in from the truck to camp.

Such distances at Holter, and the serious elevation changes there, required extra planning and unusual arrangements. During the first week we hiked together the mile uphill to the hack box to drop quail in through the chute each morning, stayed to observe the falcons to make sure they were doing okay, and to record our observations in the notebooks provided to Hack Site Attendants at each site. We took turns taking quail up to the falcons after the first week; once the falcons had been released it was important to have one person at the observation point early each day to observe the falcons, so we traded off between these two duties. While one of us went up to put out quail, the other heated water to fill our thermos jugs, and set off to hike a mile via a different trail to the selected observation point below the hack box cliff, but still uphill from camp. This observer would set up a camp chair and the scope and tripod and begin taking notes. The attendant who had taken quail up to the hack box, would return to camp to gather up whatever was needed for a day spent observing, and hike up to join the partner already on observation duty. At the end of the day, one person headed back to camp first to start making supper. The other watched falcons another half hour or so, then hiked back to camp to eat, making sure to arrive back in daylight so as to watch out for snakes during the hike. Having seen rattlers so soon after arriving at Holter Lake, we had purchased a second snake bite kit and one snake stick (mop handle) in Helena, and subsequently cut some branches to de-bark and carve so that we each had a long stick (and a couple spares) to use to beat the long grasses ahead of us while doing all this hiking. We made it a very firm rule never to hike without a day pack containing a few necessities such as water and a snake bite kit, and also to carry a snake stick to sweep through the grasses ahead of us.

Thus, on a non-town day the person who went up to put out quail would have hiked two miles for that duty and two more miles going to and from the observation point (O.P.)—a four-mile day. The person whose turn it was to "open observations" that morning would have hiked a two-mile day. On town days there was much more hiking: the person whose turn it was to "feed," i.e. put out quail, would hike two miles to and from the hack box plus a mile to the O.P. (which was actually more-or-less on the way toward our truck's parking spot), plus two more miles to the truck, then three miles back to camp for an eight-mile day, while the other person, not having gone up to the hack box, had a six-mile day. Trips to town were made twice a week, usually on Mondays and Thursdays, so adding up the miles we hiked in a week gives a total of 28 miles for the person who started the week by opening observations on Sunday morning, and 30 miles for the person who started the week by hiking up to the hack box to put out quail for the falcons on Sunday morning. Because we traded off the duties each day, the following week the person who hiked 28 miles the previous week would have to hike 30 miles in the new week and vice versa. We were at this site seven weeks so you can do the math and see for yourself that the job total was more than 200 miles for each of us. However, we also took hikes for personal pleasure; some evenings Gary hiked down to the edge of the lake to try fishing, Jean took hikes to look for more species of birds to add to the site list, and together we made several hikes at the beginning and end of our time there to explore the area scenery.

Because Holter was our second location, Jean's third hack site job and Gary's second, we were already coming up with ideas to help make our working and living conditions easier. One such innovation involved having a box custom-made for us of galvanized sheet metal, with a rain-proof lid that could be locked, and this box (15 inches high, 30 inches long, and 20 inches wide) proved especially useful at Holter. The two-wheeled hand-cart (affectionately called the mule) that Gary made for our 1991 Grave Point job proved useful again at Holter for towing jugs of water, weighing 40-48 pounds each, the half mile uphill to camp from Gull Landing, where the jugs had been delivered to us by boat, and we also used the hand-cart to laboriously tow the metal box up to the observation point (O.P.), the last 100 yards being steeply uphill on ground covered by drying grasses that made the slope treacherously slippery underfoot. We used this box at the O.P. to store our scopes and tripods overnight, along with a one-burner camp stove, one-pound propane fuel cylinders, any jugs still containing water at the end of the day, and a few other items so that we did not have to carry so much back and forth from camp every day. Often, we cooked breakfast at the observation point, and ate lunch there as well. We also left our camp chairs at the O.P., hanging them on tree branches overnight. Since that observation point was so far from camp, we also set up a very small backpacking tent nearby for shelter in a fast moving storm—there was very little even semi-level ground in the immediate area so this tent was actually set up on a game trail.

Another problem with the distances between hack box, camp and observation point at Holter was the need for more than one latrine. The ground at Holter was hard, dry and rocky; the pickax we brought from home was essential for digging a major latrine near camp and another up on the hillside near the O.P. Fortunately, during the first week while we were taking turns digging to make these large pits, it rained a couple times, softening the soil in the interim bottom of the holes each time. Until the latrines were ready we had to dig and use small "cat holes" as needed and this meant carrying a small trowel and a supply of tissue among the other crucial supplies in our daypacks. Latrines, though very necessary, were not our favorite camp facility; however, you learned to live with them. If you cannot bear to dig and use an outdoor latrine for multiple weeks, you should not be doing this type of fieldwork. And we wanted this type of outdoor work—for all the joys, enrichment, and challenges it offered.

*Phase One, Personal Stories:  Figures 11 and 12*

*Figure 11: Young Peregrine in transport box*

*Figure 12: Specialist transferring Peregrine to hack box*

## C. PERSONAL STORIES

### How we found The Peregrine Fund and hack site jobs

When we began talking about doing fieldwork, having adventures, making a difference with some kind of outdoor, environmental work, the first issue was—did we really want to do this? After that question was discussed and our intentions were clear and agreed, we had next to find suitable jobs. Jean asked a colleague at UW-La Crosse for advice, and was handed a copy of the *Ornithological Newsletter*, which in those years included a long listing of field jobs in its monthly issues in the early part of each year. This is where she first learned of the Hack Site Attendant grants offered by The Peregrine Fund. Having cousins in the Boise, Idaho, area, Jean planned a trip in summer, 1989, to visit them, and one cousin took her to visit the World Center for Birds of Prey facilities in the hills above Boise. After a tour of the Center, Jean asked for an application for a Hack Site Attendant job. The receptionist at the Center said that Bill Heinrich, Operations Manager, was in and asked if Jean would like to meet him. And so it began—Bill said all their positions were filled for that summer, Jean explained she wanted to apply for the next year, and Bill gave her an application form.

In 1990, our first year of fieldwork, Jean applied for a Hack Site Attendant job on her own. Knowing she would have to have a partner, she asked a birding friend to consider applying for the job as well. Jean had met CJ on a birding tour five years earlier and they had subsequently become friends. CJ already had some fieldwork experience, both women were experienced birders and campers, both had master's degrees and both were accepted as Hack Site Attendants for 1990. Their first assignment was to the Grave Point site in Idaho, thus Jean was familiar with conditions at this site before she and Gary worked their first hack site together there. CJ and Jean had very good experiences at Grave Point in 1990 and Jean wanted Gary to experience it too, so we requested the same site in 1991.

During the summer of 1990, while Jean would be having her first experiences as a Hack Site Attendant, Gary wanted a similar outdoor adventure, but he was reluctant to apply to The Peregrine Fund lest his lack of background in biology would affect acceptance of Jean's application. Accordingly, Gary found Boundary Waters Canoe Area Wilderness job openings, and applied to be a member of a crew that would travel a portion of the BWCAW during the summer of 1990, repairing portage trails, planting trees, improving campsites, and completing other such tasks. Gary's BWCAW adventures—and there were many—must wait to be told elsewhere.

## Physical Conditioning

Each summer as we arrived at our assigned hack site, we found that, however fit we might have thought we were back home in Wisconsin at our home elevation of 810 feet, we were in need of a couple weeks of acclimation to the higher altitude of a hack site, to the strenuous activity usually required of Hack Site Attendants, and to the unevenness of the terrain. In our teaching and engineering jobs, and life in a house, we mostly walked on streets and floors that were smooth and had little incline. Thus each summer, we had to improve our balance and sure-footedness over rough, rocky ground and our fitness for long hikes and steep slopes. Although Holter Lake in Montana was toward the low end of the 3,060-7,600-foot altitude range of our eight different hack sites, this site involved by far the most hiking. Fortunately for our sense of competence, the Release Specialists, all younger than we were, told us they too had to suffer through a period of gaining strength and stamina at the beginning of each new season. As one of them told us, the

Specialists had a term for this: "Pain is good," which they said to each other each year when they began a new reintroduction season.

*From the Journals: Grave Point – Jean*
*30 June 1990 – We find ourselves becoming less clumsy, more balanced as we gain experience in maintaining our footing on rocky, sloping terrain. I feel my muscles, heart and lungs coming into condition with all this uphill and downhill walking and am surprised to feel pleasure in using my body as it comes into fitness, a kind of "body joy."*

*From the Journals: Grave Point – Jean*
*27 July 1991 – Gary has gone down to camp for his weight-lifting exercises. He is very diligent about this. I, by contrast, am very lax, but my legs and lungs are strong from hiking the hills and backpacking loads uphill from the gate nearly every evening and uphill to the O.P.*

Spider Bite

Above we have referred to an infected spider bite Jean was treating at the start of our Holter Lake hack site in 1992. That June we had used the trip out to our hack site as an opportunity to make some visits, leaving home on a Tuesday and staying that first night with friends, visiting our daughter, Gayle, and son-in-law, Dean, for a few hours the next day, and spending the second night at the home of Jean's parents—all three locations in Iowa.

Jean must have encountered that spider somewhere in Iowa, because by the time we entered South Dakota on Thursday morning, the painful bite, located on the lower part of one breast, was already a dark red, raised area the size of a quarter, surrounded by a whitish ring, which Jean thought of as the white blood cell battlefront, and with a red, flushed area outside that. The eventual total area of the infection formed an oval about four inches long and three inches across. Thursday night we camped at the eastern base of the Big Horn Mountains and planned to spend the next day in the mountains and to camp there Friday night. However, Friday it was cold and snowing in the mountains, and Jean was becoming more and more ill and uncomfortable (apparently the white blood cell war wasn't going so well) so we went down the west side to camp at a lower, warmer altitude. By that evening the center of the bite area had developed small white blisters and several black spots. Because the topper-covered pickup box was largely filled with our gear and supplies for the summer, only Gary could sleep in the back with his "bed" made across a row of the large plastic storage tubs, and Jean slept in the truck cab on the bench seat. In these circumstances, neither of us wanted to take the trouble to dig a tent, mattress pads, and all that out of the truck, hence this plan of sleeping arrangements. Since she is a tall woman, that truck seat would have been less than comfortable at the best of times, but with a painful bite, and with a fever developing from the infection by Friday night, it was a miserable situation.

Saturday morning we sought help for those white blood cells and found it at the Southern Bighorn County Hospital, where a nurse in the Emergency department took a look at the bite and asked the Physician's Assistant on call to come in. He was very kind and thorough, giving Jean a confident diagnosis, an antibiotic injection, a prescription for a painkiller/anti-inflammatory medication, and another prescription for an additional antibiotic in pill form. He also gave Jean careful instructions on care of the bite area, required us to wait 20 minutes to make sure she did not have a reaction to the shot, and, after hearing we were headed to a job in the wilderness north of Helena for the summer starting Tuesday, he insisted that Jean see another doctor for a follow-up on Monday. We filled the prescriptions in Greybull, Wyoming, purchased sterile cotton balls and anti-bacterial soap for wound care, and then found a campground. It was necessary to boil water on the camp-stove for use in the wound care processes, and that night Jean continued to suffer pain at the bite area as well as the aches, chills and hot spells that go with fever. The next day we drove on to get closer to where we would be working, and camped again, keeping up with the medications and wound care. By Sunday night, Jean was feeling noticeably better and the fever was down. Nevertheless, being concerned about dealing with this health problem at a wilderness camp located a three-mile hike away from our truck, we were determined to follow the advice of the Wyoming Physician's Assistant, and consult another doctor before going to our hack site.

Monday we arrived in Helena, Montana, and began a search for a physician to check Jean's recovery progress. The first clinic we tried was housed in a very nice building, but the receptionist insisted they had no appointment openings that morning, and she mentioned money three or four times in the first two minutes and made it obvious she wanted to save the single late afternoon opening they had for their own patients. She suggested another clinic, looked up the phone number for us, and waved us toward a phone booth in the clinic entry. On the phone the second clinic was equally clear that we were unwelcome, and when Jean asked what a visitor in town with an immediate health issue was supposed to do, that receptionist replied, "I don't know." Though a state capital, Helena then had no walk-in clinic. By that point Jean was despairing, so Gary took the phone book and began making more calls.

At a clinic with two dermatologists, there had been a cancelation and the time slot was given to Jean; when we got there, we found a muted statement about payment posted on the reception desk and no other mention of money. The doctor and nurse that saw Jean were very concerned and kind, both saying on sight of the wound, "Oh! That is bad." The doctor took a skin scraping in the wound area and checked it under the microscope for viral damage to the dead cells (negative), gave Jean a ten-day extension of the oral antibiotic in case it should be needed, and more instructions about wound care and possible problems to watch for while on such a lengthy regimen of powerful antibiotics. The doctor made an attempt to know Jean to judge her ability to recognize problems, to follow instructions and care for the wound. He urged her to return if needed, said the Wyoming Physician's Assistant had done a good job of diagnosis and treatment, and promised to write him of Jean's visit to the Helena dermatology clinic and her status toward recovery. The nurse and receptionist at this clinic were caring, yet efficient, and we paid for the office visit from our cash supply. By this time a large white blister, which had formed over the bite area as the numerous smaller blisters coalesced, had burst to reveal a quarter-sized black circle of dead tissue underneath, so we were very glad to have been able to have this second doctor check it. Fortunately, by the following Friday, when we returned to Helena and filled the prescription for an extension of antibiotic treatment (and stood around waiting while that pharmacy insisted on calling our home clinic to check on our health insurance), healing was obviously underway, Jean was feeling much better, and in time only a scar and our journal notes and memories would be left as reminders of this adventure.

*From the Journals: Holter Lake – Jean*
*11 June 1992 – Our 27th Anniversary and Gary actually packed along a gift for me and a star map we could both enjoy while we are living in a place with very little light pollution. He baked a blueberry muffin mix in the BakePacker™ for breakfast—it was wonderful! As we had been doing each morning, we cleaned and inspected the bite-wound (I use a small mirror to try to examine the awkward location of the bite but also rely on Gary's description and opinion). With each day we are heartened by the healing progress. It usually looks worse in the evening because of the sweating I do during the day, keeping the area at the lower edge of the breast too moist. There is now an area five-eighths by one-half inch of necrosis (tissue death). The center of this blackened area is now scabbed, a good sign, but the scab is surrounded by a ring of yellow puss, then a half-inch red ring. The rest of the infected area, however, is returning to normal color but peeling as skin does after a sunburn.*

In gratitude to the Helena dermatologist for his concern and care, Jean sent two postcards to him. The first postcard told of continued improvement in the spider bite, but also included information about our Peregrine work; the second postcard informed him of our move to serve another hack site for the second half of that summer. Both times, the dermatologist replied by letter expressing his appreciation for Jean's positive comments about his care and his staff, and indicating interest in Peregrine Falcon reintroduction and our work.

*Phase Two, Post-installation: Figures 13 and 14*

*Figure 13: View into hack box through peephole*

*Figure 14: Jean observes Peregrines in hack box*

# PHASE TWO – POST INSTALLATION: week one

## A. INTRODUCTION TO THE POST-INSTALLATION PERIOD: care during week one

For each hack site, the Release Specialists not only delivered the young Peregrines, but at the same time, brought a supply of food to sustain these falcons wholly during their first acclimation week in the hack box and during their first days after release. The food supply also had to support the falcons at least partially for some weeks after release as they gained experience of flight and learned to hunt for themselves. This food supply consisted of Coturnix Quail, a domesticated species, whose small size was just right as a Peregrine meal. These quail were mainly raised at the facility outside Boise, in numbers averaging nearly 100,000 quail per year during the years when we were involved. To achieve this, about one thousand breeding females, mated by more than 300 males, produced about 100,000-200,000 eggs annually. The eggs hatched at rates varying between 62-72%, and the young were cared for so well that survivability was nearly always at 90%. Imagine the labor and facilities involved! The food production personnel also raised lesser numbers of chickens and mice at the World Center for Birds of Prey, mostly to feed other species of raptors being bred for release, although chickens were also used to supplement the winter diet of the captive breeding population of adult Peregrines there at Boise.

The quail supply for each hack site was delivered frozen, pre-packed inside a small five-cubic foot chest freezer, the freezer in each instance being placed somewhere in the vicinity of the hack site where there was a reliable source of electricity. It was part of the Hack Site Attendants' job to travel from the hack site to the freezer's location twice a week to pick up a supply of frozen quail and ice to keep those quail fresh in the large, portable insulated cooler supplied by The Peregrine Fund. Each day at the site, it was necessary to thaw a suitable number of quail before taking them to the hack box for the falcons.

When the Release Specialists arrived at a site on installation day, their first responsibility was to take care of the falcons. During the process of installation, and especially for a few hours afterward, these experts also spent some time with us if their taxing schedule of attending to other hack sites in the eight states of the northern Rockies and Pacific Northwest permitted. It was during this time that they tried to get to know Hack Site Attendants and make a judgment on our competency and dedication, if the individual Specialist had not met us before. This was also our opportunity to get to know them, to ask questions and gather information about our duties, and details about the particular site we were then working. These conversations were always very interesting and valuable to us.

During the period when the young falcons were confined to the hack box and observing their new surroundings through the barred front, it was the task of the Hack Site Attendants to feed them, observe them, to take notes and watch for problems. In order to prevent the falcons from associating their supply of food with humans, the hack boxes were equipped with a food chute of PVC pipe installed through the roof with a screw-threaded cap. When attendants opened the food chute cap sticking up above the hack box roof and dropped quail down the pipe, a baffle inside the box blocked the falcons from seeing the hands that fed them, and deflected the quail to land against the back wall of the hack box. We used the two or more small peepholes drilled into the walls of the hack box to observe the falcons, and always approached the hack box from the back or side, where the falcons could not see us.

Many birds, especially seed-eaters, but also including vultures, and diurnal raptors such as Peregrines, have a crop as part of their digestive tract. The crop is an enlargement of the esophagus located at the base of the neck just before the esophagus enters into the body cavity to deliver food to the stomach. Incidentally, birds have two-chambered stomachs; the first chamber, called the proventriculus, is glandular and produces acidic gastric juices and digestive enzymes for softening the food and aiding its breakdown into nutrients, while the second chamber, the gizzard, is muscular to grind and mix the food as it is digested. The gizzard also contains stones ingested by the bird, which help in this grinding process since birds lack teeth for chewing their food. Food eaten by birds with crops travels down the esophagus to the crop and is held there to begin being softened, until the stomach is ready to receive it. The obvious advantage of having a crop is that when a bird finds a good source of food, it can eat quickly to fill the crop and spend less time in the open and vulnerable to predators. When a bird's crop is full, it shows as a bulge in the lower neck area, and as Hack Site Attendants we made use of this fact to tell whether a falcon had recently eaten. Looking through the peepholes, we tried to observe each falcon eating, or at least note whether its crop was distended. We could count and make note of the number of quail remaining from the previous day's feeding before we dropped a new batch down the food chute. We also noted whether each bird seemed healthy, alert and active.

During this period while the falcons were confined in the hack box, we could spend time becoming familiar with the area around the hack site, take note of and report any potential problems. We were provided with a phone card and were expected to call the office in Boise during office hours twice a week to make a general report on the falcons and ourselves. In case a problem developed outside office hours, we were also given emergency phone numbers.

## B. POST-INSTALLATION STORIES

<u>Salads by Release Specialists</u>

One characteristic common among the Release Specialists we met during the summers of our Peregrine work was that they would not eat with us, even when we offered to share our supper when they arrived the evening before a release and camped nearby, or wanted to give them a piece of fresh coffeecake to go with their coffee the next morning. Eventually it became obvious to us this was part of their code or list of rules for how to interact with Hack Site Attendants they were supervising: "Do not eat Hack Site Attendants' food." We sometimes joked that we never actually saw one of these individuals eat anything. In fact, when we met our Specialist and the various members of the sponsoring agencies at the beginning of each season, we were usually asked if they could bring us anything special to eat. Based on the acknowledgment sections of the reports of other Hack Site Attendants, as published in The Peregrine Fund's annual *Operation Report*, we have read that a variety of treats such as pizza, cookies, beer, BBQ, wine, fruit, salmon and even the highly improbable ice cream were provided by Specialists, site sponsors and others determined to help attendants endure their sometimes trying living conditions. Our cravings were for fresh foods, and at Grave Point in 1991 we requested salad when this offer was made. When our Specialist arrived the night before the release, he asked to use Jean's largest cook-kit kettle. The next day he returned the kettle filled with a very large, artfully arranged salad to last several meals, and our first taste of a salad dressing made in Sand Point, Idaho. The next year this seemed to have become a competition as a different Specialist created his own version of a Specialist Salad for us.

## Gnat Problem, Green River, 1993

After installation, the Peregrines were confined to the hack box for a period of about five days to one week to acclimate to the site and finish their pre-fledging growth. This was convenient for us as attendants because it meant there would be time to attend to any remaining camp set-up tasks and allow more freedom in our daily activity than would be possible after the falcons were released. Our duties with the falcons during this period were only to feed them once a day, to observe them and their condition through the observation holes drilled in the box, to record these observations and call in reports. While enclosed in the hack box during this period, the falcons were protected from mammalian and avian predators, but tiny predators—black flies or gnats—could easily get through the wire mesh and steel bars on the front of the box and attack our birds. And in their confinement the falcons would be unable to escape.

We were familiar with this problem because for 20 years we had raised chickens on our farm in Wisconsin. Usually hatching and growing conditions for gnat populations peaked at least once each spring and we would then note some or all of our chickens cowering on the floor in a corner of the chicken house or clustered in groups attempting to deal with these biting, blood-thirsty little villains. The chickens tried to shelter their bodies away from a relentless attack by huddling together or sometimes by taking a dust bath in a depression in the ground. Our chickens would peck at and devour a few of the gnats, either off themselves or off others, but there could be literally hundreds of gnats attacking each chicken. If the gnats were numerous enough, death of a chicken could occur either through direct blood and body fluid loss or through being crushed or asphyxiated in their weakness by fellow huddling chickens attempting to shelter their own bodies. Most years all our chickens survived and the gnat population diminished to minimal numbers in a few weeks, but some years one or several chickens died during the worst onslaught. The seasonality and site variation of Peregrine installation meant some falcons could potentially encounter similar problems with gnats. By 1993, in our work with The Peregrine Fund we had seen gnats (also called black flies) hovering in the hack box at several sites prior to the falcons' release from the box when they could then escape the gnats on their own. But the density of gnats had not risen to the severe level at any site until one morning at Green River, when we looked inside the box through the peep holes and noticed our Peregrines were at risk. Gnat numbers had jumped from merely a few to many dozens seemingly overnight and we knew additional attention and action was necessary. A very serious consequence of a severe gnat infestation while the falcons were trapped in the hack box is that they would associate their misery with the location, and bolt off into the distance upon release and never come back to this, their source of food while they gained flying and hunting experience.

Fortunately, our Release Specialist knew from his experience that the willows and riverine setting surrounding our tower at Green River might result in a gnat problem for our Peregrines. Just in that case, he had left us with tightly-woven, mesh screening material to cover the front of the box and a staple gun to secure it in order to exclude the continued access of many gnats from our falcons. We paddled back across the Green River, got the screening and needed mounting supplies and tools from our camper and returned to the tower to cover the front of the hack box with it. Hoping anxiously for success, and having called in our actions to The Peregrine Fund from the ranch telephone, we were greatly relieved to learn after further checks and observation that our application of the screening was keeping the gnat numbers low inside the hack box. Released several days later, none of our falcons suffered the same end fate some of our chickens had, nor did they need fear returning to the box for food. This is one of several reasons why, even though the falcons were still confined, they had to be watched carefully and sometimes corrective action was needed from responsible on-site attendants, and why attendants needed to be able to get advice from Peregrine Fund personnel.

## Setting up Camps and Observation Positions

Of the eight hack sites to which we were assigned, three were inaccessible to any type of a camping trailer and at those three sites we spent each seven to ten week assignment camping in tents and under tarps or lean-tos. At only one of three tent sites could the observation position/observation point (O.P.) be near our camp; at the other two tent sites, the O.P. was at some distance from camp. But at five sites, even though we might be sleeping in a camping trailer, we still had observation points, either near-by (two sites) or rather remote from our camp (three sites), at which we spent most of our daylight hours. During daytime observation hours we needed to be prepared to continue observing regardless of most weather conditions. It was only quite infrequently that the weather was so bad that we literally could not see the falcons, such as during drenching downpours, thunderstorms or thick fog; on those few occasions we were not engaged in observing or serving the needs of our Peregrines, and instead sought whatever shelter we were camped in. During those times, the falcons would not be flying and we could count on them being relatively immobile, whether they were perched on a tree limb or whether they were in or near the hack box.

Never knowing the exact site terrain or conditions of a new hack site assignment until we got there, we always left Wisconsin as prepared as experience and imagination could make us to establish a comfortable and dry camp. The only thing we knew before we left home about the camp conditions at our next site was whether a trailer could be used at the site or if the site would require tent camping. Each summer we brought our favorite 9x12 green nylon tarp and two of the cheaper and more common blue plastic tarps, six sleeved tent poles of adjustable height, and four to six three-quarters to one inch diameter steel conduit poles eight to ten feet long, about 30 stout plastic tent stakes, about 30 pieces of one-quarter inch nylon rope in lengths of eight to twelve feet, and many shorter hanks of rope to secure the tarps to a frame made onsite out of the poles. For those three sites where we would have to set up a tent camp, we brought an eight by ten four-person tent to sleep in as well as one or two smaller two-person tents to be used as auxiliary gear storage or as shelter at the observation position. As we gained site experience we added a lean-to type tarp incorporating side walls which helped to minimize crosswinds while we cooked. This combination of tents, tarps and poles allowed us to set up a remote campsite in nearly any locale we might be sent to, which would meet adequately our living needs, and give shade and some shelter over our main observation point or a remote auxiliary observation point.

There were five primary questions when we arrived at each hack site and each answer was selected in consideration of the remaining questions, so that all aspects of our life on site would work well together: 1) What access will we use to get to the hack box? 2) What is the preferred observation point for viewing falcons when they are at and around the hack box? 3) What access will we use to get to our truck? 4) Where shall we establish our main camp site? 5) Where shall we position the main campsite latrine? On most sites these decisions were made within the first several hours of arriving. However, due to set-up time, often the creation of a long-serving campsite would take place over several days of our first week. And a few times, we moved either the sleeping tent after the first night or changed the location of an observation point because the first choice of location was not as suitable as originally thought. Once we even moved a camper into a more-shaded position so our cooler ice supplies would last longer.

Our tarps and poles were selected with versatility in mind in order to be able to construct onsite the exact shelters we needed. Grave Point was high on a mountain and weather in 1991 proved it could be a particularly cold, windy, rainy site. Our cooking area was under a tarp which overlapped our tent and created a corner to shelter us from the winds and rain. We extended two windward edges down low to the ground to sweep the moving air up and over us while we cooked and ate.

*From the Journals: Grave Point – Jean*
*24 July 1991 – Cumulous clouds began to build up and thunder could be heard in the east. One thunderstorm went through Hells Canyon. As the next one lined up on us, we packed our optics and came down to camp about 5:30 PM. While we prepared and ate supper under the kitchen tarps, it began to pour! We had heavy rain for an hour and camp flooding problems.*

*25 July 1991 – It rained hard again in the evening and we re-dug our trench system that deflects run-off around and away from our tent and camp kitchen area, then put in a second trench. It is not nice to have water run under the tent wetting the floor nylon and wicking up into sleeping bags and air*

*mattress covers. Next year we're going to bring a sheet of*
*plastic to line the floor of the tent.*

Our observation site at CSKT Tower was a tarp mounted within a frame of four strong conduit tubes and held six feet high in the air on four more poles to protect us from the sun and allow free air movement around us as we sat in the shade beneath it. There, our sunniest site, we saw daily temperatures in the 80's and 90's and one day it was 102 degrees. At Holter Lake we mounted a tarp several inches over our sleeping tent to keep the tent from getting so hot inside during the day and to prolong the life of the tent fabric from the ultraviolet rays of the sun. Easier and cheaper to replace the tarp than the whole tent. At the Bar None Ranch we used the lean-to as a camp kitchen and set up a shaded observation area nearby. If one had shade from an overhead tarp, one also had shelter to stay dry under during those quick mountain showers or multiple-hour slow rains or drizzles, conditions through which our falcons could still fly. At each tent site we set up a small two-person tent nearby to use as a storage tent to hold our tripods, scopes, binoculars, extra food, clothes tubs, unread books and backpacks thereby saving room in the sleeping tent for sleeping, evening lounging, or space to change clothes when we got rained on. At Holter Lake we also set up small two-person backpacking tent to use as emergency rain shelter because our O.P. was a one-mile walk away from our sleeping tent. The observation tarps and camp kitchen tarps were held taut by the long anchoring ropes affixed to multiple tent stakes. There could easily be 16 guy-lines coming out from each observation tarp or camp kitchen we set up in order to keep the assemblage rigid and tied down in heavy rains, high wind, or hail. One had to memorize where these guy lines were in order not to stumble over them in the night. Three of our main tent poles were bent in a high wind our first night at Holter and thereafter we always doubled the four main poles supporting each tent. Windy nights could cause other problems too.

*From the Journals: Holter Lake – Jean*
*23 June 1992 – Around midnight we were wakened by tarp flapping noises. I looked out—stars were visible. We had over an hour of severe winds and were unable to sleep for the noise and worry that our camp would be flat by morning and all our gear destroyed or blown away. In fact, a lot of lines were loosened, a few small things moved about and one tarp grommet badly torn—we will have to fix it with the pebble method. Finally the wind quieted and we went back to sleep. Weird country!*

*24 June 1992 – The loss of sleep last night was the last straw so I found a site for the backpacking tent (really just an old cattle trail contouring the steep hillside, we think) and we leveled it, dug out rocks and built them into a wall on the downhill side, filled and padded the low side with Douglas fir needle duff, and broke away a couple tree branches. It's a site that will have shade all but early morning. We let the soil dry awhile and Gary picked dry grass for a mat. Later we set up the old backpacking tent and I took an hour-long nap in it in the afternoon. It was great!*

At none of our sites did we ever have a campfire (too much bother, too much time and effort, some sites were very dry at times and we did not want the slightest risk of starting a range or forest fire) and in none of our tents did we ever have a propane tent heater. We became very adept at adding and removing layers to match the temperature encountered with our output of energy. During a vigorous hike to the hack box one might be comfortable in only a couple layers because of the exercise, but afterwards numerous layers had to be added in order to sit still and observe while it might be only 40-50 degrees on a cloudy, windy day. Wind resistant nylon outer layers were important as well as insulating layers of polyester fleece underneath. And at the end of the day, if one still carried a chill from a cold day outdoors, the goose down or poly-filled sleeping bags were a toasty place to return for night-long warmth and comfort while sleeping on self-inflating air mattresses.

Visitors

The different hack sites we worked in summers during the early 1990s varied in their accessibility to the public, and therefore were highly variable in terms of the number of visitors we received. At every site, we had official visitors from The Peregrine Fund and the sponsoring agencies, more in some locations than in others. The number of official visitors depended on whether a particular site was new, in which case agency representatives tended to come more often to make sure things were going well and to obtain photos and information to use in their reports and publicity announcements. Another factor in the number of official visitors was whether the falcons or attendants experienced problems during the sequence of stages of the reintroduction process. Stories of problems that occurred at our hack sites and the visits to provide advice and assistance are scattered throughout this book. We were always glad to have these agency and Peregrine Fund personnel come to our hack sites, because they could give us advice, and often told us fascinating stories as well. Sometimes they even brought treats.

On one of her routine calls to Boise in 1990, Jean was informed that in two days she and CJ would be hosting a group of volunteers who helped educate people coming to the World Center for Birds of Prey by giving tours of that facility and answering questions. This field trip to visit a hack site was organized by the Center's Education Director with the intent to help these volunteers understand more about the hacking process and the job of Hack Site Attendants. The group of five drove up from Boise the night before, stayed over in a motel in the valley below, arrived in our camp at 10:00 AM and spent six hours with us. We were a bit chagrinned at this prospect and Jean made a strong point of the fact that we would not be able to spare water for visitors. (At this site we were backpacking or hand-carrying all our water uphill from our trucks parked a distance of two-thirds mile from camp.) We felt pressured to make sure our camp was presentable, and ourselves cleaner than was usually reasonable on the job. Typically we each only took our limited-water showers the day before we were to make a town trip, and the rest of the time just used small quantities (one cup or less) of water to wash our feet before crawling into our tents at night or to sponge-bathe other limited areas. For these purposes we used melt-water from our ice containers.

When members of the general public happened by, it was part of our job to ensure that the falcons were not disturbed or endangered by the presence of visitors. We were also encouraged to use such opportunities to educate visitors, to explain what we were doing there and why our work for Peregrines was necessary and important. Often this was fun, sometimes it approached nuisance level, and a few times we encountered some belligerence to our presence or the reintroduction project. Our lowest number of "public" visitors (4) was in 1994 at the private ranch with its locked gate—the only "public" visitors in that case were visiting family members of the ranch foreman's wife. The site with the highest number of visitors (65) was CSKT Tower in 1992; this tower was out in the open in a flat valley surrounded by ranchlands with gravel roads going by on two sides. Seeing the camping trailer and our pickup parked in a grassy field, quite often vehicles turned in at the field entrance, and people got out of their vehicles to ask questions. At Wood Lake (1995) we were camped in a US Forest Service campground, and often had members of the public as neighboring campers. We were in fact mistakenly assumed to be Campground Hosts until we posted a sign in our camper window denying this and stating that we were working on a wildlife project there for the summer. We did have questions about the falcons at this and other sites, and sometimes could give members of the public a look at the young falcons through our spotting scope while we explained our jobs for the summer. The sign we crafted read:

USFS
WILDLIFE
PROJECT
VOLUNTEERS

Besides the general categories of visitors—official and curious members of the public—a number of unusual visitors made special impressions on us. At Grave Point in 1991, Vern and Rowdy were examples of the unusual. Vern was a retired local resident who liked to hike up to 15 miles in a day for the fun of it and to search for elk antlers. Vern's big dog, Rowdy, was his hiking companion and a very well-behaved visitor despite his size and name. We really enjoyed this visit, but when, a year later, we read The Peregrine Fund's *Operation Report* for 1992, we discovered that the very next year after our service there, the attendants at Grave Point had even more unusual visitors—two naked Canadians came hiking right up to their campsite!

*From the Journals: Grave Point – Jean*
*9 July 1991 – Just after Gary went down to camp I heard voices and started stripping off extra layers of clothing, especially the*

*nylon windbreaker, in order to hear better. There are people on the tower! I yelled, but though Gary heard me in camp, they on the tower did not. I began climbing straight up the hill toward the tower as quickly as I could, yelling each time I stopped for breath, but the woman on the tower did not hear me until I reached the two-track tower access road. I asked the couple to please come down and away from the tower as quickly as possible, explaining as we went, mostly after I caught my breath and we got halfway back toward camp. They were <u>told</u> to come here, especially for the view and the Peregrine project by the hosts at a campground in the area! And so they ignored the sign on the gate identifying this area and the tower access road as a closed area! We've decided to also put a sign on our camp, since the gate sign alone doesn't work.*

During the next town trip two days later, Jean reported this problem at the Slate Creek Ranger Station and one of the biologists there made two phone calls to explain that campers and others should <u>not</u> be encouraged to visit the tower during the weeks Peregrine reintroduction was in progress there.

*Phase Two, Personal Stories: Figures 15 and 16*

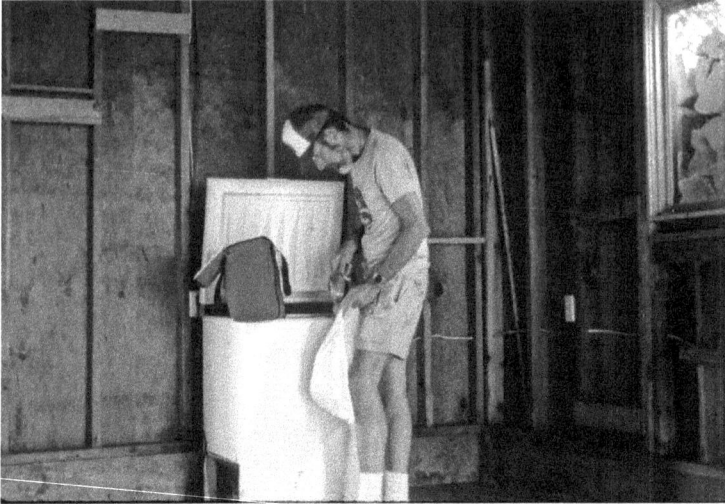

*Figure 15: Gary getting quail from the freezer*

*Figure 16: Jean putting out quail for Peregrines*

## C. PERSONAL STORIES

Atypical Hack Site Attendants

The majority of Hack Site Attendants were probably college students, or of that age group, so we were quite atypical. In 1990, the year that Gary was in the Boundary Waters while Jean had her first Hack Site Attendant job, we were 46 years old. That summer we had just celebrated our 25$^{th}$ wedding anniversary and our younger daughter's graduation from high school with a family party. Since Jean's career was teaching, she could have the summers free to seek fieldwork jobs. Gary, on the other hand, had to make complex arrangements to be away from his engineering job in order to experience his first summer of fieldwork. His eight-week job on the Boundary Waters crew was to consist of four ten-day stints in the wilderness interspersed with four-day off-periods. To make this work, Gary had to use all his available earned vacation time, take two weeks of unpaid leave, and agree to come home and go to his engineering job during all but one four-day off period. To make up the ten days for which he did not have vacation or leave time, he had to work on weekends as well when he was home during those off periods. In 1991 when Gary planned to join Jean in Peregrine work, he sought to make another special arrangement to be absent from his engineering job, this time for eight contiguous weeks. His direct supervisor was understanding about Gary's request for time off, but the company executive vice-president had been very reluctant to approve the leave arrangements in 1990, and flatly refused in 1991.

Because of official reluctance about giving Gary leave the first summer and an admonition to never ask for such special leave again, we had discussed the possibility of refusal when we decided to apply for Hack Site Attendant jobs together in 1991.

Gary did request special arrangements again in 1991, but we had already asked ourselves what we would do if the threatened refusal was given. We had enjoyed our first year of fieldwork and living in the outdoors so much, even though it caused us to be separated for 82 days, and we wanted so badly to have more such experiences, this time together, that we decided we were willing to have Gary quit his engineering job if necessary to achieve these goals. Since Jean's teaching job at that time was usually part time, and her contracts were then for one semester at a time with no contract at all some semesters, this meant we were risking having to live (and pay college fees for two daughters) on the lower, less secure, of the two salaries in our family. We knew well what we were risking. As a part-time instructor at UW-La Crosse, and lacking tenure or a Ph.D. degree, Jean's job was definitely insecure and not well paid. In 15 years since she had completed her master's degree and started teaching at UW-La Crosse, Jean had worked 28 semesters, three of them with contracts of less than 50%, and only 12 of the 28 were for full time. Worse, there were two semesters in those 15 years when she had no contract at all at UW-La Crosse, though she managed to obtain a contract to teach spring quarter at a nearby college during one of those semesters.

Gary's plan to help deal with the possibility of quitting his job was to work on obtaining a license as a Professional Engineer (P.E.), and to seek work as a consulting engineer. He began these preparations before summer 1991 and during his first summer as a Hack Site Attendant was making calls from Idaho to obtain four letters of support for his application for the license from engineers for or with whom he had previously worked. During the six-year period (1991-1996) when we were both Hack Site Attendants during the summers, Gary did find several short-term engineering consulting jobs, and eventually

100

went back to full-time engineering in mid-1997. During the years Gary lacked a full-time engineering job, Jean did continue to teach biology labs and lectures at UW-La Crosse, with five of 12 semesters on part-time contracts (but only one of those at less than 50%) and seven semesters at 100%. However, she again had two semesters without a teaching contract. The fieldwork jobs she found to fill those two spring semester gaps form stories and include adventures that may be told elsewhere someday.

Having put our Hack Site Attendant applications in the mail in early 1991 and received our acceptances, Gary again wrote a request for leave from his engineering job, but we felt we were prepared for the company to refuse to grant such leave. At the meeting when his request was denied, Gary gave notice that he would be quitting his job just before our 1991 Peregrine assignment was to begin. Although this was a momentous and frightening step for us, it also felt exciting and freeing. Thereafter, Gary was spoken of among The Peregrine Fund's personnel as "the engineer who quit his job to release Peregrines." Jean always thought she should then have been known as "the wife who supported her husband in quitting his engineering job to release Peregrines."

During Jean's semester break in January of 1990, we had taken a train trip vacation to camp in Big Bend and other south Texas wilderness areas. On the train we had made our final decision to "go for it" and filled out applications for our first field jobs, Gary for a Boundary Waters Canoe Area Wilderness trail and campsite restoration crew, Jean for a Peregrine Hack Site Attendant job.

We were at that time, 46 years old, mortgage-free empty nesters. Having gone from high school to college, married young, gone from college right into the workforce, earned one advanced degree, entered into mortgages to buy a small farm and build a small house thereon, taken up part-time farming, and had both our children, all by age 28. We were happy with our lives and happy together. Yet by 46 we felt the desire to find some adventures while we were physically able and perhaps do work that would benefit the environment. Gary had been having some back trouble and was worried about being physically limited by normal retirement age, so he wanted to hike the mountains before that could happen. We both had always lived in Iowa up through undergraduate college, and always in Wisconsin since then, but Gary sometimes traveled because of his engineering job and we had visited other U.S. states, mostly in the west, on family vacations. We had learned from all this that to really know something about another area of the country, another ecosystem with its different climate, plants and animals, the differences in culture and attitudes of people past and present, we would need to spend more than just a two-week vacation getting to know an area different from the upper Midwest.

We made several extra efforts in preparation for those first fieldwork applications, attempting to bolster the quality of our applications. Each of us took Red Cross First Aid and CPR classes and received certificates. Jean also took three different rock-climbing classes, since this skill was needed at some Peregrine hack sites. The third class was during a stopover she made in the Black Hills on her way out to Boise in 1990. Nevertheless, it was a relief not to need to use rock climbing skills at any site to which we were assigned. This may have been a concession to our ages, but it was also a trend by The Peregrine Fund away from the use of sites requiring technical climbing skills and gear.

## Food for Body and Mind

What kind of food supplies can one plan, prepare or purchase in advance, pack and transport well over a thousand miles to provide three meals a day for two people for seven weeks at a remote camp? What kinds of foods will keep for seven weeks without reliable refrigeration and also be easy to prepare into meal form with a one-burner camp stove or two? In 1990, Jean and CJ made their plans via an exchange of letters, deciding to take turns with the cooking. Having counted the number of breakfasts, lunches and suppers needed for the seven week job period and divided by two, each was responsible for planning and providing supplies for half of the 49 breakfasts (with the exception that we brought our own cereal choices), 49 lunches and 49 suppers, plus snacks. We also had to plan food for ourselves to eat during our several days of driving separately from Wisconsin to Idaho. CJ tended toward a vegetarian diet; Jean did not, but each agreed to eat the other's meals and tried to consider the other's preferences in the process of planning foods to bring. It would have been impossible to eat a healthy diet for such a long period, if all of the food had had to be purchased in White Bird, ID, and food obtained exclusively from the very limited stocks in the White Bird gas station would also have been prohibitively expensive. The only other available alternative to bringing the food from home would have been to drive more often the extra 15 miles to Grangeville and back, a bigger town with a good grocery store. That too would have added expense in terms of gas and mileage for our vehicles, but more importantly, it would have made the town trips longer, and the time spent alone for the person left behind on duty observing the falcons harder to endure.

CJ was an excellent planner and camp cook. Jean learned to eat falafel, vegetable burgers, tabbouleh and other vegetarian delights. CJ also established a very welcome camp tradition of Zakuskis, which she said was a Russian term for hors d'oeuvres, snacks, and appetizers; we served them in the middle of the long afternoon period of observations. Zakuskis also represented an opportunity for one person each day to take a mid-afternoon break to walk down to camp, prepare some snacks, and bring them up to the O.P. to share. Jean's favorite CJ meal was Bauern Frühstück (German for "farmer's breakfast"), which consisted of potatoes and onions fried first, then scrambled eggs were poured over for further cooking, and finally topped with cheese. CJ in turn, did not complain when meat was included in some of Jean's cooking, and thoroughly enjoyed every bannock variation Jean produced.

So…what is bannock and what else did we eat? What about all this preparation? Jean had purchased a food dehydrator in 1989, and set out to learn to use it in order to be able to bring at least some of her share of the food supplies in light-weight, nutrient-rich, dried form the next summer. From her own garden Jean dehydrated chopped onions, peppers and green beans, sliced tomatoes and carrots, and even sliced celery from the grocery store. On the dehydrator "leather trays" she dried rhubarb sauce, tomato paste, split pea soup, and refried beans. The rhubarb "leather" could be eaten as a snack; the other three were rehydrated with boiling water. A variety of fruits were dried by first slicing them and dropping the slices into pineapple juice to reduce browning, then laying the slices out on the dehydrator trays, fruits such as bananas, apples, pears, and fresh pineapple chunks. Some experiments—dried orange slices—were abysmal failures, but most of the dried foods were excellent. Great care must be taken to dry the foods at the proper temperature for each type, and long enough so that mold does not form because of moisture left in the foods; it is also essential to package the dried foods properly to keep them dry. It is even possible to dehydrate hamburger if you know the secrets, but this particular product was always kept in the cooler and used during the first couple weeks to be sure of its freshness and safety. The dehydrated foods were such a successful part of meals at that first Peregrine camp that Jean continued to prepare them each year thereafter.

We typically ate cereal for breakfast some mornings, and made a hot breakfast other mornings. Jean's usual breakfast consisted of her favorite wheat and malted barley dry cereal to which she added raisins and powdered milk, with water poured over to soften it all. Gary liked this same dry cereal, but left out the raisins and added some sugar; he also liked to have hot instant oatmeal for breakfast. Each morning one attendant had the duty to hike up to the hack box to provide quail for the falcons, while the other attendant was responsible for heating a couple quarts of water in the boiler on the camp stove and pouring the boiling water into an insulated jug. This hot water would be used for hot drinks (cocoa or tea), especially welcome when the morning temperatures were cool, but could also be used to make hot instant cereal. Special hot breakfasts included pancakes, bannocks, even scrambled eggs and toast, but this involved carrying the camp stove, utensils, ingredients and all up to the O.P. to cook and eat there while on duty. Noon meals were also eaten on duty at the O.P. and therefore tended to be simple, and composed of cold foods, prepared by one attendant while the other continued observations.

One of Jean's Boise cousins gave her a book on wild edible plants of the West in 1990, and she gathered edible vegetation at most sites to supplement our menus with fresh food. If we could get lettuce in town, we could add wild plants such as waterleaf, dandelion leaves, miner's lettuce and wild onions to make a salad. Little leaves of a small species of dock made a flavorful addition to a cracker spread with peanut butter; so did a piece of a green pepper if we could find such a fresh vegetable in town. We were at Holter Lake when Juneberries and the orange-colored wild currants were ripening on their large bushes. Jean carried a container and stopped on her way from camp to the O.P. in the morning to pick these berries. We had them on cold cereal or in pancakes for breakfasts prepared and eaten at our mountain-side observation position, even on crackers with peanut butter for lunches.

Supper was usually a hot meal, and if the menu required dehydrated vegetables these had to be reconstituted by pouring boiling water over them in an insulated jug several hours ahead of time. When the time came to cook supper, the vegetables would have softened and plumped up, ready to be added to the rest of the recipe being prepared. For example, from several of the dried vegetables and tomato paste plus packets of herbs, a tasty spaghetti sauce could be made. This would be a two kettle meal, because the spaghetti or other pasta had to be rehydrated too. We quickly learned to bring the water to a boil, drop in the pasta, cover the kettle and set it aside for 7-10 minutes for the pasta to rehydrate, put the sauce kettle back on to cook more, then dump the drained spaghetti in with the sauce. When you have backpacked the water half a mile or more, you do not want to have to wash very many dishes, so we tended to eat out of the kettles, and to prefer to make one-kettle meals.

*From the Journals: Holter Lake – Jean*
*27 June 1992 – It has dismayed me to discover—because of trying hard to conserve fuel in these situations where I have to backpack the fuel in to camp, that most recipes call for much more cooking, and thus fuel wastage, than is needed. For example: if a recipe says to boil pasta ten minutes, you can bring it to a boil, cover the pot, and let it sit ten minutes, then*

*relight the burner and cook two minutes more and it's done the same as if it had cooked the entire ten minute recipe time. I will be cooking it this way at home from now on too.*

Before leaving home, Jean would measure out the ingredients for pancakes (no, she did not use commercial pancake mixes back then) in several bowls and then package the mixes in plastic bags—enough mixes to allow pancakes for breakfast once a week. Syrup was always made by mixing brown sugar with water in a ratio of two to one, and heating it to dissolve the sugar. Bannock mixes were likewise prepared and packaged in advance at home. Bannock is basically a biscuit recipe, but after the dough is prepared on site by adding water, it is patted out as a large circle in a heated and oiled skillet. The bannock is fried on very low heat until browned on the bottom, then flipped and fried to brown the other side. Bannock can be served plain as bread with a main meal, but we most often used it as a camp equivalent of coffeecake. Wonderful variations can be produced by using different flours such as corn, blue corn, buckwheat, or whole wheat. (Now there are even more choices, and in ordinary camping trips in more recent years, we are trying almond flour, oat flour, and others.) Favorite variations involved mixing raisins, brown sugar and cinnamon into the dough, or dividing the dough in half, patting one half into the pan and spreading it with jam before covering it with the other half of the dough.

*From the Journals: Holter Lake – Jean*
*3 July 1992 – We forgot a couple food items we meant to bring to make things more interesting, but we can make do. It's important that food out here be good, interesting, varied since a meal may be the high point of the day, especially when falcon-watching falls off in the last weeks of the job.*

The one-burner camp stoves provided to each attendant by The Peregrine Fund saw a lot of use heating water for hot drinks, cooking meals, and heating water for dishwashing. We found that a one-pound propane cylinder lasted about six days on average, and that the rubber O-ring gasket in one of our two stoves tended to burn out about the last week on the job. The first year we were also given propane camp lanterns, but after that refused them because we preferred to be in bed by dark, since we were supposed to be up at dawn to feed the falcons and begin observations as soon as there was enough light to see. Flashlights were therefore good enough for the small amount of time that we were outside the tent in the dark, and the tents were much too small for hot propane lanterns to be used safely inside them. We were often asked if we lit campfires during all this camping and the answer is, "No, not one single time." This was an easy decision because of the amount of time it takes to gather wood and tend a fire. We always needed our sleep after dark anyway—dawn on the eastern edge of the Pacific Time Zone (Grave Point, Idaho) near Midsummer's Day came very early. Thus in late June at that site we set our alarm as early as 4:10 AM Pacific Daylight Time. As camp and the tower were located within an area of open range, we wanted just enough light to avoid fresh cow pies on the hike and yet to be up on the tower with the day's supply of quail just before sunrise and hopefully before the falcons arrived, and on observation duty by sunrise at 4:54 AM As the summer weeks passed we could gradually set the alarm later, usually about ten minutes later every other week.

We were also concerned each summer to pack along food for our minds. We brought small, battery-powered tape players and our favorite music tapes to listen to in the tent in the evenings, or late in the season when falcon visits to the tower became fewer and farther apart. We spent a lot of time writing letters to share our experiences with friends, family and colleagues, and writing of our experiences in journals. But, we brought books too, a big cardboard box of about 30 books each summer. Since Jean was on the teaching staff, she had a staff library card that allowed her to check out university library books for the whole summer. Our summer supply of books was carefully selected so that a good percentage of them would be of interest to both of us. Generally, we had only a few of the books in camp with us at any one time; when we finished a book, it was taken back to the truck and another carried into camp. Many of the books we read in those years were on environmental subjects and we thoroughly enjoyed discussing the things we were reading, but we also brought fiction for lighter reading. Some of these books are listed in Appendix Three.

We read and wrote little during the intense observation period right after release, but if all the falcons were away from the tower for a while, one attendant could read or write while the other continued observing. Even so, both of us were at the O.P. most of the time and both watched when the falcons were present. During the last three weeks of the job, the falcons were away from the tower more and more and often came only long enough to pick up a quail or, perhaps staying briefly to pluck some quail feathers and maybe bite off a few quail appendages to make it lighter, then carried the quail away to eat elsewhere. At Grave Point the O.P. was about 200 yards away from the tower and downslope, and we were seated under a couple small pines for shade. We quickly developed the habit of reading a couple sentences, then marking the place with one finger while we looked up, leaned a bit sideways to align one eye with the spotting scope eyepiece, and searched the tower and hack box for falcons. If none were present, we could read a bit more, and check again. We became so acutely attuned to the falcons, that we regularly heard their arrival in a rush of air from their wings overhead or the sound of the click of their talons as they landed on the hack box roof where the quail had been placed.

Wood Nymph, Wood Lake, 1995

The few days between installation and release at any hack site allowed more freedom for the attendants than would be possible later, when the responsibilities of the Peregrine hacking job greatly increased. We attendants needed to provide quail to our falcons once a day and monitor them several times a day to confirm they were eating and adapting normally, but apart from that the Peregrines were locked in a box and we could do other tasks to prepare for the coming six weeks: finish setting up camp, selecting and preparing the observation sites we would use, scouting places near the hack box which the Peregrines might use for roosting after they were released, re-arranging supplies and books from their transit position in the truck to being readily accessible in the weeks ahead.

On the way to Wood Lake, we should have merely pulled into a quick-lube place in Helena, Montana, as we passed through. However, as we were pressed for time and Gary was a handyman committed to saving pennies where he could, he decided to change the truck's oil and oil filter after we reached our campsite at Wood Lake. Foolish decision. Unknown to him there was a mischievous Wood Nymph who dwelled somewhere in those dark and mysterious forests surrounding our camp and the lake.

After the snow from the storm before and during release melted and the grass and ground in camp had dried, Gary parked our Ford in a level spot in preparation for changing the oil. He removed the oil drain plug and oil filter, drained the oil into a catch basin for recycling at an Augusta service station when we next had to go to town, picked up the drain plug for cleaning and lubrication from where he had laid it on the battery, and fumbled badly. Clink-clank-clunk! He did not even see it leave his fingers. All he heard was the sound of it dropping. Somewhere. But where?!? The damned thing was gone. Just plain GONE! Gary tried reaching and touching everywhere he could in the engine compartment. Looked on the ground under the truck. Removed the battery so he could search better. Used a flashlight. Shined it everywhere. Ran his fingers through the drain oil. Icky. Looked between the fender walls. Jean joined him and both searched again. Unable to start the engine without any oil in it, together we pushed hard and rolled the truck back about five feet so we could search through the grass underneath with our eyes and fingers. After over an hour of earnest searching by each of us, Gary had to conclude our drain plug had vanished, never to be seen again.

Due to the remote location of Wood Lake, we had been issued a forest service radio to be used in the rare possibility of an accident or emergency. We wondered where on the ranking of emergencies stupidity and foolishness were positioned. Damping down his embarrassment and screwing up his courage, Gary radioed into the Forest Service Headquarters and left a message of make, model, and part needed and asked for delivery at their convenience. Due to the intervening mountain terrain, it was necessary for Gary to climb a small hill in order to transmit his message out from our location; however, we could not receive transmissions back from the radio set in the office so we could not tell if anyone had received our plaintive call of distress. The following day the Forest Service delivered a picnic table for our use and we were greatly relieved to also receive a brand new oil drain plug for our idled truck.

Gary's preferred explanation for the disappearance of our oil drain plug involves a svelte, young, near naked, damsel of a

Wood Nymph dashing from the nearby trees and snatching up his drain plug for her collection of human artifacts when he was momentarily distracted and occupied in the search. When pressed he will occasionally concede the drain plug may have tumbled and bounced into the tight recesses of one of the twin hollow walls of the reinforced truck fender in front of the wheel, there to remain hidden for the duration of the truck's life. But he prefers the Wood Nymph story—it is a better explanation.

Personal Visitors

Generally it was not possible or advisable for us to have personal visitors at our hack sites, especially those sites that were most remote, or on private property, or especially difficult to access. In 1993, however, by special arrangement, it was finally possible for some of our family members to visit and to see firsthand our work as Hack Site Attendants. It was very special to be able to share this experience briefly with some members of our family, to share the work that took us away from home summer after summer. We only wish more of them could have come. Daughter Gayle and her husband, came to visit that summer at Green River, as did Jean's brother, Paul, and his wife. Friends from Missoula visited us twice at CSKT Tower, and one of Jean's cousins and her husband, in Montana on vacation, visited us at Wood Lake. Family visitors made themselves extra welcome because they provided foods for meals that we normally did not get to have in camp. Our son-in-law fished in the Green River while we were on falcon duty and gave us the trout to eat. Jean's brother and wife brought fresh hamburger and fruit for the evening meal, and huckleberries that were added to the pancakes Jean made for the breakfast we shared with them.

Since there was a US Forest Service campground at Wood Lake, Jean's California cousin and her husband, who were on vacation in Montana that summer, came for a visit and camped one night. They brought chicken, cooked it over their campfire and shared it with us along with vegetables and chocolate cake. What a treat to have such foods for a change! Our camp food was good and varied, but tended to be simple because we could not spare much time for cooking, and because it was difficult to get fresh foods, meat in particular, and to keep them safely. Nevertheless, we were proud of being able to produce meals for ourselves with one or two propane burners for weeks at a time and, if our visitors stayed overnight, usually prepared bannock in a skillet, or coffee cake or cornbread in the BakePacker™ for them for breakfast. Bannocks were Jean's specialty, but Gary became quite adept at using the BakePacker™ to "bake" various small cake and muffin mixes. Jean progressed beyond baking such mixes in camp to making pineapple up-side-down cake and even pizza with that wonderful camp cooking device.

What is this wonderful camp gadget known as a BakePacker™? It is a light-weight aluminum grid within a two-inch circle of aluminum that comes in two sizes: five and three-quarters inch diameter, or seven and three-eighths inch diameter. The small grid fits in a six-inch diameter kettle and the large grid requires an eight inch kettle; the kettles must be purchased separately. You place the grid in its kettle, pour water just to the top of the grid, cover the kettle and bring the water to a boil. Meanwhile, mix your small cornbread or other mix as directed on the package, pour the batter into a heat-tolerant plastic bag, such as an oven-roasting bag. Place the bag into the kettle, carefully rolling down the top of the bag to keep steam out of the batter, cover the kettle again and when the water returns to a boil, reduce the heat until the water just barely continues to boil. Time the mix as specified on the box. When done, remove it from the kettle, dry moisture off the bag with a towel, dump the cornbread out on a plate and serve. Yum! Turn off the stove but leave the kettle on the burner; put the lid back on the kettle, and save the hot water for doing camp dishes right after you eat.

A Day without Mail; the Importance of Mail, Grave Point, 1991

On 25 July 1991 it was Jean's turn to make the 52-mile round trip drive down off the mountain to the nearest (tiny) town for mail, laundry, phone calls (to Boise and to family), to the Ranger Station for frozen quail, water and ice, and finally to the fruit stand on the highway for peaches and treats (soda and candy bars in this case). These town trips were both a nuisance—taking time away from camp, the falcons and each other, plus costing mileage and wear on our vehicle—and a weekly chance for each of us (if we took turns going to town) to engage in human contact with people other than our partner. Our social contacts otherwise were limited to the rare cases of arrival at the hack site of a Release Specialist or other visitor. Jean's journal notes for this date have comments about her trip.

*From the Journals: Grave Point – Jean*
*25 July 1991 – This is my day to go to town so I spent the morning writing outgoing mail, and Gary wrote a letter to his friend, John. I've about exhausted my list of people to write…. Having seen no falcons yet, and Gary having returned to the Observation Point after his break for exercise and the tasks of taking a load of stuff (laundry, outgoing mail, water and ice jugs, cooler, etc.) down to the truck for me and bringing the last of the water from his Monday town trip up to camp, I went off observation duty…. I went down to camp about 10:10 AM, spent 10 minutes putting things into my pack, 10 minutes hiking down to the truck at the gate, 10 minutes changing into shorts and sandals and getting organized. I drove off at 10:40. In the Post Office I found that the Postmistress had left another*

*woman in charge without telling her about our General Delivery mail arrangements. This substitute had used last summer's forwarding address card (which I had provided the Post Office at the end of the 1990 hack site season when I worked the same site with my friend C.J.) and had sent our mail for this week home to Wisconsin! I was furious for a few minutes and the woman never even apologized.*

To understand what this miscarriage of our mail system meant to us, you have to remember that we were away from home, friends and family for 8-15 weeks for each summer we did hack site jobs, including the travel time to the hack site and back home afterward. Our only means of communication were very occasional phone calls—often we did not catch family members at home when we called and could only leave messages on their answering machines—or mail. [Note: This was the early to mid-1990s and cell phones were not in common use back then; even if we had had one of the early "bag phones" there would not have been cell towers in the wilderness areas where we worked. Thus we were dependent on finding functioning pay phone booths (fairly common then even in small towns) and in making our calls only when we were able to get to a town.] Most of our friends and family members were quite faithful correspondents and this helped us (and them) immensely to endure the long periods of separation not only from most of the people we loved, but also separation from our "regular" lives. We had to keep in touch with our employers as well about opportunities for jobs for us at the end of each summer.

Perhaps understanding of Jean's fury over the misplaced mail can be more sharply conveyed with a few statistics. In the summer of 1992 when we worked two consecutive hack sites and were gone from home from 2 June to 13 September (nearly 15 weeks), Jean kept a list of her outgoing mail, which included

115

21 letters and postcards to our daughters, nine such communications to her parents, nine to her brother, two each to Gary's sisters, nine to assorted other family members, 30 to various friends, and four to employers, a total of 86 pieces of out-going mail. She received 59 pieces of incoming-mail during that summer. And—the day in 1991 that there was no mail at all because of a post office screw-up was devastating.

*Phase Three, Release:   Figures 17 and 18*

*Figure 17:  Young Peregrine explores cliff*

*Figure 18:  Newly released Peregrines on hack tower*

# PHASE THREE – RELEASE: beginning of week two

## A. INTRODUCTION TO THE RELEASE PROCESS

Release Day was always fraught with excitement and worry; the young Peregrines would be released from the hack box and fledge, i.e. take their first flights, and, hopefully, they would rapidly become proficient fliers and to learn to hunt for themselves. From the day of release, they would continue to be provided with quail for only six more weeks, by which time they would have to be able to find food for themselves, to find safe places to roost at night, and eventually they would probably need to migrate southward to find a warmer place to spend the winter, a warmer place with a good food supply. During the first week or two, while the falcons were becoming skillful fliers, they were at risk to a variety of predators—aerial predators such as eagles and Prairie Falcons, and, at night, owls. Mammals that might find the young falcons on the ground during the first few days or perhaps even find them at night in unsafe roosting locations were another risk.

There could also be problems from the release process itself. A perfect release would involve good weather conditions, calmness among the young Peregrines so that as they emerged from the hack box they would look around and recognize their surroundings, including how the hack box looked from the outside, notice all the quail scattered on the box and nearby, and eat a good meal before "leaving home" for the first time. Ideally, sometime after eating, a Peregrine would take a first flight out from the box and circle back to land successfully again at or near the hack box. This kind of beginning usually boded well for that individual.

Of course, real life does not often include ideal events. For one thing, there were several Peregrines being released from a hack box during any given release. Some of those falcons might be calm and eat a meal, fledge without being stressed and find their way back to the hack box promptly. But another individual bird might be flapping its wings for practice and to gain strength just when a gust of wind came along, and be lifted right off its perch unexpectedly. Or, the actions of one falcon might startle another into flight suddenly. Situations like these were especially worrisome if the bird involved had not eaten since coming out of the hack box.

What kinds of weather conditions were to be avoided on release day? If the wind was too strong, a falcon might be blown far from the hack box when it fledged and not be able to find its way back before starving. Foggy conditions would make it hard for a falcon to find its way back to the hack box, and might also prevent the Hack Site Attendants from seeing the falcons on the hack box and in their flights. Rain could soak the falcons' feathers to the point of making flight difficult.

In our experiences with eleven releases, we saw smooth, successful releases and other releases when problems occurred and some of these will be featured below, but here we can summarize some of the basic procedures used to release the falcons from their several days of captivity in the hack box. Typically, the Release Specialist would enter the hack box with the assistance of one attendant to operate the door. Inside, the Specialist would spray a water mist on the falcons to help calm them and perhaps their dampened plumage would discourage them from taking flight immediately after release. The Specialist confined the falcons in one partially enclosed corner of the hack box known as the hide, by taping a piece of cardboard across the opening of the hide. Next he gathered up quail remnants from inside the hack box. Meanwhile, the attendant was placing quail on the front ledge of the hack box, on the roof, and scattered around the box. After the attendant opened the hack box door to allow the Specialist to exit, the two of them removed the barred front of the hack box and, while the attendant hurried away, the Specialist pulled a long string attached to the cardboard. This opened the hide so the falcons could emerge.

While all this was happening at the hack box, the other attendant was setting up an observation point (O.P.) typically at least 200 yards away but with a good view of the front of the hack box. Over the years we each experienced both these tasks, but in 1991, Gary particularly wanted to be at the O.P. to photograph the process and to watch the release. Working different hack sites during several years, we, Gary especially, obtained many wonderful photos that remind us of our adventures with Peregrines, though not many photos of the falcons themselves because of the necessity of keeping our distance.

The observation point was always pre-approved by the Release Specialist. We carried along either lawn chairs or small, short-legged camp chairs to use at the O.P. where we would be on duty making observations for many hours of the day, essentially from dawn to dusk in the first three weeks after release. At many sites, we had one main O.P. but several supplemental locations we could use to provide different views of the hack box area. We LIVED our days at these observation points, bringing extra clothes, bottles of water, snacks, binoculars, spotting scopes and tripods, and a variety of other items depending on the site conditions. Sometimes the O.P. was right beside our camp. If there was no natural source of shade, we learned to bring along a tarp, poles, guy-lines and stakes and to set up our own shade.

# B. RELEASE STORIES

*From the Journals: Grave Point – Gary*
*27 June 1991 – It is now 1543 [3:43 PM] and all our birds are*
*still on tower hack box ledge. There were high clouds for us this*
*afternoon and evening and it was dry, although a big*
*thunderstorm went through the Salmon River valley and up*
*Skookumchuck to the east of us. Evening was exciting for*
*falcon-watching as winds came up from east and our birds were*
*wing-flapping. RM and WF hopped to top railing. YM was*
*practicing on west end, flapping and lifting off a few inches and*
*suddenly was gone, swept over the ridge to the southwest at*
*1944. The other four falcons stayed on the tower. Jean was*
*worried about owls possibly coming in the night and harming*
*our Peregrines, and slept on the hill above the observation site.*
*I slept in camp. We did hear owls in the night but they were to*
*the south of us. It occurred to me that Edward Abbey would*
*enjoy the irony of two people sitting outside of a fire tower*
*gazing at it for seven weeks, instead of like he did, sitting inside*
*a tower for the same amount of time gazing out. The folks that*
*built these towers never dreamed they would be used to house*
*and reintroduce an endangered native bird back to the*
*environment.*

*From the Journals: Holter Lake – Gary*
*15 June, 1992 – It was certainly the ragged edge of the world*
*we were on this day. Raw life. Primitive existence. All*
*experienced by us as we tried to do our job here in the Great*
*West. The alarm went off at 0500, our intention being to meet*
*the Release Specialists on the trail an hour or two later as this*
*is scheduled to be release day. But we were rocked through the*
*night and early morn with high wind gusts and the incessant*
*flop-flapping of tarps sheltering us. Peering out the door we*
*saw the haze, the clouds, the fog. No release for a while. .....*

*Two Release Specialists arrived about noon. To our mild surprise they declared the release would go ahead, primarily because the forecast for tomorrow wasn't any better and they have successfully released in worse conditions. When the falcons are ready to fly they have to go. These birds have an optimum release point—beyond that point they may get too strong and fly too far on their first flight, not find their way back. That's OK if they fledge from a natural nest and a parent hears them begging and brings them food, but here they must only go a small distance and find their way back to the food site on their own. Still 47 degrees with fog and rain but you can see the hack box. The Specialists went up to the cliff edge to release our falcons while Jean and I hurriedly gathered our gear and went to the observation site below the cliff. Set up under our ponchos, we watched them remove the front grill, wave, and then jerk the cardboard out with a string and walk back from the cliff. It took them 25 minutes to get back down to us— obviously they used a shortcut compared to our usual route. Yellow, Red, and Blue took their first flights—lots of feeding, flapping, hopping activity. Strong winds often get young falcons all wound up. All four of us observed in the rain and wind and fog until the guys left at 1530 to catch the boat back to their truck. ..... When the guys were still with us we were treated to elk squealing, barking, whistling, and calling to one another— apparently a couple cows. Sounded like an Osprey screech when they first called out. But we could hear them moving downslope and one cow trotted past us nearby, head held high, alert and powerful. Great stuff. We watched until lowering clouds and fog totally obscured the box and then we called it quits. Came back to camp and tightened all the cords on tents and tarps. Jean put a kettle under a tarp edge to collect water, and drained ice water from the cooler. Then we retired to our tent, there to wring the water out of our socks, warm up our feet, read, write these words. On the walk back to camp, tired, weary, wet, we had looked west to the Peregrines' cliff, seeing sheets of rain and fog blowing with the wind past the bold formations of rock, intermittently obscuring them totally. Yet we felt proud for enduring the weather this day, pleased for the release, invigorated by the sharing of this wild world with the falcons, elk, coyote, mule deer, rattlesnakes, towhees, magpies, meadowlarks, this world they and we call home. Down on the lake windswept swells of waves crashed into the clay embankment sending clouds of packed soil scattering into the winds. This is raw, ragged, life lunging toward the edge of existence. The sun will bring a different beauty, a sort of indolent beauty in comparison to the wild, thrusting beauty of this storm. We admire the raw nature around us, but we know to also give it our respect.*

## Trouble during Release, CSKT Tower, 1992

Things did not go smoothly that hot, sunny day at the beginning of August 1992. Two hack boxes had been placed on the CSKT tower, each of which held five young Peregrines, aged 41-44 days, and this was planned as a double (two hack boxes) simultaneous release. Jean climbed the tower with two Specialists and closed one Specialist into each hack box to spray the falcons with water and confine them behind the hides. She spread quail about each hack box roof and tower, let the Specialists out of the hack boxes and climbed down to untie the rope after it was used to lower the box fronts to the ground one at a time. She then joined Gary at the Observation Point, as did both Specialists after the release cord pulled the cardboard barriers away from the hide entrances.

The first two falcons to emerge from the hack boxes were calm, until one was startled into fledging by the third falcon to come out onto the tower platform. Brown, a male so named for the color of his identifying leg band, was first out of his hack box

124

and, only 14 minutes later, first to fledge. However, he was not the only falcon to bolt precipitously off the tower that day. In all, five falcons including Black, another male, fledged within the first hour, flying off in different directions and landing up to half a mile away. One of these was never seen again, and none of them had time to learn the appearance of the tower and hack boxes from the outside to help them find their way back again, nor to eat, or in some cases even to notice that there was food for them on the tower.

It was fortunate we had two Specialists with us for this worrisome release; these dedicated men were vital in converting this release from potential disaster into reasonable success. One of the falcons flew south and landed near a set of ranch buildings; one Specialist went to alert the ranchers about the project and the presence of a young falcon near them. Both Specialists took walks and drives around the immediate area and by the end of the day had located four of the five early fledglings. One was perched on a fence post, one in a dead tree by the ranch, one on a power pole, one on the ground.

Brown had landed in the grasses about one quarter mile west of the tower. We kept an eye on that area and a couple hours later a Northern Harrier was seen to stoop on Brown, but was displaced by a Red-tailed Hawk also investigating the possibility of making a meal out of Brown, and scuffling with him. One Specialist took off running to try to scare off the hawks and locate Brown. This was not easy, and the other Specialist went to help. Having made note of the location and still on duty at the O.P. we were able to wave directions so that Brown was located and determined to be uninjured. One Specialist, dressed in T-shirt and shorts, remained prostrate out in the dirt and sand, poked by the sharp grasses and bitten by numerous insects, staying near Brown for two hours to discourage predators. The temperature that afternoon was 95°F. in the shade!

That night and the next night, the remaining five fledged when there was too little light for us to see them, but all but one of these had definitely been observed to have eaten from the supply of quail before fledging. Of the first five falcons that fledged so precipitously, one was never seen again, one returned the second day after release, but was not seen after that, Brown survived his experiences with other raptors on release day, returned to the tower the fifth day and was present three days but then disappeared, and the other two were present at the tower 34 or more days, long enough to be considered to have successfully reached independence. Black was one of these latter two but his survival had required special effort from us— more of his story will be told in a later section. In contrast, all five of the falcons that fledged without being spooked off the tower so suddenly, were present at the release site 29-41 days, also long enough to be considered independent.

## Red Lost in the Willows, Green River, 1993

As experienced canoeists from Wisconsin we enjoyed the requirement at the Green River site of using a canoe briefly once or twice each day to access the Peregrine hack tower on the west side of the Green River from our camp trailer situated on the opposite bank. After only a few days at this site we were already enthralled and amazed to be able to watch the smooth-flowing river going past our site, and in spite of being rationally aware the flow would always continue, were nonetheless always surprised to find the large river still gliding silently past us each morning. Having never dwelt in the presence of an endless stream, always so visible to us each waking moment, its continual, never-ending motion seemed almost magical to us.

On release day the Specialist from Boise, after a brief hello and our introductory comments on the uniqueness of the hack site box and campsite being separated by a river, took the canoe across the river with Gary while Jean set up the observing scopes and kept a camera with telephoto lens at hand to record the event. The Specialist, with Gary's assistance, wetted the feathers of the falcons, placed them behind a propped corrugated cardboard temporarily closing the hide, removed the barred front of the hack box and lowered it to the ground, and laid out fresh quail around the hack box area. Gary retreated to the canoe while the Specialist climbed down the tower, gave a firm yank on the string attached to the cardboard, thereby opening the hide, and jogged over to join Gary. The Peregrines were released, no longer entrapped or constrained by humans, and free to survive or perish in wild nature.

Jean had taken some long distance photos of the process and was watching the Peregrines through binoculars and spotting scope as Gary and the Specialist returned across the river via canoe to join her in observing the falcons' response to unrestricted access to the large outdoors. Although a cool and partly cloudy morning originally, by noon it was mostly cloudy, the breezes had increased, and it had begun to sprinkle. Release was proceeding normally: the falcons had exited the box without bolting, some had found the quail and eaten, there was wing stretching and wing flapping as the Peregrines got their first taste of all-encompassing wind passing over their feathers and stimulating them to mimic flight, some hopping up and jumping. After a short visit and viewing the falcons' initial exploration of the hack tower, the Specialist left for his other duties of the day and the site was again totally ours to monitor and maintain.

We always looked forward to having the Specialists spend time at our hack sites, and in this case were disappointed by the brief visit. A different Specialist had installed the birds at this new site, but forgotten to leave directions in Boise, so that whoever would later be assigned to release the birds would be able to find us in a site completely hidden from any public location and accessible only through a private ranch access road. In fact, our release Specialist had arrived in Pinedale the evening before and had been making calls that evening and then on release morning trying to get directions. Eventually he did of course, but this story of a single glitch we encountered serves to illustrate the magnitude and complexity of scheduling necessary each summer to get the hack boxes and hack sites ready, to make up groups of falcons at the correct ages for installation and transport them to the hack sites, to choose Hack Site Attendants and schedule them into hack sites when the sites and birds were ready, to send a Specialist back for release, and anytime there was a problem. Our Peregrine boss and others in Boise managed all of this scheduling nearly flawlessly year after year, but the toll included long, long hours and miles of travel, weather issues, sudden changes of plans and, undoubtedly, instances of missed meals, lost sleep and near exhaustion. The dedication and hard work we witnessed still astounds us.

After our Green River falcons had spent nearly three hours of gradually extending their exploration of the hack box and tower, after they had hopped and stepped out to the ends of several poles that were mounted to and extending six feet outward from the tower platform at the same level as the platform and parallel to the ground to serve as perches, the Peregrine we named Red missed a hop from the tower to the end of one of these poles and fell down toward the ground. Reflexively extending his wings, Red suddenly took flight out over the hay lands and then back toward the river and attempted to land on the six to ten foot tall willow bushes covering the sandy river bars along the bends of the river. Unfortunately, this habitat variety was second in dominance of area coverage compared to the grass and sagebrush areas, and the hay fields, but the flexible boughs and branches of the willows offered no support or secure landing site for a one to two pound male falcon; the leafy ends of the delicate branches bent under the bird's weight as Red attempted to land, his wings beating in futility and his talons grabbing hopelessly for any purchase. Red descended out of sight, down in the willows.

Two more falcons fledged later that same day but had flown far enough that we did not know where they might have landed. The remaining three falcons had all fledged by 52 hours after release (the time of each falcon's initial flight was recorded to the nearest minute for all six falcons released at this site—this level of observation and data collection being among our duties). By the end of the fourth day, all of our falcons had fledged and, except Red, all had successfully returned to the hack box to feed on the quail left there for them.

In spite of cool weather, rain, some hail, and enveloping fog at the hack site—the surrounding mountains also got a fresh new coat of mid-summer snow—we traded off searching as we continued to try to find Red over the next six days. The partner on site continued with observation as the remaining five falcons demonstrated their increasing competence at flight and consistently returned each day to the hack box for their maintenance rations of thawed quail. The searching partner would range out on hikes with binoculars in hand and check out distant abandoned ranch structures, the rare tree, the few fence lines with posts which the falcons quickly learned to land on and utilize as perches, look through the nearby willows, and attempt to find our missing Red, either dead or alive.

Recognizing the now obvious danger of the surrounding willows as a trap for our falcons we collected some ten foot long poles left over from a rancher's abandoned wooden hay-buck, a type of ranch implement used more than fifty years earlier, and mounted these poles vertically in fence rows to provide additional landing and resting perches for the young Peregrines. Our efforts were rewarded by the falcons' quick adoption of these taller, more rigid options for perching.

As interested students of wildlife we had each heard of cooperative hunting behavior observed and recorded by some outdoor biologists, but one day while on the lookout for Red, we had the rewarding opportunity to witness it for ourselves. Gary was returning from a walk to the west hayfield when a large badger came trot-trotting, always moving, never slowing, advancing toward him down the same worn field trail, apparently intent in its pursuit of small rodents to consume. Flying above the badger, circling over the same area being covered by the badger, was a Red-tailed hawk. Several times the hawk swooped low above the sagebrush to the same spots over which the badger had hunted, searching to capture a creature that might have eluded the powerful badger. Behind the first badger a second, slightly smaller badger was following the same path trod by badger number one. The chances of small prey species eluding this tripartite alliance, one of them airborne, must surely have been reduced considerably. Eventually spotting Gary coming from the opposite direction, the three predators veered off through the taller sagebrush.

Six days after release we made one final push to locate Red where we last saw him, going down in the willows. We loaded the canoe into the back end of our truck and Jean drove up to a bridge spanning the Green River, several willow-bound river bends and half a mile above camp. While she brought the truck back to camp and resumed observations, Gary paddled the canoe downstream stopping frequently to plunge into the tall willows looking intently in the many branches and leaves but mostly observing the ground between the bushes looking for feathers or any sign of Red or any predation on Red by other predators. The chief hazard in this effort was encountering a distraught bull moose, or worse yet, an angry female moose with calf at her side. We had seen several different moose individuals and pairs in the mornings and evenings as they came out to feed in these times of lower light levels. Once he was inside a willow perimeter, forward vision was quickly reduced to a few yards as Gary stepped and twisted and wended his way through the tangle. Several times Gary heard moose while searching the willows. Each time the moose went fortunately crashing away from him instead of toward him, and the search gradually came full circle back to our camp. Red was permanently gone and recorded as having last been seen on his first and only flight two hours and 46 minutes after being released.

Although Red was permanently lost and we had to record his release as unsuccessful, the pattern of watching the emergence of the falcons from the hack box, and trying to see their first flight, and then observing where they landed was repeated at each site. Often we were able to observe and record fledging flights and first returns of our falcons to the hack box, but some first flights happened after the end of observations on a given day or before we started observing the next day. Occasionally, their initial flights took the Peregrines away from and out of our immediate observing area. A few times, fledging occurred during a severe storm while we were seeking our own shelter. Each early morning after release we anxiously observed until we identified that every Peregrine had successfully returned to the hack box, and then breathed a sigh of relief.

On a day after release when we could not see a particular falcon, we would trade off to take short hikes around our release site hoping to find and identify any wayward falcon still alive and hopefully trying to make his or her way back to the hack box and its convenient food source. Other Peregrines we did spot early in their learning-to-fly stage at Green River were two falcons that had landed on the roof of an old abandoned ranch site building a good half mile south of the Green River site. At Grave Point we found an early fledgling high in the branches of an old dead tree, but the tree was in back of the fire tower and so was not visible to us while we were at our normal observation point. At the Bar None Ranch, Holter Lake, and Wood Lake we hiked up and down along the base of the local cliff faces searching for our birds. It always felt good to come back to our partner and report, "Found another one! It's over there by the ….," and then a day or two later, even better to see that individual Peregrine back at the hack box eating a quail. If they made it back to the hack box at least once in the early days after release there was a better than 50-50 chance we would see them often.

Little Baby Ducks on the Green, Green River, 1993

During the week following the loss of Red, Gary was walking back from the ranch, still keeping a half-hearted lookout for Red. As he approached the river's edge from the dusty driving trail he had been following for one more peering look into the willows, he accidentally startled a mother Blue-winged Teal and her six little babies from the shelter of the overhanging grasses gently sweeping the surface of the river's current. Mama Teal quickly entered the rapid flow of the river from her calm sheltered cove, followed closely by her six very small brown and tan balls of fluff paddling with all their tiny might to keep up. Gary quickly sat down so as not to scare the brood further but to no avail as the mother Teal continued guiding her young charges toward the opposite side of the river, away from that hulking, frightful human.

The last baby in the short line squeaked in alarm as he fell further and further behind his siblings, swept away from his family by the current and bobbing downstream from them as well. There was no way the little duckling could battle such fast current and work his way back upstream to Mom and the rest of the family, but he at least was still heading for the same side of the river where the other ducks were located. Gary watched in silent alarm willing for a happy ending but the spread between lost baby and the rest of the group was lengthening while the downstream drift was speeding up. Gary, in the process of trying to save the life of one bird, our lost falcon, valued in terms of its production and transport to this point in human financial measurement of several thousands of dollars, had placed another bird, an un-costed "free" product of nature, in danger of dying. While on a mission to save a Peregrine, he was chagrinned to be causing the death of a wee duckling. He was sure at that moment of anxious observance that Mother Nature and the gods of humans did not consider one life was any more or any less valuable than the other.

Finally, swept along by the current and its own frantic paddling the little Teal made it to the slow current within the reeds of the opposite shore and stopped its drift downstream, squeaking for help all the while. All this time the parent Teal had kept talking to her little one in in a motherly constant quack of deep concern, while harboring her five remaining little ones 20 yards upstream from the wayward baby and over 20 yards away from Gary. The baby recognized Mom was the ultimate safety and was slowly making headway to join her as it paddled in the reduced, slow current within eddies and reeds and hanging grasses. From the far shore it appeared to Gary the mother Teal was telling her other babies to stay hidden and where they were and she would paddle downstream and fetch the squeaker because all Gary could see was the mother duck approaching the lost baby. But as the angle of approach subtly changed relative to Gary's position he noticed the five other babies were paddling in concert with mother, stuck like a blob of fluff with five little heads immediately on her far side, protected from the human watcher. The floating family fleet rejoined the still squeaking baby, the full family was together again, the squeaking was replaced by a gentle motherly murmuring quack, and mother and her brood drifted downstream out of sight and only the flowing whisper of the river's current remained. Mother Nature had implemented a rescue mission. Biologists and Ornithologists call this drama the survival instinct in action. Calling it the survival instinct and seeing it in action are two different parts of the human brain trying to comprehend the same thing. One is a rational explanation, the other, an emotional reaction. One was Gary's scientific explanation of what had happened. The other was revealed by the smile on Gary's face as he remained a few moments longer sitting quietly on the riverbank and later as he reported the duckling story to Jean when he got back to camp.

## Golden Eagles, Wood Lake, 1995

Release at Wood Lake in 1995 did not end well at all for one of our young Peregrines. Our Release Specialist had arrived at camp the night before and he and Gary went up the cliff early the next morning, while Jean set up her spotting scope and other equipment at the near-camp observation point below the cliff. The release of six falcons was straightforward and went fairly well. The Specialist disassembled and stored the bear resistant electric fence while Gary went to his selected observation point above the cliff. The Specialist laid out quail around the box area to sustain our falcons for the next few days and wetted down the feathers of the falcons. Then the Specialist quickly removed the front of the hack box and ran for the trees so the falcons would not see him. Now exposed to the wider world outside the box, all the falcons quickly exited the box and became excited by their unconstrained freedom and the fresh morning winds at the cliff edge, flapping their wings as they sensed new possibilities. At such a time, we and the Specialist would wish each falcon to first become fully cognizant of its surroundings and linger near the box long enough to get a good visual sense of its new broad environment but one falcon leaped into the air within the first minute after release and commenced its maiden flight. The remainder of the falcons for the next eight hours acted as one could hope for on this special day of their and our time at the hack box—testing the air, lifting their wings, hopping, exploring the cliff edge, eating some on the quail strewn about; several of them took short flights of just a few feet or elevated themselves into the air momentarily before settling down again and they cacked at a Red-tailed Hawk flying high above.

After seven hours of observation with Gary up on the mountain, the Specialist was satisfied with the falcons' response to their new freedom and, needing to get to his next assignment, came down off the cliff while Gary remained to observe the falcons until near dark. Five minutes after Gary saw the Specialist's truck driving away down the valley, tragedy struck and one falcon met death at the talons of a Golden Eagle.

At this time in the late afternoon, there were some scattered rain showers and an overcast sky. Suddenly there was loud cacking from our Peregrines as two large raptors rapidly winged in from the east. This is a perilous time for young falcons when they are not yet flight-adapted and are potentially-catchable prey for Golden Eagles. One Golden Eagle quickly power-dived, flaring his wings near the cliff edge, forcing three of the Peregrines into premature flight, one of which the eagle grabbed in its powerful talons. With swift, strong wing beats intermixed with a graceful glide, the eagle returned down valley carrying away its catch. Gary jumped up and stood with binoculars to his eyes as he witnessed this emotionally powerful display of raw nature. With a three-foot wingspan a falcon is not a small bird, but our falcon looked small under the mass of a predator with a wing span in the seven-foot range. The eagle, with his fresh meal carried below him, rapidly disappeared from sight and there was not a thing Gary could do, and not a thing he could have done, to prevent what he had just seen.

Given the unique site characteristics of the Wood Lake cliff site, Jean observed falcon activity above her on the front side of the cliff from an observation point near but above our campsite. In order to see hack box and cliff perspectives not visible to Jean, Gary observed the falcons below him from a position above and behind the hack box and well above both Jean and our camp. Shortly after absorbing the drama of a simultaneous, forced fledging of three falcons and capture of one through actions of the Golden Eagles, Jean signaled Gary from camp for him to return off the mountain and join her for a parley. We compared notes and deduced the bird we called Silver had been captured and was unlikely ever to be seen again, but we continued to observe the cliff and perimeter surrounding the hack box, hoping to be able to confirm that more falcons than the one still perched by the hack box had survived the attack. Because of his concern about eagles at this site, our Specialist had given us his home phone number. After dark we collected our notes, driver's licenses, and telephone calling card, drove 24 miles to Augusta to find a public phone at 10:30 PM to let our Specialist know what happened and seek his guidance and suggestions in case the eagles would return; his wife took our message and, at our request, relayed it both to her husband and to Peregrine Fund personnel in Boise. When we returned to camp at midnight, we knew we would not soon forget this release day and we knew we had better get some sleep before our Peregrine observations commenced again at sunrise.

Yellow Needs Help, Wood Lake, 1995

During the attack of the Golden Eagles at Wood Lake on the first day (14 June) of our young falcons' release, the female which we identified as Yellow was amongst the three falcons which had been forced into a rapid fledging and early dispersal from the safety of the hack box. Late in the morning we had seen Yellow feeding on a quail but by 6:00 PM that day, after the eagle attack, we could not see any falcons anywhere. We were depressed over the major event of the day and feared the worst but based on our experience we did know it was possible that most of our falcons had in fact survived and were merely in hiding or in some spot which would assure their safety but was hidden from our view. After our midnight arrival back at camp, we were tired enough to fall asleep quickly but yet anxious to wake early the next morning and hopefully confirm some of our falcons' return to the hack box for their necessary feeding.

The following morning (15 June) we left camp when it was just barely light enough for Gary to climb up to his observation point and for Jean to mount the hill close to camp to look up at the clifftop; we were in position for viewing as soon as it was light enough to read color bands on falcon legs with our spotting scopes. By noon, we had confirmed the sighting and return of four of our remaining five falcons back to the hack box and breathed a sigh of relief. While Gary could not see Yellow from his position above and in back of the cliff, Jean had found a falcon that was likely Yellow near some rocks and scrub brush on the face-portion of the cliff, some 30 feet below the place on the edge of the cliff where Yellow had last been seen prior to the eagle attack. Our Specialist was able to return in the afternoon, also for part of two subsequent days, to help us keep watch for eagles. On this day, as well as several other days during the first week following release, occasional thunder storms crashed overhead releasing rain and pea-sized hail, even some marble-sized hail for short periods of time. When that happened Gary would retreat from his open hillside observation point to a small shelter he had erected from a plastic tarp and some aluminum poles. Instead of getting soaked during a half-hour hike back to camp, this tarp arrangement enabled him to seek good temporary shelter to wait out the passing of short-term storms, and thus return to close monitoring of the falcons as soon as possible.

On 16 June Jean was able to confirm by leg color band, that the falcon on the cliff-face was Yellow; however, although Yellow had exhibited motion, her position on the cliff face had not changed since she had been spotted the day before. Furthermore, Yellow was perched on a steep face inaccessible to us attendants. Late in the day Jean observed that a local recreation site visitor or camper had begun target shooting or shooting at ground squirrels down near the lake with his gun pointed near the same area and trail system that Gary used to ascend or descend through the trees between camp and his upper observation point. In a matter of unfortunate timing Gary had closed down his observation up on the mountain and was returning to camp for a late meal when the shooting was taking place. This was confirmed when Jean and the shooter heard a rather thunderous and otherworldly voice, amplified by the concave shape of the hillside in back of Gary, as he yelled to the shooter that there was a person on this trail and the shooter better not be shooting without knowing what he was shooting at. The shooter quickly cased his gun, hopped in his truck, and "got out of Dodge." As Hack Site Attendants we knew we faced a number of real possibilities of danger and injury but we did not want, "got shot" to be among them.

On 17 June Gary drove the 26 miles into Augusta, Montana, where our freezer was located in the Ranger Station in order to replenish our supply of quail for the falcons. Over the time we were stationed at Wood Lake this gravel road generated three flat tires for our pickup truck as the very hard and dense crushed flint and granite knifed into and cut through our tire treads with its extreme edge sharpness. Because of this, Gary took on the responsibility of most of the town trips at this site. Anxious to learn from Jean the latest status of our cliff dweller, Yellow, Gary was relieved not to have to change a tire this time around. Back at camp Jean expressed her concern for Yellow to both Gary and the Release Specialist who had joined us again for some eagle watch duty. Yellow had not yet flown nor even moved from her solitary spot on the cliff face and was showing signs of weakness and lethargy. Then throughout that night a cold rain was falling robbing Yellow of more of her shrinking energy.

The following morning, 18 June, we finally saw and identified all five of our remaining falcons (after the loss of Silver) and so we knew all had survived the release and were now into their fourth day of independent freedom. Seeing all of the hack site's falcons simultaneously was the easiest way to know the site's falcons are all present on that day. The other option was to individually identify the color band on each falcon, a much more difficult goal. Not only were the color bands small and difficult to see but often the bird was engaged in activities where you could not see the lower portion of the leg. Obviously, the bands were nearly impossible to see when the falcons were in flight. At 8:00 AM Gary saw Yellow's leg band and confirmed again she was the falcon on the cliff face that likely had not eaten a quail now for more than three days. Although weak and not appearing very alert she was working her way ever so slowly back up the cliff face. At 10:00 AM we observed Yellow's right eye was closed, not a good situation for a predator such as a falcon. But it also helped explain why she might choose or be forced to be nearly immobile. We speculated an injury to her eye could have been caused by the eagle directly hitting Yellow on release day, or maybe she flew or ran into an object in her haste to escape, or perhaps it was even possible she had been struck by a piece of hail in a thunderstorm.

Gary, Jean, and another Release Specialist that had come on the 18th, conferred and all agreed we had better try to get some needed food to this valuable falcon if we wished to save it from starvation or a predator. We did not want to have Yellow see Gary as the food source, so the Release Specialist on the hillside above Gary, and Jean, located below Gary, guided him to the correct location on the cliff edge with hand signals so as to position Gary for tossing quail to Yellow without Yellow seeing the quail come from a human hand. At the same time, because of the relative positions of Gary and Yellow on the cliff, Gary would not be able to see Yellow. This effort required Gary's final approach to be done via crab-walking, then hand-and-knee crawling, and finally stomach-slithering while carrying two fresh quail and observing hand signals from his partners in this effort to save one of our falcons.

At last in position and having been shown where and how far to throw, Gary lobbed the first quail where directed over the cliff edge. That quail landed eight feet east of Yellow. Not a bad toss. She should be able to see it. With one last try, Gary redirected based on more hand signals and lobbed one more quail in Yellow's direction. This effort was near perfect as the Release Specialist reported that the quail had almost hit Yellow and she had ducked her head. We had all done what we could. Gary slithered and crawled back to the safety of flat ground and firm footing before standing up and sneaking back to the upper observation site where he rejoined the Release Specialist and waved down at Jean to assure her he was back in observation position and safe again.

An hour later we were disappointed to notice yellow had made no move to eat the quail tossed for her convenience. But nature has its own time schedule and after another two hours Yellow had finally fed, worked her way back up to the cliff edge, taken a couple of short hopping flights, was back near the hack box and had joined with two other falcons there in some minor squabbling over quail remnants. After four days we were finally feeling better about Yellow's chance at survival. Later that day one of our falcons stooped (attacked aerially) a Red-tailed Hawk from above and we recognized how quickly any young predatory bird can attain the competence to protect its own territory and how important it is for them to master the skies. That evening, as the sun was setting, a band of seven bighorn sheep came off their bedding area on the hill behind Jean and passed with 55 yards of her observation point on their way down to cross the valley floor. Later we observed them ascending the nearly vertical cliff face in hops and jumps as though they were on an invisible elevator. As the sky faded to night, we saw them bed down about 30 yards away from the falcons, who neither cared nor reacted to these large neighbors sharing their cliff top. Later in the summer we eventually saw bighorn sheep right at the hack box and one even hopped up and stood on top of the box briefly. Sheep behavior—just another rock to stand on top of.

On 19 June, with Yellow spending most of her time within the vicinity of the hack box where we could most readily observe her actions, we could tell she was at last feeding adequately as evidenced by her extended crop. However, her right eye was usually closed and she was the poorest flier of our group, often seeming weak and faltering and reluctant to fly. Late that day Yellow was again in the wrong place at the wrong time as a strong and rough Prairie Falcon flew into the hack box area with extended talons forcing Yellow to flight at the last moment before striking her. This was perhaps evidence of Yellow's inability to see her surroundings on her right side. Two days later Yellow was acting more like an assertive falcon instead of a sick bird and holding her injured eye partially open at times.

On 22 June, until an intervening mule deer crossed Jean's line of sight from the east observation point, Jean noted Yellow's eye was nearly fully open and could tell there was no clouding of the eye. During the next few days Yellow's eye continued to slowly improve, i.e. she held it open more often. And although preferring to land on the cliff and nearby snags than amongst the trees, she was now flying more with the other falcons. By 28 June, 14 days after Yellow had emerged from the hack box, her right eye was finally in the same good shape as her left and matched Black's appearance. For us it was a long worrisome recovery period, but perhaps typical of the self-healing all wildlife might at some point encounter during their lives in the wild.

On 26 and 28 June, members of our falcon group stooped and repeatedly attacked Golden Eagles entering the dome of airspace our falcons now claimed as their territory. No trespassers permitted. During the first few days after release our Peregrines could barely fly and were the unwilling potential victims of other powerful birds that thought they owned the territory wherein they found these young falcons. It was most reassuring for us to note that within two weeks of flight time, our falcons could readily defend themselves and defend their territory. That in turn meant we earthbound partners in the Peregrines' claiming of the skies in this lovely setting could relax our concern and instead focus on documenting the Peregrines continuing activities and encounters with life.

*Phase Three, Personal Stories: Figures 19 and 20*

*Figure 19: Our camper and the tower at Green River*

*Figure 20: Latrine with camouflage privacy netting*

## C. PERSONAL STORIES

*From the Journals: Bar None Ranch – Gary*
*3 August 1994 – This morning, still early in our assignment*
*here, I walked up a small feeder-valley that enters into our*
*valley from the north. It was an interesting walk, but as walks*
*can be at this time, slightly spooky. As one walks up an old road*
*or trail now covered with grass, there is usually a grass-parted*
*trail for you to follow. What large creature made this trail?*
*There are no cattle here but this is lion and bear country. And*
*so one slows behind the sweeping snake stick, carefully using it*
*and your eyes to search for that hidden, elusive rattler. Or,*
*something bigger. Then there is the silence, and walls of the*
*valley closing in on you. And the large over-turned rocks, done*
*recently, where Brother Bruin has been searching for insects.*
*And an eight foot tall fir tree stripped of nearly all its branches.*
*Some critter bigger and stronger and more woods-wise than I is*
*the one who has done all these things. That critter is out here*
*too. The facet of unfamiliarity of course is probably one of the*
*main fear-inducers. More time spent here and repeating each of*
*these walks will allow me to finally declare, "I have come to*
*know this land, I call it mine, I know what is here and how to*
*deal with it." But not now, not yet.*

### Good Sanitation Requires a Pickaxe, multiple sites, 1990-1996

At all of our field sites, except one, we lived each summer
without access to a bathroom or a flush toilet. The one
exception was Wood Lake where we enjoyed the luxury of a
pit-toilet type outhouse in the adjacent public campground area.
Luxurious because it had four walls and a swinging door that
functioned and could be locked while one was inside and
convenient in inclement weather because it had a roof that shed
rain and snow. Our usual fieldwork latrines had none of these
features. But it was still very important to provide for

appropriate sanitation and disposal of normal bodily waste products. Over those Peregrine summers we built a lot of latrines.

Because we were already experienced wilderness campers we always brought with us a home-fabricated wooden toilet seat built of plywood and 1x2 wood strengthening members approximately 16 inches by 16 inches square. We also brought a full-size farm dirt shovel with five foot handle. Digging a latrine to last a summer is serious hard work and you need the utility of a full-sized shovel, not a mere army surplus folding trenching tool or a plastic trowel. The plastic trowels were only used in an emergency on a long hike or for simple back-filling and daily covering at the latrine site.

In our first joint summer at Grave Point we supported the toilet seat with two long natural wood poles or tree branches which in turn rested on two piles of carefully selected and gathered rocks positioned at each end of the trench latrine. The latrine was always constructed in a narrow trench configuration because this meant we could dig it once and by moving the toilet seat laterally along the wood branches could gradually allocate usage and filling from one end to the other as one ran out of room in the trench portion one was hovering over. After Grave Point, however, we always brought our own six to eight foot long stout 2x2 wooden support beams so that they would be straight and we would not have to find the supports on site or risk not being able to find suitable tree branches.

Personal needs for privacy dictated where the latrine site would be positioned. Each site offered its own challenges for positioning. All of our hack sites would have at least a few visitors so we always selected a latrine site away from and on the opposite side from where visitors might first approach. At

Grave Point trees and brush were thinly scattered so it was located in back of a small rise in the hill and then the land contour and remoteness was our privacy screen. A peculiar item of note for our Grave Point latrine site: it offered a spectacular view into the dominant immensity of Hells Canyon, far better than what we could see from our campsite, far better than what we could see from our falcon observation sites. One did not lack for awe-inspiring wonder of earth's formations when seated at our Grave Point latrine. At Holter Lake, Bar None Ranch, and CSKT Cliff a small copse of trees, tall willow-type brush, or a somewhat hidden grove of pines provided security. At CSKT Tower we were located in the midst of broad open fields of cheatgrass, wheat stubble, and native prairie grasses, nothing taller than 12 inches for hundreds of yards around. But there were naturally-formed prairie potholes, dry all the while we were there, around 50 feet across, and four to six feet deep. Accordingly we chose one well positioned, not too far from camp, into which we could descend, and dug our latrine in the middle of it. When seated on our latrine nobody could see us from the road or our camping trailer and parking spot. We had all the privacy desired until two times when hot air balloons with their passenger-carrying gondolas passed overhead, on one of which occasions our latrine was occupied. Green River found us camped on open rangeland where the nearest latrine site hidden by brush or land contour was judged to be too far away to be practical. Therefore, we chose to dig along a fence line and then to string a camouflage net we had brought with us to shelter us from any prying eyes in the ranch house or on the road and bridge about a half-mile north of us. At Willow Creek Reservoir we were in the middle of an expansive short grass prairie range and pasture land area, again no trees, rock piles or convenient hiding spots for hundreds of yards. Our solution was to park our camper beside the large corral system built there for the sorting convenience of the local ranchers and to dig a latrine right in back of our camper inside the corral with a small hill to one side of it and our camper and truck forming additional privacy screens on two other sides. Where to put the latrine was always a significant question when we arrived at each camp site. The decision was always perplexing when we first arrived, but at each site we were satisfied with our eventual choice.

Sanitation needs dictated how the latrine was constructed and defined its final location after privacy of use was considered. We did not dig in or near a watercourse or where water erosion might occur. Depth and size needed to be sufficient to allow bacterial breakdown and aerobic action on contents while still being able to control odor with total soil coverage after each use. Our main campsite latrine would be about two feet wide at the top, four or more feet long, at least two feet deep, and with sides as vertical as the soil would allow. It was easy to wear ourselves down physically during the digging and cheat on how wide the trench was at the bottom, but narrowing at the bottom would severely impact the total volume of the trench and what it could contain as it gradually filled over the summer.

Although it provided a fantastic view, our latrine at Grave Point was physically exhausting to dig. The ground was very dry, very solid, and very rocky. We were making scant progress on its construction with our spade. Fortunately, Jean remembered there was a genuine, heavy-duty pickaxe in a storage building under the fire-watch tower. Apparently other personnel in years gone by had discovered the same impenetrable characteristics of the soil there. We trudged up the hill, retrieved the pickaxe and swung away. Dug out what was loose. Swung away. And repeated those steps over and over until we were worn down and had a satisfactory new latrine. After that summer's experience we always brought our own pickaxe as a supplementary digging tool and found it of immense value on the hard and rocky soil structures of several more of our hack sites, Holter Lake among them.

The campsite latrine was not necessarily the only latrine needed within a hack site assignment. At two of our sites we utilized remote observation points hundreds of yards or more, up to a mile, away from our nightly campsite. For these locations a supplementary smaller latrine was built near each observation point in case nature called while we were on observation duty. And over a summer's time, nature did come calling, and we were always glad we already had accommodations suited to the need of the moment.

At each latrine we had a water-tight container holding a roll of toilet paper and either an old tin can or small trowel. We used the can and/or trowel to cover our wastes with dirt, dipping dirt from the pile of soil, rock, gravel, which we had removed from the latrine trench during construction. It was important to fully cover the waste and used toilet paper with some soil because this hastened the biological breakdown and controlled odor. Once at Holter we became a little lackadaisical about adequate coverage while trying to prevent the need for digging a second latrine. We discovered how unwise and disgusting that was when we came back to our campsite latrine one day after a long day on the mountain observing falcons to find magpies, a bird related to crows and jays, had gotten into the latrine, scratched around and pecked at the exposed toilet paper, tearing it into shreds, and making a general mess.

Another disgusting issue ranking right up there with magpies in your latrine was the presence of carrion beetles at the CSKT Tower latrine. A carrion beetle's role in the environment is to recycle dead bodies, carrion, back into the earth. The beetles at

CSKT, perhaps descendants of those which had helped decompose the bison of past centuries, seemed to us to hone in on the odor of smelly things, decomposing flesh certainly, but available cow pies and our latrine also attracted their presence. In the hottest parts of the summer several could often be spotted crawling in and over the backfill in the bottom of our latrine. We hoped they would not take flight at an inopportune time. At other times one of us would be sitting on the latrine and then glance up to find one or several beetles in their slow buzzing flight about three feet over the ground surface headed erratically in twisting flight upwind to our vicinity. Or look down and see them slowly crawling on the ground, up and down and around the hummocks of grass, marching inexorably toward our latrine, then tumbling freefall at the edge of the pit to end up upside down at the bottom, their legs kicking in an attempt to right themselves and keep heading toward their goal. Carrion beetles are a diminishing species, not many bison to munch on anymore, so we tried hard to ignore them. But it wasn't easy, or pleasant.

At the end of each assignment we would finish back-filling our latrine and cap it off allowing for some settling but basically trying to retain the ground contour of its surroundings, remove and scatter any support structures, and put the support rails and toilet seat back in our truck ready for another use at another site. Sometime after we had left the Bar None Ranch site, we heard back through The Peregrine Fund, the ranch foreman's compliments for a total camp site well-tended and cared for; he, a skilled outdoorsman, had inspected our campsite several weeks after we left and had difficulty determining where the tents had been set up, where the latrine was and where we had parked. In spite of the extended use we gave to each site that was always our goal: to leave the site looking as much as we found it as possible. We tried to consider the admonition expressed by Wendell Berry in his book, *The Long-Legged House*, "A man should be in the world as though he were not in it, so that it will be no worse because of his life."

## Getting Cash from the Ranch Foreman's Wife, Green River, 1993

In 1990 when we began our biological fieldwork the banking and financial institutions were just beginning their transition to the electronic and digital transactions we now take for granted. During our first field assignments our monetary transactions happened with cash, a personal check, or a Travelers Check. Credit cards were used but reserved for large purchases and not all stores accepted them. Having stocked up supplies at home and brought them with us, most of our purchases while away from home for fieldwork were for small amounts of food or single items of clothing or camping gear and supplies that were unexpectedly needed at a specific site or as required replacements for something worn out or broken. Furthermore, once we were at our hack site location and making local purchases for the seven or more weeks on assignment, the communities where we made nearly all our purchases ranged in size from a population of less than 100 to less than 2000. Several of these communities did not have a bank or a full-service grocery store.

Except for our truck, our summers were spent without having secure premises to keep our valuables or our cash. Even the locked truck was sometimes at risk of being broken into because at some of our hack site locations, it was parked out of our sight and in remote rural areas. This made us reluctant to carry very much cash and we counted on a personal check or a Travelers Check for replenishment of our cash needs. But Travelers Checks were going out of vogue at that time and becoming difficult to cash, even if we could find a bank big enough to accept Travelers Checks. And personal checks were little better, not all banks accepted those from people from out of state as we were, and those that did usually required a burdensome vetting, sometimes involving contacting our credit union, and often requiring an additional fee.

It was with some small sense of relief that our credit union began issuing cards which we could take to a new device called an Automated Teller Machine (ATM). But guess what, once we left our service area in Wisconsin only a limited number of machines were accessible to us, and again only in the bigger cities, cities we only passed through once in a summer. About the mid-point of our fieldwork career, 1993-1994, we learned we could go to our credit union and determine a list of the locations of the nearest approved ATM's on our intended travel route. Most of the small communities where we worked did not have an ATM, let alone a credit union-approved ATM. So we acclimated to taking a larger amount of cash with us as we started each summer. How much does it take to get through a whole summer? That depends. Some expenses while we were on a hack site assignment were expected and somewhat predictable, i.e. coins would be needed for doing laundry, postcards would be purchased and postage expended to communicate with friends and family back home, we bought local detailed maps once we arrived in our assigned area each summer, and we photocopied our reports and some group-letters for family and friends or colleagues. We also budgeted for some recreational items including fishing licenses for Gary, occasional newspapers, magazines, even books, for reading material. Other expenses were not predictable beyond knowing there would be some. What will happen to you that summer? Flat tires, truck breakdown, food supplies damaged by mice, tent poles bent in high wind? We guessed as best we could and rolled with the punches.

The summer we drove into Pinedale, Wyoming, nearest community to our Green River hack site and located 25 miles and one hour from where we would be camping, the first thing we did was to look for an ATM machine to stock up on cash for our seven week Peregrine job. On our way west we had visited Gayle and Dean who were then located in Sheridan WY. After the visit, as we continued west we enjoyed a stop at Independence Rock Wyoming State Historical Site, and the scenery along the highway that followed the Sweetwater River and the route used by pioneers heading west in covered wagon trains. We even made a small side-trip to see the Lander, Wyoming area. Leaving for the next long (135 mile) stretch of driving, we did not realize for many miles that we had forgotten to visit an ATM in Lander. This made looking for one in Pinedale fairly urgent. Pinedale did not have one. Oh-oh, hadn't even started the summer job and the financial planning had already gone awry. Next stop, the local bank. No, they would not give us cash for our personal check. Not having any easy options and needing to set up camp at the release site we decided to stretch what cash we had as far as we could.

After four weeks on site we had become good friends with the ranch foreman and his wife. Good enough to ask for monetary help—you can always tell a good friend by whether they are willing to give you money. After four weeks our available cash was mostly gone so Jean meekly asked the foreman's wife if she would be so kind as to pick up a few grocery items and some cash for us the next time she went to Pinedale if we gave her a personal check. She, a very nice woman, readily agreed. Whew! Short-term cash problem solved. Until near the end of the summer that is. By then we were down to four dollars available between both of us. Time to somehow replenish our cash and we wanted to avoid embarrassing ourselves by asking our good neighbors for more help.

By this time we were close enough to the end of our assignment that the falcon watch duties had declined a bit so we decided Gary could take the time to go to the next-closest community where our credit union assured us a working and acceptable ATM existed. The nearest usable ATM was in Jackson, Wyoming, the next-most populous community, about 110 miles one-way down the road. Good thing Gary had enough gas in the truck to get there! Besides getting cash in Jackson, Gary found a nice bookstore to visit and was able to get all the laundry done in preparation for our upcoming journey home.

Green River was our fourth hack site out of eight. After Green River our financial guesswork got a little better and the developing American financial system became a little easier to deal with when we were traveling as non-residents through communities we had never visited before. We never again got down to our last four dollars.

It is perhaps appropriate here to remind our readers that by summer 1993 when we were at the Green River site, it had been two years since Gary quit his engineering job in favor of Peregrine work. Jean had had a teaching contract at UW-La Crosse for fall semester 1992, plus a Bald Eagle field job February through mid-June 1993 that paid about $5000 before coming to Green River. Gary had obtained some engineering consulting work to supplement our family income also. We felt were doing okay so far on our financial situation, but it was a relief when a letter came about a teaching contract for fall 1993. We still had a daughter in college after all.

*From the Journals: Green River – Jean*
*31 July 1993 – Found a letter in our mail today from my department chairman that there is a full-time fall semester job for me. We are celebrating the economic surety of $13,000 in salary and $2000 in health insurance benefits!*

Perhaps an example of the sort of expenses we encountered in doing fieldwork would be of interest at this point. In 1992, the summer we did two seven-week hack site assignments with only 24 hours between them, Jean kept a precise list of our expenses, subdivided into several categories. Food expenses to stock up before heading west are not included, nor certain other supplies purchased ahead before leaving home, such as propane for the camp stove, film for the cameras, and the like. Gasoline for the truck was purchased with a credit card, so that expense also does not appear in her record.

Food Expenses (including treats such as sodas, candy bars, ice cream)
Holter Lake job                         $110.14
Restock in Missoula between jobs  $181.45
CSKT Tower job                       $118.28
Fieldwork Expenses (tent pole repairs, 2$^{nd}$ snake bite kit, photocopying, etc.)                     $114.29
Medical (WY E.R., Helena Dermatologist, medications, supplies for spider bite care)       $196.50
Clothes (jeans)                           $ 19.99
Recreation (fishing license, reading materials, post cards & postage, photo developing)          $145.11

Total expenses for fieldwork summer 1992  $885.86

Did we make a profit during these fieldwork jobs? No. Not really, or at least not much. But then, that wasn't the point.

*Phase Four, Intense Observation: Figures 21 and 22*

*Figure 21: Gary observing falcons with spotting scope*

*Figure 22: Jean using scope at an O.P. with shade tarp*

# PHASE FOUR – INTENSE OBSERVATION PERIOD: weeks two, three and four

## A. INTRODUCTION TO DUTIES DURING INTENSE OBSERVATION PERIOD

The time period directly after release is most crucial for the successful transition of a nestling falcon to a free-flying, self-supporting falcon. At the time of release the falcons are essentially full-size and fully feathered, and they have spent their last week or so of captivity becoming increasingly restless. This restlessness is visible in increased movement inside the hack box, intense interest in the world outside the hack box, and wing-flapping sessions that serve to strengthen the flight muscles. It was always amazing to see these birds, though having never flown before, yet possessed of the feathers, muscles, nerves and instinct for flight, take off and usually fly quite well their very first time. They were, however, not nearly as good at "sticking" their first landings. And, very often that first landing was not made back at the hack box.

Since the young Peregrines had been fed all the food they wanted until the day before release, they had a supply of stored fat and were thus not desperate for food for a day or two. Nevertheless, they were denied food the day before release, and sprayed with water to make their feathers wet and heavy, in hopes that they would come out of the hack box calmly, eat another meal, look around and dry off before fledging—i.e. taking their first flight. Before the moment of release a large supply of quail, about 6-7 per falcon, was scattered out on the hack box "porch," the top of the box, and also on the tower or cliff around the box. This supply of food was provided so that the attendants need not approach the hack box during the period immediately after release. To do so would be to flush the falcons into precipitate fledging instead of allowing them to fledge in their own time if possible. After those first three days post-release, we headed up to the hack box to clear up the remnants (quail bits) from falcons dining there and also pickup up any leftover, uneaten quail—all this remnant food was rather rank by then. Putting out a fresh supply as we would then be doing daily from that morning until the last week, we always left the hack box (tower or cliff) area quickly so any hungry falcons could return.

It was our job to try to observe the first flight of each falcon from the hack box, and note where it made its first landing. In order not to miss these first flights we were expected to watch from dawn to dusk and make at least one note per hour in our observation notebooks for two weeks starting on Release Day, i.e. during our second and third weeks on the job. Since the falcons would begin to show weakness after three days without food, we also needed to make note of which falcons ate before fledging and how much, since this information would predict how soon an individual would be desperate for food.

*From the Journals: Grave Point – Jean*
*27 July 1990 – Alarm: 4:20 AM. I jerk awake from heavy sleep, quickly remember it is my morning to hike to the tower, sit up in the tent so I won't fall back asleep, and peer out the tent window—aah, clear skies at last. Hurrah! 53°F. I hike the half mile uphill, climb the tower, place nine quail on the hack box about 4:42 AM and rejoice in the morning. My world is bounded by a circle of mountains around a mystic tower, cut by two great river valleys. The grassy top of tower mountain is open to the sky, a baldpate surrounded by treed slopes in Ponderosa pine and Douglas fir. As I start down, I see CJ arriving at the O.P. Sunrise waits for no one. And neither of us wants to miss a single one of our turns at tower duty.*

Obviously, sometimes we needed a bit of time off now and then for such necessities as preparing food and visiting the latrine, but during these intervals the other attendant stayed on watch. We took turns at these tasks, and usually ate meals at the O.P. Experience had shown The Peregrine Fund, that independence in hunting and providing its own food began to be reasonably reliable in a Peregrine three weeks after release. Since we had to have notes on the last sighting of each of our falcons to be able to record that date in our report at the end of the hack site job, we decided for ourselves to keep a modified intense observation period during the third week after release (fourth week on site). Our goal in this extra week was to record a sighting, and preferably also evidence of consumption of quail, for each of our released falcons. If each of the falcons came to the hack box for food on a given day in the third week post-release and we saw and recorded them for the day, we sometimes watched less intensely for the rest of that day. Occasionally there was enough daylight after we had recorded all our falcons on one of these days that one of us could take a hike around the area. Certainly such an opportunity was welcome after so many hours of sitting in a camp chair watching the hack box for the appearance of falcons.

## B. STORIES FROM INTENSE AND SEMI-INTENSE OBSERVATION PERIODS

### Black's Personal Hack Site, CSKT Tower, 1992

As previously described, the release did not go as smoothly as usual at CSKT Tower on 1 August 1992. The tower held two hack boxes and from each box five falcons were released. One of the females became upset early and her constant cacking seemed to cause five males to fledge precipitously without eating. By the end of that day, the two Release Specialists had located four of the five fledged falcons at various points around the area, and the other five had eaten and remained on the tower the rest of Release Day and overnight. The Specialists stayed with us several days at this site to help sort out this situation. The other five falcons fledged individually and more normally over the next few days.

Gradually as the days passed, two of the precipitously-fledged falcons, named Brown and Black for their colored identification leg bands, settled down to small regular territories. Brown's story concluded in a few days, but Black's story continued much longer.

Black's territory centered on a large flat rock in the ditch beside the gravel road about half a mile to the west of the tower and he was observed making use of fence posts near that rock for perches at first. A small stream passed through a culvert under the road and flowed by Black's rock, providing him a water supply. Early each morning and late in the afternoon one of us walked west toward the road, carrying a spotting scope so we could check on Black. Soon he improved his perching locations to include a line of power poles that paralleled the road, and the roof of a small, abandoned wooden building in the field near his territory. Some of the falcons, after successfully flying out from the tower and back several times, began to range out further and found Black on his power poles and roof. These falcons interacted with Black thereafter, a development we found encouraging.

Since a large supply of quail was always placed on the tower on release day, the falcons could be left undisturbed for a few days. It was on the fourth day after release that attendants were scheduled to put out fresh quail. This was also an opportunity to remove any leftover quail and to clean up remnants and refill the water pan that was provided for falcons at this hot, dry site. Although this was a normal procedure, it also flushed all falcons from the tower and we then had to wait in suspense and hope that they would all get back. On 6 August, Black attempted to return, but a vigorous wing-flapping practice session going on among other young falcons on the tower as he approached, caused Black to abort his landing. Instead, he looped around and came in to perch on the understructure of the tower, which held no food supply for him. Again the next day he landed on the understructure of the tower, and from our observation point 200 yards away, we could hear his piteous food-begging calls. These failed attempts to return to the tower to feed raised agonizing concerns for Black; his obvious fidelity to his territory along the line of power poles led to the decision to put out quail for him on the rock that seemed to be the center of his territory. In effect we were hacking him from the rock instead of from the tower. It was very good news when Black was observed as having taken a quail up onto the top of one of his poles, and as already having a full crop—now that he had a food supply, he was keeping it close! At first Brown, and later several of the other falcons, perched frequently with Black on the power poles that lined the west road, sometimes more than one falcon on a single pole, but often on individual poles. And, these occasions led to roosting on the poles overnight. Thus, our morning and evening walks west to check on Black became an opportunity to record roosting places of several other falcons as well.

Brown had begun trying to return on the third day after release and Black on the fifth day, but both merely circled the tower or landed on the support boards underneath the platform, rather than landing on top of the tower where the quail were provided. Brown successfully returned to the tower for food on the fifth day, but Black took much longer to work it out. He did begin

161

coming to the tower almost daily, often begging for food from the support boards underneath, but did not succeed in landing on top and consuming quail there until the 19$^{th}$ day after release. When he did finally land on the tower, he grabbed a partially-eaten quail abandoned by one of the others and hunched over it very defensively for five minutes before he became calm enough to eat. After that, Black was soon coming regularly to the tower for quail and after a few more days to make sure of him, we stopped putting food out on the big rock that had served so well as his personal hack site.

*From the Journals: CSKT Tower – Jean*
*14 August 1992 – I spent a couple hours walking around by road to put out four quail for Black, and then sitting under the fence-row apple tree by the irrigation ditch to watch for him. Eventually I got to see Black circling over a field, stooping over a Red-tailed Hawk and landing on a pole. Pink came and sat on the same pole with him, and two other falcons flew in and perched together one pole away. No cacking occurred amongst this group so I know Black is accepted by them and accepting of them. This is encouraging.*

## Remnants, Site Exploration, and Moose Confrontation, Green River, 1993

We were over a week past release of the Peregrines and awoke early with the hint of dawn beckoning in the far east as the sun began to kiss the far slopes of the Wind River Range 50 miles beyond. From our bed, using a binocular always placed in a handy position, we had seen a Prairie Falcon making an early visit to dine on some left over quail before the Peregrines returned. We dressed for another cool but pleasant morning and went out to set up our scopes and camping chairs at our observation position in front of our camping trailer. As the Green River continued its slide off the mountains and its silent flow past our camp, we logged the Prairie Falcon's visit into our spiral-bound field notebooks and wrote down the first morning visits by our Peregrines to the hack box.

We spotted the pickup truck driving down the access trail skirting the high bank of the river and stood to meet our visitor. The local state wildlife agency nongame biologist was obviously pleased to see we were already at work and asked, "Don't you folks ever sleep!?" He was on his way to survey for adult Peregrines farther up the valley and had dropped by to check in with us and learn a bit more about our latest observations. The good news for us was he brought us some fresh fruit. Great! Anything fresh was always welcomed by Hack Site Attendants dining mostly on dried food, boxed products, and canned items. The biologist listened attentively and took his own notes as we told him about the Trumpeter Swan with neck band that we had observed several times on the river near the lower hayfield.

After the biologist left and while the tower was temporarily vacant of any Peregrines, we paddled across the river in the canoe and replenished the quail. It was Gary's turn to climb the tower, retrieve any quail remnants, and lay out a fresh supply. Peregrines appreciate fresh food too—fresh from the freezer and thawing cycle.

For each day we supplied quail to the hack box for the Peregrines to feed on, the other half of this responsibility was to pick up the "food" left over from the previous feeding. These left-overs we always classified as "remnants" but, depending on how much our Peregrines consumed, whether there were any non-Peregrine aerial visitors, whether the Peregrines carried the quail bodies away to eat elsewhere, how much wind there was that might blow off the quail wings generally not consumed by the Peregrines, the quantity of remnants was always variable in volume and aesthetic appearance. That is to say, it was a messy and icky process to gather stinky pieces of quail and quail heads and legs and various abandoned piles of internal quail organs including clusters of yolks from the ovaries of the females and sometimes even a completely formed egg, and to note the insects which the rotting bodies would attract. But, in that sense Peregrines are like people: given a choice they would rather eat "fresh" quail than to eat left-overs. In addition, if the remnants were left on the hack box they might attract other predators like owls or the putrefaction might cause illness or disease in the Peregrines.

At our very first hack site, after briefly trying various techniques for final disposition of quail remnants we quickly deduced our preferred method was to discard them a long walking distance from camp and the hack box and put the remnants in contact with the soil, there to become recycled by natural means of decomposition, insects, worms, or any other living fauna that could gain advantage from our deposit. A different option was to gather the remnants in a plastic bag and periodically take them to an approved garbage collection point but after a few days' time in the plastic bag or in a garbage can this was a smelly, distasteful process for both us, the attendants, and for the garbage handler when they found the "surprise" we had left in a municipal or agency garbage can. Another possibility was to bury the remnants—of course we tried this— but it was a time-consuming and difficult labor in rocky or hard soil conditions. In addition, if the remnants were not buried deep enough a coyote or skunk could and did find them and dig them up. Bear in mind that disposal of remnants was a daily requirement for many weeks on site. Far easier and actually more sanitary to let nature do the recycling and to assist nature in this by a broad and random dispersal of remnants, never returning exactly to the same spot for following days' deposits. We wanted to assure nature's decomposition processes did not take place near our camp or the hack box.

Because he had plucked them off the hack box and tower meant this day it was also Gary's obligation to dispose of the remnants. Picking up the bag of quail remnants he crossed over the barbed wire fence and walked off into the nearby rangeland dominated by sagebrush. The ranchland to our west largely consisted of hayfields of meadow grass growing near the rich and the more moist alluvial soils of the river bottom. The ranchland to our east was on a slightly higher bench beside the river and had dry, rough soil, and from a modest distance appeared to be growing nothing but sagebrush. As one got closer though, or walked into the sea of sage, one could then discern the grass and other forbs growing in between the sagebrush plants. It was this combination of living plants that sustained the local Greater Sage-Grouse in the winter and provided nourishment to their chicks in the late spring and early summer.

Sagebrush has always been a bit of a magical plant to us and we have long admired its tenacity to grow where other plants fail and, of course, the pleasant aromatic odor of its leaves. At this site it was growing robustly, several feet tall, with lower branches as big in diameter as one's wrist, and the plants were thick in density, so thick you could not walk a straight line but had to weave between the bushes and push your legs through the spreading branches. The ground surface was hummocky and roughly contoured from many decades of sage growth. Occasionally a small pothole or depression or swale with no outlet for any rain that might fall appeared in the general land contour. This depression was often covered mostly in grass, was the preferred grazing area for cattle on this rangeland, and was also preferred by us walkers for its easy transit.

Finally, reaching a point largely inspired by a feeling of "this is far enough," Gary tossed the remnants on the ground and wove a serpentine path back through the sagebrush, the path determined by multiple obstructions of the branches of the intervening sagebrush, or sometimes coming upon a worn cattle trail going in the right direction.

In the afternoon, after confirming Jean was agreeable and willing to take on solitary observing duties for a while, Gary put a five-gallon jug of water in the front of the two person canoe to serve as a counter-balance weight in lieu of a second paddler, and put into the river to paddle solo downstream. Although his personal goal for the afternoon was further exploration, specifically of another area near our release site that he had not yet visited, he could justify it as being one final attempt to learn what might have happened to Red, our missing falcon. This because he would be going through locations reachable by Red in flight but which we had not had the opportunity to visit. He paddled down to where Mud Creek enters the Green then ascended Mud Creek as far as the draft of the canoe would allow. After paddling and poling several hundred yards of a much slower, smaller stream he was stopped by a three to four-foot high beaver dam, water trickling over and through the many branches and sticks and mortaring mud. He pulled the canoe out on a convenient shallow creek bank, and examined closely the engineered construction of the beaver dam (damn fine work, well-chosen location, high and stoutly built).

With the canoe parked on land but very near to the naturally occurring ground water level, Gary walked toward the short butte overlooking this area of creek meeting the river. He encountered the typical obstruction of this flat river valley terrain, that being standing or drainage water in varying sizes of pools within the concealing vegetation, ranging in depth from a mere quarter inch to as much as six inches. By the time you see and know you are in water it is too late to avoid it. Looking more carefully after that to avoid standing water, Gary picked a meandering path through the driest or shallowest areas until he topped the butte and found there a small concrete marker designating the location of the grave of Alexorama Hill. It is a particularly remote and solitary location for a grave; no other clues were in the area to hint at an explanation. Little is known historically, but two children are rumored to be buried there as well. Coming upon a marker of death in such a vast and open panorama gives pause for some reverence and deeper contemplation. Gary left three wildflowers by the marker and wandered back to the canoe.

Returning to the canoe by a different route Gary again encountered some inevitable standing shallow water. This time he elected to run and hop while quickly trying to choose the shallowest water in the false hope that if his feet are in contact with water but briefly then he would not get wet. It almost worked. The problem was while Gary was focusing on choosing his water path he neglected to look up toward his final destination, that of the beached canoe. When he did finally look up, standing near the canoe were a mother moose and her large calf that had been startled from their grazing by a two-legged water-hopping human. Oops! Down to a 20-yard distance from mama and baby when he noticed them, Gary put a quick halt to running and went into slow cautionary mode. By this time both moose had drifted into the willow bushes and momentarily were hidden from sight but reappeared 20 yards on the other side of the canoe. As he stood there staring at the moose, remembering how protective a mother moose is of her baby, as the mother and baby stood there staring back, Gary asked himself, "How fast can I run and get into the canoe before she decides to bring this gap between us down to zero?" Given the length of her legs this was not a good situation. Gary looked at her. She looked at Gary. Then Gary thought of the eye contact dilemma that wilderness travelers are advised to remember with cougars and grizzly bears. With one you are advised to look into their eyes, with the other you must look away to avoid appearing aggressive. Gary asked another question, "Do I make eye contact with moose or not? Have not read about moose eyes!" Gary backed up slowly. The moose backed up slowly. A truce! Soon the moose turned around and went deep into the willows to escape this strange intruder in their land. With his escape path now cleared Gary hurried back to the canoe, launched, floated down Mud Creek and paddled back upstream to camp.

As dark came on that evening the pleasant breeze of the day diminished and the mosquitoes came back to pester us, we put away our scopes and shut down falcon observation for the day. We retreated to our trailer to eat supper, read some, write in our journals, and, from Gary's particular day's exploratory activities, to record P46 as the swan identification neckband number for the biologist when he visited us next time. We knew he would be pleased.

Foul Weather, Kayak, and Curlew, Holter Lake, 1992

*From the Journals: Holter Lake – Gary*
*19 June 1992 – Sitting on our side of the mountain, the lengthening sun-drawn shadows tell us the afternoon is waning. The day has been calm and warm with the hot breath hint of summer days to come—days that will call for further shedding of our garment layers. But at this time comes the soft breathing of the conifers in back of us, the increasing whisper of the hillside, a precipitate waving of the fronds of grass suddenly kissed by this gentle wind of late afternoon. A tenderly spreading blanket of fresh moving air envelopes us within the*

*sound of subtle whispering magnified by its passage through the needles of these trees we shelter in.*

*Now it is gopher time again. Late in the same afternoon we heard the crunching of sun-dried balsam root plants. Then we saw one seed head wiggle and another seed head literally descend into the ground. Putting our binoculars on the spot and slowly walking closer we at last spied the source of activity. It was a small dark hole in the ground which yielded a white furry face furtively popping out, nipping off a stem of whatever was near the hole, and quickly pulling it down into a subterranean lair. A white pocket-gopher!? Yes, when at last, after many looks by us at his "secret" activities, we could return to our guidebook of mammals, we confirmed the potential color variation of white for these rarely observed mammals. Another rare gift. Granted by the mountain. To those who have the time to seek and wait for such a gift.*

The reader can tell by now that we made many interesting "discoveries" during these summers, our Peregrine Summers. Discoveries within ourselves, discoveries of our relationship, discoveries in nature and the outdoor world surrounding us at the time. But interesting to us through the writing of this memoir was the discovery of our latent reaction to some of our experiences, one of which is our altered perception of the Holter Lake hack site. While we were there, Holter Lake presented numerous challenges and struggles and within the time period of our hack site adventures we had classified it as one of our least favorite sites. With the passage of several decades since that experience and re-considering the Holter Lake site from the perspective of writing some stories about it, we now find it is the site of which we are most proud.

The struggles and challenges of the Holter Lake site included caring for Jean's spider bite upon our arrival, the remoteness and distance involved in accessing the site and providing food and water to it, the incessant roar and distraction of power boats on the lake below where we sat each day, the wind-driven rain and thunderstorms we endured, the disgustingly hard soil in which we had to dig our latrine. But in retrospect, as can happen with specific life struggles, we feel so much satisfaction at having surmounted those challenges that Holter Lake has become one of our favorite sites. We have now the pride of accomplishment plus the numerous "positives" of the site: good success at the life-launching of our Peregrines, wonderful photographic opportunities, meadowlarks we could individually identify by their songs, mule deer who calmly passed within five yards of us while we were sitting quietly in our camp, dramatic vistas, and privacy befitting mountain recluses.

Because Gary had read several editions of the Lewis and Clark journals and studied their great western exploration rather extensively, he was fascinated to be able to live adjacent to a path they had traversed as part of their voyage up and down the Missouri River. From our mountainside hack site observation point, Gary would look down at the river's path and try to imagine what they saw, because nearly all of the physical form of the mountains and the path of the river yet remained as Lewis and Clark had seen them. What was different was that the water level they traveled upon would have been 100 feet lower at the point where Holter Dam now stands and 14 feet lower at the point of the renowned "Gates of the Mountains," named by Captain Lewis in 1805 and located about six miles south and upstream of where we spent each day.

Imagining the pristine and quiet wilderness which Lewis and Clark and their men passed through, and in spite of our own remoteness and never being visited by any casual stranger utilizing the lake adjoining our side of the mountain, we were nearly daily disappointed by our fellow man and his treatment of what we considered a near-sacred place. The mountain-rimmed bowl in which Holter Lake was situated acted very much similar to a megaphone in echoing and amplifying the sound of the power boats and multiple jet skis traversing to and fro upon the lake surface. One Sunday we counted more than 50 different powered watercraft visible at once from where we sat high above the melee, but not out of reach of the noise. We were always pleased when the weekends ended, for it meant fewer manmade sounds would distract us from the natural sounds we wanted to hear. But then the following Friday the noise again would intensify. Admittedly we were somewhat misanthrope as we passed some conversation time in concocting various mean-spirited methods of ridding our end of the lake of these disturbingly loud noise makers, one of which involved imagining a long cable strung across the lake. But it wasn't just the noise and the boats that disturbed us about the utilization of this lovely resource—if one walked close to the shore you occasionally found piles of human waste and toilet paper strewn about, along with garbage left over from shore-side picnics. Discarded fishing lures lay at water's edge and several times we found the dead bodies of gulls, their legs and wings tangled with monofilament fishing line.

Although the majority of outdoor enthusiasts using this lake would be opposed, we could imagine how different it would be if only human-powered watercraft were allowed on the lake, and how avidly our fellow silent-sports advocates would support such a move. We tried to set a small example: because we knew we would be situated on or near this lake for our Peregrine assignment we brought along a boat, a folding, 17-foot long, two-person kayak weighing 62 pounds. The kayak packages, one of poles, one containing the treated canvas "skin," fit into the back of our pickup truck while still allowing room for all our camping supplies. Instead of hiking out along the lake to our truck for supplies, water, food, and quail for the Peregrines, several times we assembled the kayak and paddled the several miles between our truck and our camp. We discovered that although the kayak saved our legs, it did not really save any time in terms of transit or time away from our assigned hack site duties compared to walking. But it did offer variety and a different perspective on not only the stunning visual scenery, but also on what it takes to supply a wilderness camp. We gained a revised respect for the boat voyage of Lewis and Clark and their men traveling in this same locale, also by human-powered boat, also having to carry along gear and supplies.

On the lower end of the large peninsula on which we were camped was the breeding and nesting territory of a Long-billed Curlew pair. This largest sandpiper nests far to the west of our Wisconsin home and so we were unacquainted with its habits. The species is very possessive of its nesting territory and one of the pair would fly shrieking toward any visitor who got too close, but its size and actions invited several attempts on Gary's part to get some image-filling photographs. The biggest challenge was to adjust the manual focus on the long lens barrel with high magnification while the Curlew was rapidly approaching and then to judge when it was best to duck out of the bird's flight path. The image of a large bird rapidly approaching in the view finder was quite intimidating and inevitably Gary would duck before he needed to. Better safe than sorry and Gary did not persist as he valued the Curlews' right to nest above that of his desire for a striking photograph. The Curlews were special neighbors and the peninsula big enough to share.

As we re-read our extensive journals from the Peregrine Summers, even we are somewhat amazed as we remind ourselves of not only the grand and great memories, but also of the miserable conditions we successfully endured. Early in the Holter Lake hack site stay endless days would pass where we yearned to see the sun once again. One day the temperature just kept hovering around 44 degrees while we sat observing our young birds in the rain and mist. After a 2-mile hike up to feed the falcons and back to camp, and a third mile to reach the observation site, our feet were inevitably cold and wet. Under thick overcast skies the breeze would come up and without a good wind layer your body chilled quickly once the exercise of the hike had ended. Rain pants could keep the outside moisture off your legs but during three plus miles of hiking your sweat produced enough condensation that your legs still got wet. Commiserating with each other we fought to keep our spirits up in spite of how our bodies felt and Jean came up with a saying we sometimes repeated to ourselves: "Elitism, self-righteousness, and pride will get you through a lot." It helped. Eventually, with patience and self-will we saw the sun return and welcomed its warm radiance back into our lives knowing we could handle the next time it disappeared under rain and clouds.

## Visual Communication between Observation Points, Wood Lake, 1995

*From the Journals: Wood Lake – Gary*
*21 June 1995 – When the thunder is not around and only the rain comes down, I have had several recent opportunities, as I have also had at other sites in other years, to stay in my position and pull the poncho over me and my few belongings, and sit out the rain. It is a simple but satisfying act to tuck my head and wings in and to have this small thin shell of fabric*

*protect me from the elements, I am in them, the elements, but protected and sheltered, perhaps like the shaggy buffalo or feathered falcon might feel. I accept it. I feel the drops, watch them pool in front of my eyes, but I am not wetted. I feel more OF nature instead of watching it.*

*Jean has had several bands of Bighorn Sheep walk past her within 20 yards. One batch of three I signaled to her via semaphore from my hill to hers and she stood and saw them. The other group was seven. Both groups also made their way to the hack box, the group of three startling three Peregrines to flight as the sheep crested the cliff from below having climbed straight up the very steep slope. They look as though they do those things (climbing, jumping, going up vertically) because they can.*

*The weather continues unseasonably cool. We are thankful for the heat of the sun when it shines and the shelter of the trailer. It is remarkable what we can endure. With the proper layering (four on the legs, six on the torso) I sat through ten hours of 35– 45 degrees and was quite comfortable. Nonetheless, after repeated hours of this, the immobility we sustain during observation, we eventually get bone-chilled and need to exercise or hike for at least 15 minutes or seek artificial warmth.*

*One lesson we've learned this summer we kind of picked up from one of the Specialists. He said he could sit for hours and do nothing, nothing but observe. He seemed to hint variously at guilt and at pride for being able to do this. Due to our observing obligation plus the fact that books are heavy to carry, we also can find ourselves sitting on a hill for 8, 10, 12, and pushing 15 hours and, except for eating, just observe and think. For multiple days. No journal writing (except for mandatory*

*Peregrine Fund entries), no reading, no TV, just be out there sitting, observing, pondering. Perhaps again more like the animals. The feral in us coming out and being content to be, without being busy. It was easy. I might not have predicted that.*

The hack box at Wood Lake was several hundred yards away from Jean's normal observation point (O.P.) close to our camper in the valley, and the box was positioned at the edge of a flat-top cliff. The cliff edge was above the valley and above her O.P., which meant Jean would look up at the hack box and be able to see activity on the valley side of the box and at the cliff edge but could not see any activity behind the box or any of the falcons on the ground unless they were at the valley edge of the cliff. During the first one to two weeks of pre-fledge and early flight action of the falcons we decided Gary should set up a second observation point above the cliff and in back of it so that at least one of us would be able to see the falcons no matter where in the hack box vicinity they chose to spend some time. Given the rough and mountainous contours of the area, we located Gary's O.P. on a grassy open area of the mountain above the hack box and several hundred yards from it so that our birds would not be disturbed by his presence there. This gave Gary the opportunity to observe the falcons' daily activities at the box that Jean could not see from her O.P., and Jean could see falcon activity that Gary could not.

The three lines of sight established between us two observers and between each of us and the hack box thus formed a rough triangle, each side of which was several hundred yards long, with the three tips of the triangle being Jean at her O.P. not far above the valley floor, the hack box on the cliff above her, and Gary higher yet at his O.P. up on the mountain side. Although we could see each other we were separated by more than 300 yards and Gary's walk back to camp and then to Jean's O.P. was about one-half mile; the route was indirect because of elevation changes and the rough terrain, and it involved first descending to the valley floor, then climbing up the smaller hill of Jean's O.P. We did not have a set of two-way radios or any other wireless communication between us but knew we would want to compare notes and signal one another regarding falcon counts or daily planning. The question thus presented is, how do we accomplish the communication we want and need?

We both had very good binoculars, we each had a powerful spotting scope with magnification up to as much as 60X, and, along with our daily needs such as water and snacks, we each always had with us our Peregrine Fund 5x7-inch spiral notebook. We would communicate visually. We agreed that on the hour, each hour of our observation periods, we would turn our spotting scopes toward one another and observe the other partner. We each held our notebook in our right hand beside our head when we were ready to communicate, one to give a message visually, and the other to receive it visually while peering through the scope. We would raise our notebook vertically in the air above our heads once for each falcon we could see. For example, two pumps of the notebook meant that viewer was looking at two Peregrines. After we lost Silver to the Golden Eagle, we still were observing five falcons, the goal being to see all five falcons each day. We could compare our notebooks when we got back together at the end of the day to see if, between us, we had seen all five falcons. The other option, or if one of us had a question of who was seeing which falcon, was to write in the air with our handheld notebook, the first letter, or two letters, of the name for each falcon: Y for Yellow, BK for Black, W for White, R for Red, and BU for Blue. The sender of the alphabet transmission had to spell the letters backwards, or in reverse visualization, so that the receiver could read them as they would normally appear on a page. If Jean wanted Gary back in camp for any reason, she could signal that with arm and hand motion. We got fairly practiced at concise, but clear messaging. Years later we felt that in our Peregrine summers, we had invented a sort of precursor to the digital texting that eventually developed on personal cell phones. We referred to our methodology as "Semaphore Signaling." Our visual communication over remote distances would prove a valuable asset at the CSKT Cliff site the following year.

## Bear Troubles and Semaphore Communication, CSKT Cliff, 1996

There were bears at our first 1996 site; not only did we see them, or evidence of their presence, often but they formed the basis of a couple of the most-often-told tales of our Peregrine summers. The day after release of the falcons at this site, the Release Specialist who had released them was still with us because of potential problems from a resident pair of Prairie Falcons and their young. The Specialist's concern was appropriately well-founded because we observed an adult Prairie Falcon dive and purposely strike our Peregrine identified as Yellow in mid-air while Yellow was still a new amateur flier, and on other occasions, closely chase Yellow. We also were hearing Great Horned Owls at night, and having an adult Peregrine take quail from the hack box supply daily from the first day of release. With so many concerns at this site, Gary and the Specialist were watching the falcons from a location below the hack box and cliff, while Jean was observing from upon a lower portion the cliff some distance away from the hack box. As Jean finished noting the arrival of the adult Peregrine to the hack box and prepared to rotate her spotting scope and aim it at Gary for the hourly exchange of semaphore signals, she saw a bear on the cliff only about ten yards from the hack box, but back from the cliff edge where it could not be seen by Gary and the Specialist from their location near the base of the cliff. Obviously, the bear might be a direct threat to the young falcons, but it was also very important that it not become aware that the hack box was a source of food. Bears had also been known to attack and seriously damage hack boxes because of the associated odors.

It was then just 1600 hours (yes, we were required to use the 24-hour method of designating time in our observation notebooks and reports) and, though she knew he would be soon training his scope on her for the hourly communication, Jean stood waving her arms in hopes of attracting Gary's attention quickly. As soon as she saw him lift his notebook to head height, indicating his attention was on her, she began to move her notebook through the air in large motions to spell out

B    E    A    R

in reversed letter shapes so Gary could easily read the message, while simultaneously pointing emphatically with her other arm toward the hack box. As soon as she finished the one-word, one-gesture urgent message, she repeated it for emphasis. In the scope she could see Gary turn to the Specialist and begin to speak.

Gary: "Jean says there's a bear at the hack box."
Specialist: "What? How do you know that?"

Gary repeated the message and said Jean had signaled it to him. The Specialist took Gary's word for it and immediately began to throw his gear into his backpack. Jean could not hear any of the conversation, but could see the Specialist getting ready and setting out to come up to her location. Meanwhile, the bear had disappeared from Jean's view, perhaps disturbed by all her arm-waving and about 20 minutes later, Gary saw it moving away northward along and then down the cliff.

The Specialist got Jean's report in detail and continued to observe with her until dusk, but the bear was not seen again on the cliff. Leaving us both on watch, the next day the Specialist went to town to get more quail and some noise-making gear for us to use to discourage the bear if it returned.

Even though the bear left the hack box and cliff area that afternoon, it wasn't the end of the bear story for that day. When we ceased observations in the failing light at 1956 hours (7:56 PM) and returned to camp we discovered a bear, presumably the same one, had also visited our camp. We found its big muddy paw prints up high on the big cargo door at the back of the camper, indicating that it had stood upright leaning on the trailer. The bear repeated this action on the right side of the trailer and there poked its paw through the screen of the small window. Feeling around inside, the bear caught its claws in Gary's canvas briefcase and dragged it out through the window. The briefcase was tossed around a little, and since the main zipper was open, Gary's magazine reading material was scattered. Fortunately the zippers to the smaller compartments were closed so those contents were undamaged—good thing too as most of our summer supply of money was in that part of the brief case! The bear continued along the side of the camper where our water jugs were lined up, tipped over several and chose one six-gallon jug to maul and bite with claws and teeth, poking it full of holes so that all its water drained away. The only other things the bear found to its liking were the foam bumper for our entry door and the wash basin resting on the trailer tongue—the bear chewed the bumper half away and ate the soap bar from the wash basin!

Bear sightings were common at this site; in one case the presence of a sow with two cubs feeding at a berry bush

179

blocked Jean from returning to camp until the trio departed. With such experiences, especially the situation of a bear approaching so close to the hack box, confirming the potential hazard to our Peregrines and to ourselves in our protection of them, our Specialist drove to town to consult with the site sponsors, other relevant agencies and the local bear biologist. The following day we were issued two cans of bear spray, a shotgun, and four rounds of rubber bullets to use in the gun along with careful instructions on when and how to use each. Bear spray was not to be used against the direction of the wind or it might disable the user instead of the aggressor. The gun was to be used only in the event noise and distraction did not deter the bear and then only aimed at large muscle mass from some distance away, the intent being to "hurt" the bear and dissuade his encroachment without causing any lasting injury or skin perforation. Although we continued to have several more bear sightings, the bears were focused on the continued ripening of local berries as they moved down off the mountain in back of us to berry-rich terrain near and below us. As attendants, we quickly learned to recognize the bears' likely intent and direction and fortunately never had to use either bear spray or the gun, although these items probably bolstered our confidence in making proper decisions regarding our interaction with this impressive, large, and self-willed species. We had heard of other sites with bear problems, even one year when a bear had to be destroyed for the safety of attendants and Peregrines at another release site in these Rocky Mountains, and we did not want that to be a possible outcome at our site.

*From the Journals: CSKT Cliff – Gary*
*16 July, 1996 – I was at my observation post (O.P.) and waiting to signal Jean at 1100 when several tall fronds of a Juneberry bush began waving. I thought it was likely a wind current until, upon standing, I saw a smaller bush shaking and the brown face*

*of a young bear facing my way at 20 yards. Adrenaline rush, heartbeat hit, quick shot of anxiety. I bent over and collected my bear spray—armed it—held it in one hand, grabbed a handy rock with my other, and was preparing to advance, but signaled Jean first. Tossed the rock over in the direction of the bear but never saw it again, so went back to falcon duty. Life in the outdoors. Real zest. Henceforth, having had about five other bear sightings down there, I have named it Bear Valley and the Bear Valley O.P.*

## Thunder and Lightning at Remote Observation Point, Wood Lake, 1995

In spite of the loss of our Peregrine at Wood Lake, estimated to be worth a few thousand dollars as measured in human economic terms considering cost of production, distribution, and hack site management, we had to recognize in this particular experience it was the eagle who acted "naturally" and the Peregrine who was "artificial." This is a prime example of the risks and dilemmas faced by wildlife organizations attempting to re-balance what was the natural ecosystem in the past by re-introducing species that have been missing from the ecosystem for a period of time. Ideally the young Peregrines would have been protected by a pair of adults, but ours had no aerial protectors. We just had to hope that within a week after release they would gain their own aerial competency to avoid an attack by eagles. Three days later, after the loss of Silver, our young Peregrines were already better fliers and were able to avoid capture in another rather determined raid by an eagle. After two weeks our Peregrines were themselves skillfully stooping and chasing Golden Eagles from the hack box cliff area. Our subsequent sightings of eagles were of eagles passing over the area at a greater height.

After we reported the taking of Silver by an eagle, a Release Specialist immediately rejoined us the following day to do what little humans can do to discourage a determined aerial predator from destroying any more of our small group of Peregrines. Jean was far below at the lower observation point with a good view of the front of the hack box, but would be of no consequence to a Golden Eagle from there. The Specialist and Gary occupied the upper observation point and greater cliff area hoping their presence would deter returning eagles from their potential food source of more young Peregrines. In addition Gary and the Specialist each carried a noise-maker to use to attempt to thwart an eagle's advance upon our birds.

While a hilltop prominence of the mountain holding the cliff was the preferred observation point looking down upon the hack box, in case of rain or storms Gary had constructed a rain shelter slightly down slope but still overlooking the hack box. The shelter was a tarp supported by a series of five aluminum poles, two trees, and numerous guy lines to stakes in the rocky soil. This shelter, fondly referred to as "The Hilton," was immediately accessible whereas retreating to the lower observation point or camping trailer entailed a hike of one-half mile and elevation change of about 800 feet.

During the afternoon of our Eagle Watch, a short but severe thunderstorm rolled down our valley and Gary and the Specialist quickly sought shelter from the storm under the tarp. The shelter was pummeled by hail and large rain drops as thunder and lightning crashed and boomed, cracked and lit up the whole area. Gary tried to maintain his German stoicism and gripped his rain jacket tighter but the Specialist admitted to being just plain scared of lightning. And that response is actually more appropriate to what was taking place around them. Still, Gary was chuckling inwardly to himself as the

Specialist threw his expensive, heavy-duty tripod farther down the hill away from the shelter on the assumption the aluminum legs of the tripod might attract a lightning bolt to himself if the tripod remained near him in the shelter. What Gary had simultaneously remembered as the Specialist tossed his tripod downhill, was that the shelter under which they sat was constructed of vertical aluminum poles. Swaged down at their upper ends, these poles took the same shape as lightning rods. Gary and the Specialist endured as best they could, as well as they each could, waiting for the lightning bolts and thunder to roll past. Suddenly a terrifying vertical flash split the sodden sky, the immediate pressure wave hurt their ears, and the brilliance was momentarily blinding as lightning struck the small mountain valley floor BELOW and in front of them. Not good. Not supposed to happen. But it did explain Gary's vague notion of arm hair rising, slight tingling, and a sense of negative ions building up around them. Fortunately, the storm at last receded. With the thunder finally echoing farther away, the Specialist retrieved his tripod, he and Gary exchanged glances of relief, and both went back to Eagle Watch duties.

Great Horned Owls, Grave Point, 1990 and 1991

*From the Journals: Grave Point – Jean*
*8 July 1990 (only six days after release) – I woke groggily*
*about 1:00 AM hearing an owl, heard it again—Great*
*Horned!—and jerked awake, grabbing clothes, unzipping the*
*tent, yelling at CJ. She finally woke when I ran into the dining*
*area fly guy-rope and swore. Owl continuing to call, CJ*
*dressed, we got binocs and flashlight and hurried up to O.P. in*
*the full moonlight, urgent to try to protect our falcons. Our*
*arrival apparently sent the owl on its way, for its calls, which*
*had been coming from the direction of the tower, fell silent.*
*After much discussion, we decided I would bring up poncho,*
*pad and sleeping bag and sleep in full view in moonlight and CJ*

*brought me her boom box so I could play a vocal music tape which I did about 2:00 AM. I slept after that until about 5:00 AM when I saw two falcons arriving at the tower. CJ arrived soon after with optics to open observations. Knowing that Great Horned Owls are a great threat to newly-released young Peregrines, it was an anxious morning for us until we eventually knew at 8:35 AM that all five young falcons were still present.*

*At evening we set up in tiny adjacent gullies on the slope in front of the tower; ponchos for ground cloths, pads, sleeping bags, binoculars and other gear under a tarp beside us. From there we watched for falcons in the last of the day's light and prepared to protect our falcons again by sleeping out near the tower, filled with overwhelming awareness of our great fortune in being here. CJ said we went to heaven without dying as we watched the moon rise full above a mountain and through a tiny, thin cloud, watched the shadows climbing a mountain east across the Salmon valley through wind-waving grasses around our beds, on top of White Bird's world in complete human silence and windy pines.*

It was CJ's turn to make the town trip the day after this owl scare and she spoke to Bill in Boise to ask for advice. While CJ was gone and Jean was on watch alone at the O.P., three adult Golden Eagles, another major threat to young falcons, flew over the tower headed north and later two flew back again in the opposite direction. Feeling besieged on behalf of the Peregrines, in both cases Jean tore off her shirt and walked back and forth waving it over her head on the slope below the tower, trying to stay far enough away not to set off "cacking," the sound Peregrines make when disturbed.

*From the Journals: Grave Point – Jean*
*9 July 1990 – Sighting yet another eagle flying over, leaving my*
*chair in the shade to go out into the clearing and wave my shirt*
*again, I saw one of the falcons briefly give chase, cacking, and*
*this deflected the eagle into a U-turn back in the direction from*
*which it had come. I was really glad to see that because it*
*seems to mean they will soon be defending themselves.*

CJ brought back instructions from Bill to clear left-over quail
and quail remnants off the tower every evening before dark
thereafter. Since the falcons were quite innovative in leaving
behind quail remnants—plucking feathers, biting off wings and
legs, pulling intestines out in long strands and draping these
over the edge of the hack box roof, avoiding eating eggs or
yolks they found in female quail—there was quite a mess, an
odiferous mess, on and around the hack box. Therefore, we
actually took soapy water, rags and other equipment and
scrubbed off the mess at the beginning of this new chore of
removing any remaining food before dark so as not to attract
owls to the tower at night.

Owls were a concern at Grave Point again in 1991. We heard
them calling at night often from 27 June through 17 July, most
worrisomely all during the night before Release. We cleaned
quail off the tower regularly in the evenings after the first three
days of the release period when we were not to approach the
tower lest we force a falcon to fledge—a large supply of quail
was provided on release day to make possible this three-day
undisturbed period. Because of the owls, the Specialist had
advised us to watch into the long summer evening hours on
Release Day and Jean slept that night, as the previous year, on
the hillside below the tower. Laying her down-filled liner-
stuffed sleeping bag on and under ponchos, wearing a lot of

clothing layers to bed, she kept owl watch through the first
night of Release.

## Clouds and Fog Flowing Like a Slow River, Grave Point, 1991

Living outdoors as we did for seven or more weeks at a time,
and in remote locations difficult for the average traveling public
to readily access, we were privy to some remarkable visionary
and auditory feasts which we will long remember. There were
of course the brilliant nighttime flashes of lightning displayed
upon the tent fabric over our heads and illuminating a 180-
degree dome over our until-then darkened world, the lingering
image dancing in our memory as if it were an instantaneous
photo, only briefly shown. Of course the flashes were followed
by either the deep growling rumble of thunder muffled through
a rain-thick cloud deck; or the intense sharp crack of a lightning
bolt escaping the clouds, a cleaving force bound for the closest
point on earth where the opposite charge had accumulated. And,
lying there awake, waiting for the storm to be over, we
wondered where that point would be. Sometimes we
spasmodically jerked when a flash/crash came, unable to control
the automatic reflexes of our bodies, and felt the pressure wave
of a strike too close. Other times we could coldly, knowingly,
count the seconds, "one-thousand one, one-thousand two, one-
thousand three," and know that last strike was over half a mile
away. We always felt greatly comforted by being able to get all
the way up to one-thousand ten.

Far better, far preferable were those sights, which became gifts
we carried into the future feeling as though we were the only
ones to witness them. The ones which made us feel we were
bearing witness to Life and to what it could offer. One such
sight was the fog that flowed like a slow-motion river in a
noiseless syrupy cascade over an unseen embankment and

descended, unbroken, unfettered, like a riverine slow-loris down to the Snake River Canyon far below.

*From the Journals: Grave Point – Gary*
*12 July 1991 – Sitting at the Observation Point from 5:00 AM until 9:00 AM before any falcon comes and staring up at the tower—the tower always there, looming over us silently and large—one gets odd feelings about the falcons ever returning, or perhaps ever even having been there. Like a dream you think you can remember seeing them perched there and flying around the tower, but this morning hour after hour there is nothing, nothing to look at, no living thing to tantalize or dance with the soul, just the tower, the tall, looming tower. And after wondering if they will ever return, if there will ever be a life form on the tower again, those elusive mysterious falcons with no pattern, no regularity, and us essentially giving up and saying, "Well, I'll just read a while," and doing so, and then you casually look up. Then, inexplicably, out of nowhere one has materialized and is sitting on the tower guard rail, silently looking about with great intentness, and appearing as though he, the falcon, is in charge of the moment. He decides, not you, when, or if, he will appear. You, only the watcher. He, the Peregrine, the event maker.*

The day before was a busy one, lots of falcon sightings, lots of recording in our notebook. Our supper routine was a little later than normal, but dark was coming on a little earlier than usual because of dark and thickening clouds building overhead as we prepared our bedding for a night's rest. It did not look to be a stormy night but a gentle mist had developed, causing exposed surfaces, the tarps, the tent fly, the water jugs to glisten when our flashlight beams passed over them as we made our way into the tent for the night, the beams made conically visible by exposed mist droplets almost hanging in the air. Wakening occasionally and rolling over in the night, we sensed the mist had turned to a light rain as it whispered in a soft brushing sound on the fabric roof inches over our heads. Nearer to morning a soothing deep hush enveloped our ears as we reached down and pulled one extra layer over us, the mist and rain ending as some weather front passed over and cooled the world outside our sleeping bags.

Arising in the morning to the sound of our alarm, our world was about as bright as it normally was; we could see the last of the bright stars fading away overhead, but something was different. The light was different, our place on the mountain seemed different, and as we came out from under our tarp to gather up quail for the morning's falcon feeding, we saw what was different. We were above the clouds and our hill was suddenly an island in a new sea.

We knew it was an island because, as we walked up toward the tower, we got clearer view of our world and noticed other islands around us in the same sea. The weather system passing over us in the early morning had converted last night's moisture into fog. Or a combination of clouds and fog. The cloud fog sea before us and below us appeared to have a tightly delineated upper surface, not wispy or effervescent but appearing more substantial, as if one could almost wade into it and sink into the magical fog sea only a few feet. Our Grave Point mountain top and the tops of several high, tree-covered mountains and ridges to our south were above the fog level and the far ridge of mountain tops to the southeast firmly held our seemingly solid grey fog sea in place against the shores of the black-green mountainsides. The utterly calm and clear morning around us held not a breath of moving air. The normal Salmon River valley bottom scenes we took for granted from our elevation were buried beneath a 3000 foot thick layer of impenetrable fog and we gazed in quiet admiration of the stunning fog sea beneath us.

As the sun rose above the sea and mountains and trees and began to lightly kiss the fire tower behind us, a new wonder slowly developed out of the fog sea below where we stood. The rays of the sun began to reach and warm the fog, brightening and whitening the top smooth waves of the sea, generating some slight wisps of gaseous radiance, diminishing the former firmness of the top surface of the sea, but also causing it to expand, and the upper level of the fog sea rose against its far mountain shores and swallowed more of the treed beachfront. As the fog heretofore trapped in the Salmon River valley to the east expanded and rose from the morning's increasing heat, it began to crest the ridge below our camp and flow like a river over a dam into the valley of the Snake River, some 4000 feet below us. But this was a slow motion flow, almost sacred or at least mystical because again there was no sound. A flow like thickened syrup, a molasses-type flow, but bright silver-grey fluid of a whimsical texture. And down it flowed, down about 500 feet in a single lingering glide until the fog river passed out of sight to the west, now hidden behind intervening flanks of the mountain, our fog river flowed out of the Salmon River Valley into the Snake River Valley and up against the mountain shores of Oregon. The fog sea gradually rose and thinned, emptied and evaporated until the sea bottom was revealed once again. We were favored by a shared vision such as we could not hope to see again. No, not in our lifetime.

Flower Beauty, Grave Point, 1991

At our Grave Point observation site on the hillside below the tower we marveled that we sat in the midst of a profusion of wildflowers as they seemed to leap up from the rocky soil to get in their growth before the grasses tried to drown them in their turn at life on this mountain. The flowers competed in their show of loveliness, some in vivid and bright and dark shades, and some in tempered pastels. Our eyes could focus on the defined singularity of a particular flower but most often we saw the overriding multiplicity of their hovering all at once, all together, like a thin cloud rising over the surface of the ground and the lower haze of new growth green grasses helping to support the gently swaying flowers and new buds. The brilliant red of the scarlet gilia was a temptress to the hummingbirds as they could buzz into the nectar of the blooms swaying gently and horizontally to the hummingbirds approach. Adjoining colors captured our vision equally, beauty profound enough we could declare no favorites, the rich blue and deep purple of the lupine and larkspur, blue hyacinths, yellow sunflowers, and one that Gary called white lace in his notes that we all these years later have no actual name for, all lightly dancing and waving and vying for our attention. In competition with our admiration of any single flower was the enhanced view offered by the telephoto compression of our spotting scopes as we looked uphill and saw through the lens the single-plane proliferation of flower colors, individually distinguishable but yet on the verge of being mixed into a Technicolor dot matrix of variable spacing. We were reluctant to rise from our chairs and step amongst the many flowers, some level of guilt accompanying our necessary movement, the flowers were so abundant.

It was as though we sat inside a garden, a garden without weeds, surrounded by purposely selected flowers and grasses. There was no plant we would pull or cut down or willfully destroy as we would a weed in Jean's garden back home and so there were no weeds. Having recognized that we had not willfully planted any of our surrounding foliage, we could also recognize that weeds are a fabrication of our minds. If we accept that which naturally surrounds us, then there are no weeds. This is likely an important lesson to apply to all aspects of reality and living.

As the morning warmed with the sun rising higher, the intense color of individual blooms dimmed slightly. Photographers recognize colors are more intense in shaded light or slanting light and we saw the same result on our flowers as the day lengthened. They were best admired in the early morning or late day. During midday our senses shifted a bit from recognizing the visual to instead recording the audible, from noticing a low background murmur to identifying individual sources and types of sound. Multiple flies buzzed in the air, ranging from those we could hardly see, to those big, ugly black flies, which were not numerous but bit ferociously. Most common were what we called little brown biting flies, smaller rascals also prone to biting and doing so as soon as they landed on exposed flesh. There were several different types of bumble bees and other pollen and nectar-gathering buzzers. One was the hummingbird moth which, with its delicate proboscis, would hover in front of deep narrow flowers and probe in without landing and then move on to another flower, and another, and another. Our favorite buzzers were of course, any of the several species of hummingbirds at Grave Point: the Calliope, the Rufous, and the Broad-winged. On some cool mornings when Gary wore his red stocking cap, one would often buzz up to his hat and inspect this large bright flower-seeming "bloom" and Gary would freeze motionless while the little hummer roared loudly in his ears, the wings and sharp bill just millimeters from his head and cap. Jean tried sitting quietly by a scarlet gilia plant with her camera at the ready in hopes of photographing a hummingbird at one of the flowers. Her only photo that captured a hummingbird is dark, the bird merely a silhouette, because the flower and photographer were in deep shade and the camera aperture incorrectly set. Nevertheless, the fun of the attempt lingers in memory.

*From the Journals: Holter Lake – Gary*
*11 June 1992 – More rain so back in camp for supper a bit early today. A bee alighted on our rain-wetted tarp with a load of pollen on his legs, got his wings wet, and couldn't fly off. Jean went under the tarp, flicked the tarp upward with her fingers, and the bee flew away and disappeared. I observed that the bee was lucky Jean was here because he consequently made his escape courtesy of her. However, on reflection, the bee would never have gotten stuck on the tarp if we had not been camped here and put up the tarp in the first place. There's a lesson there. At least I thought so after my afternoon whiskey. It's an allegory to a supreme being, you know, and how he might be running the show. It's a little hard to grasp now that I am sober again.*

*Phase Four, Visiting Falcons: Figures 23 and 24*

*Figure 23: Adult Peregrine visits Holter Lake hack box*

*Figure 24: Celebrating identifying visiting adult falcon*

Visiting Falcons, Various Sites

The visiting falcons described in this section are various Peregrines that showed up at some of our sites, yet were definitely not members of the young groups being cared for and released at those sites by the hacking process. In addition to those individual visiting Peregrines described below, it is important to note that, native to the western United States, there are several species of raptors in the Falcon group; in ascending size these are American Kestrel, the smallest species, Merlin, Prairie Falcon, Peregrine Falcon, and Gyrfalcon, the largest. Of these, only the Gyrfalcon, which does not breed in the lower 48 states but may sometimes be seen during winter in the northern tier or two of states, was not seen at any of our hack sites any of our summers. [Note: We served at Grave Point two years (1990 and 1991), and at two sites in two of our Peregrine summers (1992 and 1996); counting all the sites and all the years gives a total of nine opportunities for us to have listed a species of falcon on our reports.] American Kestrels were seen during all nine of our jobs, as were Prairie Falcons. The second smallest falcon in the United States is the Merlin, seen during only two jobs. Peregrines (other than the young ones being released at these sites) were seen at five of our hack sites.

Having other falcons visit our hack sites was always interesting, sometimes worrisome, and sometimes very exciting. Prairie Falcons, almost the size of Peregrines, but lighter in weight, were competitors for the food supply, both the quail we provided at the hack box and the wild birds our young Peregrines were supposed to learn to hunt. They could also be a danger to freshly-released young Peregrines not yet flying strongly, and were believed to have killed some of the young birds we were observing at one site. Peregrines were the most exciting of the visiting falcons, and it is these that are featured below.

Visiting Peregrines: Three Subadults at Grave Point, 1991

In early July 1991 we began to see subadult Peregrine Falcons at the hack box, recognizable by plumage differences from our young falcons. Birds in their hatch year are called juveniles or immatures; at this age Peregrine plumage is brown and tan and the feet are gray, while adult plumage (from age two on) is white and blue-black and the feet are bright yellow. In the first year after their hatching year, Peregrines usually show a mix of new blue-black feathers coming in to replace the brown and by this time the feet have become yellow; thus it was possible for us to recognize we were seeing one-year old visitors to our hack site—subadults. Over several days we also noticed that there were at least two—then three—different subadults, all males, coming to the hack box, individually recognizable by plumage details. One of these had a large white area on his throat and upper breast—looking rather like a bib—with a few thin black streaks and was seen only on 3 and 5 July. A second subadult had a very small white area at the throat and was seen almost daily 5 July-8 August On 6 July, a third subadult, also male, began appearing at the tower and was distinguished by having a large white bib-area with clusters of the juvenile tan feathers remaining among the new white feathers.

These subadults showed no aggression toward our young falcons or each other, but were usually consuming or carrying away quail when they visited the tower, making it necessary for us to increase the number of quail we put out each morning to ensure that our young birds would not go hungry. This supply of food, their age and the fact that the visitors made use of it, suggested that they were likely Peregrines released by The

Peregrine Fund somewhere in the general vicinity the year before. Clearly they recognized the white hack box top as a feeding station.

During our twice-weekly phone calls to The Peregrine Fund offices in Boise we began reporting our sightings of these subadults as early as 5 July. Bill, our Supervisor, was eager to have us try to identify as many of these one-year old birds as possible and instructed us to enter the tower and observe through observation peepholes. On Monday, 8 July we looked for the peepholes from outside the tower and found none. On some occasions when we called Boise, Bill was unavailable and we gave our twice-weekly reports to anyone who answered the phone, but eventually Gary got to talk to Bill again on 16 July and learned we had to remove the plywood window shutter that covered the tower window behind the hack box. We did this in the evening of 18 July, thus exposing one of the glass windows of the old tower structure. From inside the tower we found this window covered with brown paper in which two small observation slits had been cut.

Early on the morning of 19 July, Gary entered the tower to spend the morning watching through the peepholes to try to identify the visiting subadults should they visit the hack box to take quail. Gary was on duty in the tower from 5:45 AM until 12:35 PM (six hours and 50 minutes), but during that time period none of the Subadults visited the tower. However, Gary was able to get a couple of wonderful close-up photos of one of our own juvenile Peregrines by holding his camera lens up against a peephole. This was a male juvenile we had named Red for his red color band, and when Red first arrived at the hack box to eat he appeared uneasy because of light reflections on the glass window that had, before that day, been covered by a plywood panel. After Gary came out of the tower and we had

had lunch, Jean entered the tower at 1:35 PM to spend the afternoon hoping one or both subadults that were regulars at the tower would come for quail.

At 2:11 PM the subadult with the tan feathers mixed with white in his "bib" arrived. Without an official name for him, this feature caused us to refer to him as "Dirty Bib" in our field notes to distinguish him from the other two subadults that were temporarily named "Big Bib" and "Small Bib" in our notebooks. Jean was easily able to read the red identification band code while Dirty Bib plucked a quail before flying away with it: X over A. At 5:37 PM a few minutes of high suspense began as a Peregrine came over the tower roof, landed on the box top and immediately flew off again, probably startled by the window reflections as Red had been in the morning. At 5:38 PM Jean heard a falcon land on the north side of the tower roof and walk over the roof to the south side where he would be able to look down on the top of hack box. By 5:50 PM Small Bib was eating a quail on the hack box ledge, from which position his leg bands could not be seen by Jean. At 6:13 PM Small Bib came up onto top of the hack box, cleaned his beak and flew off, but not before Jean noted his identification code: X over T. Eureka! Jean exited the tower at 7:26 PM (five hours, 51 minutes). [Note: There was no bathroom in that tower; hence we chose to drink very little in preparation for our stints of inside-tower duty. There was also little ventilation inside the tower so it was hot being cooped up in there.]

Because the behavior of both our juvenile falcons and the visiting subadults was being disturbed by the light reflections on the glass window, on our own initiative we resolved to move the plywood shutter back into position to cover the window and did so on the morning of 20 July when we went up to feed. We would report this action two days later on our next call to The Peregrine Fund offices in Boise.

*From the Journals: Grave Point – Jean*
*23 July 1991 – Gary got to talk to Bill today. Bill was very pleased and excited about our identifications for two of the subadults and said, "Say, I sure hope you two are planning on coming back next summer" and offered us a new site in Washington in sight of Mt. Rainier!* [Note: We chose not to take that site; by preference, all our subsequent sites were closer to our Wisconsin home than Grave Point.]

As we had with us The Peregrine Fund's 1990 *Operation Report* that Jean had received after her 1990 Hack Site Attendant job, we were able to look up the identifications of these subadults and their history. Dirty Bib (X over A) was named Gordon by his Hack Site Attendants and released from the Hells Canyon, Oregon, hack site in 1990, some 35 or more miles south of our Grave Point site. Small Bib (X over T) was identified as Left Green and he had been released at Grave Point in 1990, while Jean and CJ were the Hack Site Attendants— how exciting and gratifying to see these direct, positive results of the reintroduction program! For Bill and The Peregrine Fund this was excellent information about the survival and success of some of the many Peregrines released to the wild with so much effort by so many people.

The Peregrine we called Dirty Bib visited the Grave Point hack box often enough that we began to notice a characteristic and repeated flight path as he flew off the hack box after each of his visits. Sometimes carrying a scrap of quail, sometimes not, he would leap off the hack box, plummet straight down to gain flight speed and temporarily going out of our sight behind the contour of the mountain on which the fire tower was constructed, until he reappeared flying low and fast following the contour of the mountain, about 10 feet above the ground and 20 yards away to either side of our observation post, until he disappeared just over the tree tops farther down the mountain. What an awesome flight display! Sometimes we could hear the whoosh of his feathers as he quickly appeared and then was gone. Gary desperately wanted to capture this moment on film, knowing full well it might not be possible.

The fact that Dirty Bib had a repetitive pattern when leaving the hack box meant Gary could ready his camera and move a few yards out from under the trees where he usually sat on observation duty, into the opening in front of him. Jean would watch Dirty Bib finish his meal while Gary knelt in the wildflowers and grasses ready with his manual-focus, high-magnification lens, 35-mm film camera. Gary tried to pre-focus on grasses at about the distance he expected to take the picture. There could be only one photo per Dirty Bib visit. The odds of getting a great picture were not good. As soon as Dirty Bib took flight, Jean would yell, "Here he comes!" Then Gary quickly put camera to eye, "whoosh," hopefully "click," and then the flight path photo effort of a sub-adult Peregrine flying close past us over the mountain terrain was done until another day. Gary had a lot of fun trying, sometimes laughing at his missed opportunity, always admiring the speed and grace of this well-experienced flier, but he never did capture the perfect photo.

Visiting Peregrine: One Subadult at Willow Creek Reservoir, 1996

A single Subadult, probably a male, was observed on the tower deck, sheltering from winds in front of the hack box. Its feet were yellow, but it retained many tan feathers on its breast. Details were hard to discern that day with the scope vibrating in the strong winds, and it was not determined whether this bird was banded. It was not seen again.

Visiting Peregrine: One Juvenile at CSKT Tower, 1992

Hearing a long whooshing sound of wings, Jean stepped out from under the shade-tarp, where she had been sitting and observing falcons on the tower through her spotting scope, to see a juvenile Peregrine in a stoop on a gull. The falcon failed to make contact with the gull, and the gull began a desperate effort to climb with strong wing-strokes in a tight spiral, screaming all the while. The young Peregrine also climbed upward but in a bigger spiral, both continuing until the gull was too high for Jean to see against the bright sky. The Peregrine finally gave up the chase and glided off in a west northwest direction, out of sight into the distance. This young falcon was far too strong and skilled to be one of ours, which had only been released from their tower hack boxes the day before. Yet, its back and malars (facial markings) were brown, its underside, terminal tail band and wing linings were tan—he was definitely in juvenile plumage. There were no other, earlier-released hack sites anywhere in the vicinity to explain the presence of this juvenile, so our speculation that this was a wild-hatched young falcon was accepted by the Release Specialist when he returned and heard the story.

*From the Journals: CSKT Tower – Gary*
*2 August 1992 – Jean got a good sighting of a juvenile (not ours) Peregrine Falcon attacking a gull right over our trailer. The gull got away by flying upward in tight circles. This is probably a wild juvenile from an adult pair released earlier by The Peregrine Fund with an undiscovered eyrie in the Mission Mountains or the Flathead River area. Jean said it headed west. Exciting! One of the Release Specialists said this would be the*

*first mid-summer sighting of a wild Peregrine. Other sightings in this area are of migrants in spring and fall.*

Visiting Peregrine: An Adult Male at Holter Lake, 1992

At Holter Lake, we had an adult male Peregrine present for several days; as some adults that visit hack sites could be quite aggressive toward the young birds, this was a concern. However, our visiting adult never offered any harm. He was first observed on 5 July with our three remaining juveniles, all flying well, having been released 20 days earlier. Much vocalization, chasing and crabbing—a clash between falcons in which they grab each other's feet—carried out by the adult with our young falcons engaged our attention. Our first description of this visiting falcon indicates our uncertainty with phrases like "no apparent dark axillaries so Prairie Falcon unlikely....very light underneath" but other sightings through 19 July convinced us this was a full adult (at least two years old), and we soon referred to him as "The Stranger" in our field notes. All three juveniles displayed defensive posture if the adult appeared while they were eating quail at the hack box. If our young male was present when The Stranger arrived, the adult "eechiped" (a vocalized greeting) loudly. This young male became secretive, coming to the hack box only when The Stranger was not present and usually taking a quail and quickly diving off the hack box and flying away below the cliff edge and just above the trees. The juvenile females continued to perform aerial interactions with The Stranger, and sometimes one young female flew away south with him. The Stranger often circled over the hack box when he arrived and, if a juvenile was at the hack box feeding, The Stranger perched in a nearby tree. As though waiting politely, The Stranger vocalized occasionally and only came to the hack box to eat or carry away a quail after the juvenile left.

Obviously, we were anxious to try to identify The Stranger. Since our regular observation point was well below the level of the cliff and below the hack box, identification of individual falcons was very difficult due to distance and the fact their leg bands were often out of our view because of our position so far below. To counter this problem, we had placed rocks atop the hack box and often a falcon would perch there, bringing its legs and leg bands into our field of view briefly before feeding, or hop up there before departing. As another aid to identification, a few simple leather tethers were attached to the hack box top, into which we could insert the legs of some quail, thus assuring that at least some of the quail would be consumed on the hack box, rather than being carried away. The next morning after The Stranger's first visit, we hiked together up to the hack box to put out quail and then went further up along the cliff seeking a temporary observation point at a level above the hack box and closer than our usual place. We clipped tips of two tree branches to make a small, clear opening between us and the hack box. Several mornings were spent at this upper observation point in our attempt to learn The Stranger's identity. On 7 July, from observations at this upper location, Jean was able to sketch The Stranger in her field notebook.

*From the Journals: Holter Lake – Jean*
*6 July 1992 – This upper observation point is wonderful. The view is great! From where I sit, the hack box is viewed against the lake below, thus it appears to have water both above and behind it and so the falcons too are observed against the lake. Sometimes boats go by "above" them! When I went further along the cliff to make a one-use latrine, I discovered great chunks gouged out of the thick moss growing there—probably we spooked an elk or deer when we came up here today. We identified all three of our juveniles, but The Stranger did not*

come this morning, and at 1:00 PM we had to leave to make our town trip.

*7 July 1992 – At the upper observation point again, we observed one of our females come to eat. About noon she left and the young male arrived and claimed a quail, but then seemed to doze. A falcon flyby and vocalization wakes him to hunch protectively over his quail and begin to eat. As we and the young male were finishing lunch, a display began. One of our females is chasing and crabbing and screaming with the light male from 5 July. Very vigorous interactions and loud screams, but our female is at least part of the time the aggressor. Eventually she broke off but by then we had definitely seen The Stranger has yellow feet and appears to be a full adult. He perched and eechipped at the young male, but came to the box only after the young one left. The Stranger wears a red Peregrine Fund band on his right leg, and a black Federal band on his left. We tried to sneak close enough to read the red band, but he was standing with his right leg hidden, and then flew away. <u>What a thrill</u>!*

*8 July 1992 – Again this morning, we set up on our closest clifftop observation site and used the blind as a concealing drape over me and the scope. The other of our young females came to eat first and she ate leisurely. She defended her quail and the hack box against The Stranger when he arrived. He tried to take a quail off the box, but her presence and the tether on the quail prevented this. Eventually the young female left and The Stranger came to eat. Both of us were individually able to clearly read his red Peregrine Fund leg band code and we are anxious to call in this coup to Bill tomorrow and find out where and when this falcon was released and whether there have been any other reports on him. [Note: Bill wasn't in the office the*

*next day but eventually we learned that The Stranger, code WP,*
*had been released from the York, Montana, hack site in 1990.]*

Visiting Peregrine: An Adult Female at CSKT Cliff, 1996

On the first day of release, an adult female Peregrine came to
the hack box and made use of the quail supply put out for the
newly released falcons; on that very first day she took two
quail. The young birds cacked (made defense calls) whenever
the adult was present, but she was not seen to make any
threatening moves toward them. This adult wore a dark band on
her left leg, and a red band on her right. She was therefore
presumed to be a previously-released Peregrine Fund bird and
Jean spent 3 ½ hours one afternoon under a blind Gary set up
for her nearer the hack box in an attempt to read her
identification code on the red band; however the adult did not
come to the hack box during that time. Unfortunately, we had
significant problems at this site with bears, heard owls
frequently, and there was a threatening pair of adult Prairie
Falcons with young in the immediate vicinity as well. Our
young Peregrines began to disappear, i.e. we stopped seeing
them and the number of quail left over at the end of each day
confirmed they were not coming to the hack box. In
consequence, this site was closed early and we failed to identify
this adult.

## C. PERSONAL STORIES

<u>Work Ethic and Observational Differences between Jean and
Gary</u>

It is normal for two people to have different approaches to the
fulfillment of perceived job or work requirements. Such was the
case for the two of us. Gary will readily admit that Jean was the
more devoted of the two of us in terms of adherence to The

Peregrine Fund's overall objectives and to the needs of the Peregrines, whose care and responsibility at the release site was fundamentally ours. In general, most of the time the difference between us as applied to our work was very little and thus insignificant. We shared a similar overall work ethic from our youths and delighted in performing our roles for the re-establishment of the Peregrine as a species in the Rocky Mountain West. But in a handful of incidents there was some consternation and frustration on Gary's part in dealing with Jean's priorities for the needs of the job compared to Gary's priorities as applied to his own needs.

By the time we began working summers for The Peregrine Fund we had been married 25 years and had time and experience enough to understand differences of opinion and how to work them out well enough to move forward from those differences and still stay committed to each other. Every release site always had two individuals assigned to the site. In the majority of sites this would be two people, often of college age and unmarried who had perhaps just met when they arrived at their assigned hack site. In our case one could declare The Peregrine Fund actually got a bonus in who was responsible at sites where we worked in that there was not only Jean and Gary, but a third concerned party—the couple. And thus we had a mutual desire to present a united front to site visitors or representatives of The Peregrine Fund.

Another factor helping us in the process of meeting our release site objectives was that Gary willingly assigned Jean as the final authority in all matters related to doing our job on site. She was the "Boss," the final decision-maker. Gary did this because it was Jean who found this job helping reintroduce Peregrines, because she was the trained biologist and this job would enhance her work teaching university biology courses and increase recognition of her skills by her university colleagues. And—she loved the opportunity to perform this work with Peregrines. Gary had no desire to diminish any rewards she might find. This was very similar to the way we ran our mutual household in Wisconsin—one person typically took the lead in decision-making in a particular aspect of our partnered lives. For example, due to Jean's study and comprehension of biology as applied to the human body, she was the family decision-maker in matters of health and her counsel was sought and listened to. Gary, on the other hand, due to his interests and training in Engineering, was the family expert and final decision-maker on matters related to machines and construction. Successful relationships draw on efficiently using knowledge and skills that are available. None of us are experts at everything and appropriate deference to who knows the most about a subject and then applying that knowledge is fundamental to meeting job or project, family or marriage requirements.

But what are the requirements? And how does one perceive or interpret them? For the Peregrine assignments Jean's interpretation was rigorous and slanted in favor of the Peregrines and meeting her perception of what our boss at The Peregrine Fund would expect. Gary's interpretation was a bit looser and slanted in favor of meeting his own comfort level while still meeting his interpretation of job requirements. In the few instances where Gary admitted to a certain frustration or mounting tension regarding his disagreement with Jean on Peregrine work duty issues, as noted in his personal journal, the most common irritant was time—the amount of time we should devote to continued observation toward the end of a day or in the face of possible inclement weather. Gary was always willing to give in easier and first and call it a day and head back to camp and the obligations there or for a precious little "free time" which might be yet available away from our observational and falcon duties. Jean was nearly always ready to give it her all—until near dark allowing just enough time to get back to camp while still able to see the trail adequately, or until the storm was nearly on top of us. Nearly always we came to an equitable agreement on when quitting time would be each day (highly variable according to weather, day length, site characteristics and viewing conditions). On the those occasions when Gary had a differing opinion of what was appropriate, he nonetheless sought to understand Jean's position and tried to keep his frustration to himself and his journal, a handy outlet for expressing feelings without impacting one's partner. At other times Jean could sense what was happening, that Gary was getting anxious, and she agreed to finish up observations if Gary wanted to head back to camp or take an exploratory hike as a break from the falcons. Another accommodation between us was that Gary took more than half the town trips, and Jean accepted that he might take a little extra time on such trips, after the intense observation period was over, to visit a local museum, scenic wonder or other point of interest.

We are now, at this writing, 20 years removed from our exciting days of Peregrine releases, and still engaging in environmental activities. Apropos to this discussion of should there be, is there, a final decision maker, and Gary's obsequiousness to Jean as the "Hack Site Boss" of our Peregrine jobs, is our recent ten-year history of prairie burns as we work to re-establish some native grass and forb prairies on our farm in Wisconsin. We took training in the management and control of planned burns, and we file our burn plans with the State of Wisconsin and with the local Fire Marshall for the periodic controlled burns on our prairie fields. Explicitly stated and expected in each burn plan and executed burn is the demand for a "Burn Boss" to be listed, along with all contact information for that sole individual. It is too important a function and too dangerous to have split responsibilities for such an important action—there can be only one "Boss," one person who makes the final decision. We had the same philosophy for the care and concern of "our" Peregrines, which, by any measurement standards, cost some thousands of dollars each in terms of raising the falcons in captivity, raising the quail to feed them and their captive parents, building the hack boxes, transporting falcons and hack boxes, the facilities for all this and funds to pay all the staff.

## When the Tent Zipper Breaks, Grave Point, 1991 and Holter Lake, 1992

Tents housed us at Grave Point (both years), Holter Lake, and Bar None Ranch. A tent provides shelter from weather, and we increased its effectiveness in most cases by adding a layer of tarps above the tent and its rainfly. Having a tarp above the tent helped protect against the rain since the tarp setups covered a larger area than the tent's rain fly, thus directing the rain farther away from the tent, but the tarps did more than that. Tarps protected the fabric of the tent from damage by solar rays and kept the tent and its contents a bit cooler on hot sunny days. Tents and tarps also protected our gear and supplies: spotting scopes, binoculars, cameras and film, clothing, books and writing materials, outdoor cooking area, food stocks, O. P. locations and so on. What only the tents could do, however, was keep the insects out and give us a place to get away from insects for a nap and the nights, and to keep insects out of at least some of our gear and supplies.

*From the Journals: Grave Point – Gary*
*12 July 1991 – While sitting here in the bright sun, and sunning myself amidst the flies and mosquitoes and bees and the buzzing of this myriad of insects, swatting, and chasing, and twitching*

*and acting like the cow in the pasture with her permanent ever-encircling cloud of insects, a real cloud passes over. Rather a large, grey, and thick cloud. And, as though a switch were slowly thrown, the buzzing noise dies down, not all of it, but a large and noticeable measure. And it is more silent. When the cloud passes over and the sun slowly appears again, the reverse happens. Like a magnetic dynamo slowly starting and winding up to full speed, full crescendo, the buzzing, humming, whirring sound of the insects re-establishes itself.*

We were each issued a small, 2-person tent the first couple years by The Peregrine Fund. Jean and CJ each slept in one of these in 1990, and used an extra tent CJ brought for gear. But, when we (Gary and Jean) began working together as Hack Site Attendants, we brought a 4-person tent we already owned for our sleeping tent, and used the 2-person tent issued to us for gear. Our 4-person tent was a good one, but we had already used it some years for camping vacations. So, we should not have been surprised when, on 3 July 1991, the lower of the two zippers at the tent doorway gave out—after all, we opened and closed those two zippers several times every day. But, surprise or not, we were confronted with a problem. Tents in those days had only one door, and we still had to go in and out of our old tent several times a day. Our awkward, temporary solution was to use safety pins and clothes pins to hold the front tent wall/door semi-connected to the floor. We also laid a nylon-covered fleece bag, which we had along to use unfolded as an extra cover over our sleeping bags as needed, across the opening at the bottom of the front wall of the tent to block the opening a bit more.

The first available town trip after the zipper broke was two days later, 5 July, and it was Jean's duty that day. She made the 52-mile round trip in a record time, six minutes less than four hours, partly because she never enjoyed making town trips so kept them as brief as possible, but mostly because the contact biologists were not at the ranger station to answer her questions, Bill was not available so she could only leave a message for him at the offices in Boise, the fruit stand was still not open, and she did not reach either of the family members she tried to call. In the end Jean just left a phone message for her sister and brother-in-law about the zipper problem.

*From the Journals: Grave Point – Jean*
*4 July 1991 –Gary says I have to make the trip to town tomorrow so I "don't entirely lose touch with society." I still do not like the town trips—remembering everything, being efficient and quick so my partner will not be left on duty alone too long, worrying about the truck and its tires on the narrow, twisty, gravel mountain road—I get all stressed from these pressures and yearn for my simple, quiet mountain life!*

Pretty quickly we found out how much the tent had been protecting us from having insects in our "bedroom." Each night before bed it became a chore to search the tent for spiders, ants, daddy-long-legs, and flies and escort them out of the tent, then pin the two edges of the separated zipper together and block the opening with the extra bag. Early in this zipper-failure period Gary had tried rubbing a bar of soap along the zipper to make it slide more easily, but instead the zipper just separated more.

When Gary drove to town on 8 July, he found a package from Jean's brother-in-law containing two very long, strong-looking metal zippers that had been purchased for a project, but never used. Gary sat for long periods over the next two days slowly sewing one of these zippers into place. To make this task easier, we elected not to remove the old zipper, but just to sew one side of the new zipper to one side of the old, separated zipper, and then sew the other side of the new zipper to the other side of the old one. It worked and once again we could go to bed without insect searches, and without whatever insects the searches might have missed still in the tent with us for the night.

At Holter Lake in 1992, we again used the old 4-person tent, but brought along the second of the long zippers Jean's brother-in-law had given us—just in case. We had only been at the windy camp by Holter Lake five days when the upper door zipper separated just as the lower one had done the year before. This time it was Jean who sat tediously sewing the replacement zipper in by hand. We did vow to give up on that tent after that summer as it was showing other signs of wear after so many weeks of continuous use in two consecutive summers. In fact, the next time we were assigned a tent hack site (1994), we asked if The Peregrine Fund would consider issuing us one 4-person tent, instead of the usual two 2-person tents, which we had stopped taking after the first couple years anyway. They agreed.

Holter Lake was hard on tents and tarps because of strong winds and frequent windy thunderstorms that often prevailed there. On our very first night in our campsite there, such a storm blew up soon after we entered the tent for the night, and the wind bent two of the tent poles. We went out into the wind to reinforce the tent poles with duct tape and two extra poles we had brought to support a tarp over our camp kitchen area—as this tarp hadn't been set up yet, the poles were available as immediate help for the tent. Installation of falcons occurred the next day, and a few days after that, but before Release, we made our first town trip to call in to The Peregrine Fund. Since the falcons were still confined in the hack box, we took the time that day to drive beyond the tiny nearest town to Helena. There we purchased a long handle (meant for floor mops) to use as a snake stick since we had already learned the Holter Lake area had numerous snakes, a second snake bite kit so that each of us could always carry one, the second round of antibiotic pills for Jean's infected spider bite, and four lengths of 2x2-inch lumber to use to reinforce the tent poles.

*From the Journals: Holter Lake – Jean*
*12 June 1992 – We parked again by the sheep shed under the pines. I loaded my pack with 16 pounds of water and ten pounds of ice, putting the ice inside a hard-sided cooler (which itself added 4.6 pounds to the weight in the pack), plus mail, odds and ends of food and a book. In one hand I carried the soft red cooler with another 10# chunk of ice and my other hand held the snake stick for sweeping through the grasses ahead of me. Gary carried eight pounds of water in his pack along with all the clean, wet laundry, additional odds and ends of supplies and a bag of 35 frozen quail to supply the falcons until the next town trip. He had wrapped duct tape around the four 2x2s near each end to form them into a stack and around the middle to create a handle so he could carry all of them with one hand. We had eaten our lunches on the drive back, and now shared a can of peaches beside the truck before setting out on the hike. Despite these heavy loads, the 3-mile hike back went better than we expected and we reached camp in 70 minutes with one brief rest. We beat the approaching rain storm just barely. (On this day we got mail, but we did not notice the Post Office's open hours; the next time we went to town, we were too late—the Post Office there closed at 3:45 PM!)*

Back in camp, Gary patiently, tediously drilled a hole through each end of each 2x2 with the awl on his pocket knife, inserted a length of cord through each hole and tied pairs of the 2x2s into two V-frames to strengthen the poles at each end of the tent. Though we had several more windstorms, the tent frame held up very well with this reinforcement.

Jupiter Comet Impact, Bar None Ranch, 1994

Good spotting scopes, specially adapted telescopes used most often by birders and hunters and generally in the 20X to 45X magnification range, were a necessary tool of the Hack Site Attendant. Attendants were charged to observe, identify, and report on the daily activities of the falcons under their care using their visual sight and, as necessary, augmented through the use of binoculars and spotting scopes. Observations had to be made from far enough away so as not to disturb the normal development and behavior of the Peregrines, yet attendants needed to be close enough to identify each individual bird through noting the color of its identifying leg band, sometimes even by reading numbers and digits on the leg band. Leg bands were approximately one-half inch in diameter and one-half inch wide while the identifying letter and digit were one-quarter inch wide. From a practical perspective this meant that most or our Peregrine observations took place from a distance of 200-400 yards away; a distance of 200 yards was quite manageable for discerning band colors except in conditions with high heat wave production or against the rising or setting sun. The 400 yard distance at the Bar None Ranch site would have been impossible without the unusually powerful scope we were loaned for that job. Identification and good visual observations were deemed so important by The Peregrine Fund that attendants were issued a Peregrine Fund spotting scope at each site.

Although we owned and brought a spotting scope ourselves to our early assignments (to supplement the scope The Peregrine Fund could supply on loan for each hack site), so we could each have access to a scope during our observations, we soon realized we wanted to purchase an additional scope. This would assure each of us would have a good quality scope of our own to use on our Peregrine assignments. But how good is good enough? Spotting scopes can easily range from several hundred dollars to several thousand dollars and eventually the increase in cost and features will no longer be justifiable, especially with the risk of damage when used in outdoor work for seven or more weeks at a time. We owned and used what we could afford and be comfortable using. Inevitably, at least once at each site, sometimes more than once, we wished we had a better scope, one with higher magnification.

At some of our sites, such as Green River, CSKT Tower, and Willow Creek Reservoir, the ground contours were level enough and site conditions suitable for us to position our observation area very close to the "sweet spot" between too close for the Peregrine's comfort and too far away for good identifications. At other sites, such as Holter Lake and Bar None, the location of the hack box on top of the cliff meant we would be viewing from down below and with severe mountainous limitations on where we could position our viewing point. At those sites, we felt too far away and often wished we could be in a silent, invisible hover craft able to float about 100 yards closer in mid-air in order to be able to identify the falcon currently eating in the poor light conditions that existed at that particular instant.

In 1992, while at the CSKT Tower, the local area biologist had loaned us a high-quality spotting scope with a 60-power, 80 millimeter diameter objective lens for several weeks to utilize on our Peregrines. The biologist used this scope to view and take a census of Grizzly Bears high in the Mission Mountains nearby as they fed on insects under boulders. Every year the bears tended to return to a particular location where they could get nutrients from eating the insect larva, but the hatch and development of the grubs was tied to a point on the calendar which allowed some use of the high quality scope by us until and after that time. We were very appreciative of this loan as it was our first opportunity to use such a wonderful scope for an extended period of time, not just a quick glance offered by a fellow birder. We were able to compare the large refractor-type scope directly with our own, less-expensive refractor scopes aimed at a Peregrine perched on the CSKT Tower and could readily tell it offered superior optical enhancement.

In his youth Gary had enjoyed studying some astronomy as a hobby and had become familiar with the planets and constellations. Knowing Saturn was bright in the sky, one evening we put off our normal nighttime getting-ready-for-the-next-day activities and, after full dark, aimed the big, on-loan refractor at Saturn in the southeast sky over the Mission Mountains. It was an awesome view and we had it as long as we wanted it, all to ourselves! Saturn was remarkable and beautiful, appearing just brilliant and super gold and crisp through that fantastic scope. Saturn was oriented in its classical shape, rings roughly parallel to our horizon but slanted obliquely enough that we could see their orientation encircling the planet. We could also see a moon about two ring diameters to the right of the planet. Up until then we had thought such personal views were limited to the true amateur astronomer using astronomical reflector-type telescopes. We were pleased and impressed that we, despite being in the rural mountainous landscape of Montana, had been privileged to personally witness such a phenomenon. We pondered the contrast between using the 60X spotting scope to identify individual Peregrines by their leg bands and observe their behavior across a couple hundred yards of atmosphere often distorted by heat waves, with using the same scope to marvel over the rings of Saturn across a vast distance of hundreds of millions of miles of space.

Almost all of our experience using spotting scopes in the field was with the refractive-type of scope in which the image is focused by use of optical lenses. However, suitable locations for observation sites in 1994 at the Bar None Ranch were all at a distance of well over 300 yards from the hack box, because of the height of the cliff, the shape of the valley below it, and intervening trees. The Release Specialist knew the distance and elevation could cause problems for our ability to identify individual Peregrines and so had arranged for us to borrow one of The Peregrine Fund's finer and most expensive scopes, a reflector or mirror-focus type scope of 120X magnification. Wow! Very nice scope. Very high power. However, its high power and design construction meant it had an eyepiece mounted perpendicular to the axis of the scope, making it difficult to locate a falcon in the field of view of the scope until we gained experience. And images viewed through the scope were right/left reversed because of the internal reflector mirror. This meant that the viewer looking through the scope had to mentally perform a recalculation and reprocessing of the image seen in the scope before the individual identification of a falcon could be recorded in our notes. For example, when we saw a falcon in the scope, what appeared to be a green leg band on the left leg was actually a green leg band on the right leg of the falcon. We had to be accurate, because at that site we had a double sequential release and so we had two falcons with green leg bands, one with its green leg band on the left leg, the other with its green band on the right leg. Initially it was quite a challenge for each of us as we took turns using the scope, but we gradually got quicker at performing the mental gymnastics in order to correctly record which falcon it was we were seeing.

We owe it to our falcons and the Bar None Ranch location that we were able to bear personal witness to one of the astronomical events of a lifetime while utilizing that powerful mirror-scope on the impact locations of the comet Shoemaker-Levy9 on the surface of Jupiter in July of 1994. Although we purposely never listened to any commercial or public radio while on location at our Peregrine assignments, Gary would occasionally buy a newspaper on a trip to town or to the quail freezer. In early July we had learned from a newspaper report of the intense excitement then building in the astronomical community as to potential results of an impending impact of the comet into Jupiter. The comet had only been discovered in 1993 by Carolyn and Eugene E. Shoemaker and David Levy, but by the time of our Bar None Ranch assignment predictions were being made as to when the comet fragments would collide with the surface of Jupiter and whether those collisions or their results might be seen from earth, and if so, what would be the magnitude of the impacts.

On several clear dark nights in early to mid-July we focused The Peregrine Fund's mirror scope on Jupiter to observe and memorize the appearance of the planet through our scope at the pre-impact stage. During our bi-weekly call to The Peregrine Fund, Bill had eagerly told us the comet fragments had struck the planet and were indeed visible. Both he and our Release Specialist advised us of how excited the astronomical scientists were to see such results. On 22 July we were fortunate to have a dark, clear, calm evening and once again set up the mirror-scope to view Jupiter. There! Big gray smudge marks, purportedly equal to the diameter of earth or more, now appeared on that huge planet. Amazing! We could plainly see the results ourselves. Quite a marvelous and unique sight and we would not have had the pleasure without that powerful scope and the chance to see it from the Bar None Ranch location with its lack of light pollution. We fell asleep that night once again appreciative of the opportunities presented to us, courtesy of Peregrines and The Peregrine Fund, and pondering the size of the Universe and our role in it.

*From the Journals: Bar None Ranch – Gary*
*22 July 1994—Perhaps we are all like Bill Kittredge (author of Owning It All)—just trying to work at or work out our role, our place, our justification, in the world around us, for if we do not do that, then there is no justification for our existence. It can be hard, it can be difficult, frustrating, but you have to do it. Do we write, or want to write, to leave a legacy? No, we write to put down answers we think we've found for ourselves, or at least the questions, and the search for answers. The search being the Quest, the Quest being reason enough.*

*Phase Five, Relaxed Observation: Figures 25 and 26*

*Figure 25: Jean on hike at Grave Point site*

*Figure 26: Hells Canyon scenery from Grave Point*

# PHASE FIVE – RELAXED OBSERVATION PERIOD: weeks five and six

## A. INTRODUCTION TO ACTIVIES DURING RELAXED OBSERVATION PERIOD

After the required two-week period of intense observations and note-taking that began on Release Day, and our own self-imposed, nearly-as-intense third week of observation that gave us clear data for the required reports on how many of our falcons were still in the area and doing well, we next entered into a more relaxed period of observation for weeks five and six on site. By three weeks after release, the Peregrines were spending more and more time away from the tower, exploring the surrounding area and practicing their hunting skills. Individual falcons might skip a day or two and then return to take a quail from the daily supply we continued to place at the hack box.

Having been so restricted in terms of free time since week one when the falcons were safely confined in the hack box, we now finally had some free time to do more exploring. Most of our exploration came in the form of hikes in the immediate area. The Grave Point site was especially good for such hikes. There were little springs and cattle tanks supplied by bigger springs and these "watering holes" attracted birds and other wildlife, not just cattle. Gary loved wandering, finding long-distance views, and taking photos. Being required to develop lists of bird, mammal and reptile species in each hack site area, and having been a birder (bird-watcher is an "old" term) since her youth, Jean relished the excuse to look for bird nests, sit by water sources or berry bushes to observe birds, and to hike to find new habitat variations where she could search for new critters. As a biologist, she also studied the plants, especially wildflowers and kept lists of the species she was able to identify. The US Forest Service biologists at Slate Creek Ranger Station near White Bird, Idaho, provided us with a list of plants that were considered rare or species of concern and asked that we report any we found. These biologists had access to much more detailed plant identification manuals, which Jean was allowed to consult in their office. Jean also submitted drawings of some plants she could not identify with her own plant books in hopes the biologists at the ranger station could help.

This relaxed period also gave us more time to read, or to pursue other activities. It was at Green River that Jean began a new hobby, one that continues to the time of this writing, of making earrings. She had brought along some necessary tools and supplies, including a silver bracelet given to her in childhood, but which had since broken. She drilled holes in two of the pieces and turned them into earrings. She also crocheted "turtle" soap bar covers to give as gifts.

By this point you will be wondering how successful the Peregrine Falcon program was in general, and how successful our release sites were in particular. This is hard to quantify. The Peregrine Fund used three weeks from the day of release as a reasonable prediction of independence, i.e. if an individual falcon was being seen at the hack box through at least the 21$^{st}$ day after release, it probably had had enough time to learn to fly well, to hunt for its own food, to find safe places to roost at night, and to learn to avoid danger. This three weeks-to-independence prediction was based on expert knowledge and past experience with Peregrine Falcons. Using this time span and data from multiple release sites over many years of releases in the Eastern US, the Midwest, California, and the Rocky Mountain/Northwest regions, The Peregrine Fund and cooperating groups could assess the success of the overall reintroduction process. Those data available to us in The Peregrine Fund *Operation Report* 1989-1997, and through our personal experiences, indicate a wide variation of results, from 0% of falcons reaching independence to 100% at a given site in a given year. Young Peregrines released through the hacking process had humans serving as "surrogate parents" to provide food, observation and limited protection, but the protection Hack Site Attendants could provide was different from and less complete than protection adult Peregrine Falcon parents can provide to their young in a natural nesting situation. Hack Site Attendants of course were unable to fly and thus unable to attempt to attack and drive away predators threatening young, newly fledged falcons on the ground or otherwise perched in risky places, or in their early days of flight when they were not yet very fast or skillful. If a fledgling could not find its way back to the hack box, attendants might not be able to find it, while parent falcons might be able to hear food-begging calls of a fledgling lost from the nest after its first flight, and then carry food to that young bird until it could fly and hunt on its own. On the other hand, if attendants did notice a falcon in trouble, weakening from hunger because it had not found its way back to the hack box, or had been injured in some way, attendants could call The Peregrine Fund for help from one of the Specialists. Sometimes it was possible in such a case for a Release Specialist to recapture an injured falcon and return it to Boise for veterinary treatment and, if it recovered, it might be able to be released again later. Bad weather soon after release was sometimes a big problem because falcons became lost from the hack box and attendants had little chance of locating them. Predation on the young was a major hazard to hacked falcons, especially if there was an active nest of other raptors such as Golden Eagles, Prairie Falcons or Great Horned Owls undiscovered nearby until the release process was underway.

Any specific hack site might be very successful one year and yet be a miserable failure another year. Some sites seemed to become less successful with subsequent use; perhaps one reason for this was that predators in the vicinity of the hack box became accustomed to the quail and/or the young falcons as a possible food source, or the young falcons may have been perceived as a threat to the offspring of the other nesting raptors. Returning Peregrines from previous releases at that site or another site in the area might steal quail from the hack site, harass the newly-released falcons, or even find a mate and attempt to claim the hack box area as their territory.

We had one hack site with 100% success; all five of the falcons at that site were seen and identified for 33-38 days post-release and therefore all were considered to have successfully attained independence. Does this mean that all survived to adulthood and subsequently were able to produce their own young? Probably not—life is risky. But, it does mean those five had a good chance of making it on their own and reproducing themselves. We also experienced the other extreme; one of our sites had 0% of the falcons reach probable independence. This was devastating to us. All five of those falcons returned to the hack box from their first flights but all five disappeared between three and six days after release. An active Prairie Falcon nest with fledging-age young was discovered only a few yards away in a niche of the cliff below the hack box; Great Horned Owls, Golden and Bald Eagles, Cooper's Hawks and Northern Goshawks were also heard and seen in the 19 days we were present at this site. We reported to The Peregrine Fund when our falcons began disappearing and we ourselves searched for them. We were horrified to find the remains of one falcon, including a leg with The Peregrine Fund's identification band still in place, and to also find two other locations within the forest on the cliff top where there were piles of juvenile Peregrine feathers. After no sightings for a full week, we and The Peregrine Fund could only conclude that all of our falcons had been killed, probably by avian predators. We had one site with 50% of a group of six falcons reach independence, and the rest of our sites ranged between 64% and 91% successful. No matter how many sites we worked, it was always worrisome to watch our young falcons go out into the world, and always upsetting when some of them disappeared.

How does this compare to wild Peregrines raised by their parents? Various sources indicate that average clutch size (number of eggs laid in one nesting) for Peregrines is 2.5 (range 2-6, but usually 3-4), and average survival to fledging for the offspring of a nesting pair is 1.5 (reduced because some eggs are infertile and because of predation at the nest). Even more difficult to obtain are survival rates, i.e. mortality, in the first year of life. Avian mortality is generalized from various field studies to be about 80-90% for the first year of life, with small birds that breed at one year of age, perhaps laying several clutches of eggs in one breeding season, and having average adult survival of only a very few years, being at the upper end of this first year mortality range. Larger birds such as raptors, which may not breed until age two or more, lay fewer eggs in only one batch per year, and have a longer average adult survival, have a first year mortality rate at the lower end of the above range.

In captive breeding, the hatching rate and early survival rate of young Peregrines could be higher than is typical in a natural nesting situation because of extra human care. For one thing, the clutch of eggs laid by the female of a captive pair was removed for artificial incubation. If dummy eggs were not given to the female at once, she would often lay a second, perhaps smaller, clutch of eggs, thus increasing that pair's potential reproduction for that year. And, the second clutch of eggs could also be removed for artificial incubation, while the adults "incubated" dummy eggs given them. This laying of a second clutch replicates those cases in the wild when a clutch of eggs is lost early in incubation by predation, eggs breaking because the shells are too thin, or from some other accident. A wild female may lay a second clutch in such situations. Thus in captive breeding, the females typically produced more successfully-hatched eggs per year than wild females do.

## B. STORIES FROM THE RELAXED OBSERVATION PERIOD

### Peregrine Behavior

During the period of their young lives that we knew Peregrine Falcons, we could observe changes in their behavior. During their first day or so after installation in the hack box following a long journey from Boise, the falcons were rather subdued. Very soon, though, they became intensely interested in the world outside as seen through the barred front of the hack box. These falcons, though young, were very alert, watching the scene before them, especially any birds that flew by within their view. They also always were aware of our arrival at the hack box even though they could not see us, and presumably did not know us except as sounds approaching them. When we placed an eye close to a peephole, we always saw falcons looking back, no doubt because that little hole in the plywood, previously letting in light, suddenly darkened as we leaned close. We could see them quite well; they could just see a big eye at the opening. During their confinement in the hack box, restlessness set in, usually in the males first. Behaviors that indicated restlessness included moving about in the box, hopping up on a perching rock and back down, and displacing each other in favored positions. We often saw them engaging in wing-flapping—exercising the flight muscles they would soon need.

Once released, the alert behavior continued and various explorations began. At first some falcons set off on foot along the cliff or around the tower platform, depending on where their hack box was located. More wing-flapping occurred and sometimes this led to a falcon rising by wing-power a foot or more into the air before dropping back down on its former perch. Occasionally, a gust of wind coming just at such a hovering moment would blow the falcon away from its perch and into its first flight.

Flight usually appeared to be wholly instinctive, but landings did not go so well at first. The Grave Point fire-watch tower roof was particularly useful as a landing zone for beginning fliers. There were beam-frames around the edge of the roof that had been used as places to attach the big plywood shutters when they were open in the days when the tower housed fire-watchers each summer. The Peregrines used these beams, and the railings of the tower walkway, as additional landing and perching places. Jean once saw a newly-fledged Peregrine miss its landing on one of the walkway railings and smack into the "wall" (actually a closed window shutter) of the tower cabin, slide down the plywood and end up on the walkway of the tower. Jean held her breath for a moment, but the falcon merely shook itself and proceeded to explore on foot the walkway which extended around all four sides of the tower.

After their first trial flights out from the hack box and back, the young falcons quickly began to work at perfecting their new skill. Since they would soon have to catch their own food supply on the wing, this was very important and their progress seemed rapid to us. For practice they chased each other, they flew low over the ground and "footed" grasses or grasped balsamroot or thistle flower heads in their feet, or grabbed at cones as they flew past pine trees. We found a variety of these objects on or near the hack boxes and towers, even pieces of horse droppings and baling twine at CSKT Tower, which was set in ranching/farming country. The baling twine concerned us in case a falcon might become entangled in it. Thereafter, on our exercise walks around the grasslands of the site, we picked up any twine we found and disposed of it. They grabbed each other's talons in flight—this involved one bird flipping upside-down below the other briefly—a behavior called "crabbing," a technique with many uses in a Peregrine's life. Crabbing can express aggression or be used in capturing prey, or during food transfers; it can even function as part of courtship and formation of a bond between a breeding pair.

As their flight skills improved the falcons began chasing other birds. Although we never saw an actual kill, we saw many hunting behaviors. One day in mid-August, 1992, at CSKT Tower we heard the wing-rushing sound of a stoop over the shade tarp where we sat; suddenly three European Starlings were trying to hide near us, either under the camper trailer or our truck located on either side of our O.P., one starling even perching briefly on the edge of the half-open truck window glass as the Peregrine circled overhead.

During courtship and nesting, an adult pair will execute aerial transfers of food items from one to the other. Usually the male, bringing a bird he has killed, will call to the female; she then comes off the nest and flies to him for the transfer, coming in below to grab the prey as he releases it. The young falcons we observed made some, usually unsuccessful, attempts at such transfers with various objects they collected. We also noted occasions when a young falcon dropped a quail it had taken from the hack box supply. Often this appeared to be accidental; sometimes the falcon would follow the dropped quail down to the ground and try to find it and/or retrieve it.

*From the Journals: Holter Lake – Jean*
*27 June 1992 – The best falcon episode of the day was Blue carrying away the first quail and what followed. Blue flew a loop to the north with his quail, then a loop to the south, finally landing on the cliff edge and beginning to pluck the quail before eating. Oops! He has dropped the quail over the edge of the cliff. He is looking down. He acts like he can see it below in a bush. He walks along the cliff, tries to get into the bush, looks up and down the cliff face, studies the situation—fascinating to watch this! With another approach, Blue finally gets behind the bush—he has GOT it! Blue flies off the cliff carrying his quail, circles, tries to land, goes around again, and appears to land on the cliff just out of our view. As he did not return to the hack box for another quail, we can reasonably assume, Blue was able at last to consume this quail.*

While a Release Specialist visited with Jean at Bar None Ranch on a day when Gary had gone to town, he saw a young male Peregrine stoop at a swallow. We were always strongly impressed by the excellent observational skills of our Specialists and strove to improve our own diligence and skill. That day another falcon, having taken a quail from the hack box, was observed to drop it in midair, quickly dive after and recover the quail in flight—excellent practice for hunting and for food transfers with a future mate.

At the same site on another day, a male named Red Yellow for its two colored bands, carried a quail from the hack box in strong winds and was chased by two other males and one of the females. All four falcons perched briefly in a snag (dead tree) and then resumed their chase. Coming up toward Red Yellow and his quail from below, the female grabbed the quail in her talons. Both falcons held onto the quail for several seconds and were borne aloft in an almost stationary position by the strong winds rising off the west side of the ridge. At last Red Yellow yielded his rights to the quail and the female landed on a rock and ate the quail she had won.

It is worth mentioning here that winds in the vicinity of cliff sites tended to be stronger, more erratic, and to promote lift for bird flight better than winds by hack towers placed in more level terrain. Of course, wind is invisible to humans; we can only observe its effects, e.g. by noting leaves or other objects carried in the wind or the waves of motion wind creates on water and grasses, or by studying the way wind affects the flight of birds. In the situation in the paragraph above, the fact that two falcons and their contested quail were held aloft apparently in one place in the sky reveals that a "standing wave" of wind had formed on the lee side of the cliff for a time that day, just as a standing wave can be formed in the water by a sub-surface rock in a white-water stream. We could "see" the standing wave of wind and its strength by seeing the falcons and their quail floating in one position in the air rather than falling. Likewise, if a standing wave of water is strong enough, a boat such as a kayak can be held in one position in the rushing stream with skill from the paddler.

Another behavior that developed during the hacking period was defense of the hack box area as the falcons' territory. The first vestiges of this were usually loud "cacking" calls when one or more of the falcons observed something they regarded as threatening. As they became more proficient fliers, they would give chase and attempt to drive away aerial intruders such as Common Ravens—which at some sites became a problem because they stole quail—and other raptors. It was especially thrilling to watch Peregrines that had only been flying for a few days or weeks try to drive away raptors larger than themselves. At Bar None Ranch there were two raptor families being raised near the hack cliff, a family of Red-tailed Hawks and another of Prairie Falcons. It was at this site also that we had the most trouble with ravens; therefore we saw many interactions between our falcons and these three species. At several locations we saw our Peregrines give chase to much larger Golden Eagles and they often chased Turkey Vultures. Although Great Blue Herons certainly did not offer much threat, still the falcons chased one when it flew over their territory. At Holter Lake we even saw two falcons rise to a single-file line of nine American White Pelicans flying over the hack cliff; these pelicans have nine-foot wing spans, and a Peregrine looks pretty small in comparison, yet each of the falcons chose a pelican to harass, and to our amazement, two of the big birds gave up following their group and turned back the way they had come.

*From the Journals: Wood Lake – Gary*
*6 July 1995 – Suddenly they come. Out of nothing, something. The falcons burst silently upon the canvas of the sky above the cliff like a noiseless burst of artillery. One sits gazing thoughtlessly at the firmament, the canvas is clear and unfettered. The next instant a dancing scene of wing and body and the crabbing of two falcons grasping for each other's talons, suspended briefly in the air, before they dance some more, gliding, chasing, flying, pirouetting against the blue. It seems to me a fitting image for the Ancient Ones of fundamental creation. First there is nothing. Then in an instant the artful bodies of two falcons are dancing in the scene, in the midst of nothingness. And now there is something. Life exists. It was not, our memory tells us that, and now it is. Writing this, having recently read some more of Joseph Campbell, I could get lost in*

*the scene. The Seer becoming the Seen. One instant I am not in the falcons' vision, nor are the falcons in mine. The next instant we are within each other's vison. Are we dreaming one another into existence? No matter. No answer required. What is important is to enjoy the journey, to bear witness to your surroundings. And when awe appears on the journey, relish it, ponder, and travel well.*

The better the falcons became at flying, the less we saw them. The more mature their behaviors, the more hope we felt that they would be able to take care of themselves when the hacking period ended. Thus the maturation of behavior engendered feelings of both sadness and gladness in us as each hack site job wound down toward the time when we would close the site and leave for home.

## Release Specialist Finds Jean in Fire Zone, Bar None Ranch, 1994

On a Thursday afternoon at the Bar None Ranch hack site, we crawled into our tent to endure a severe electrical storm that actually dropped only scattered, light rain showers. On the following Monday morning, when Gary hiked up to put out quail, he discovered a column of smoke rising from a fire started by the electrical storm 2 – 3 miles northeast of our camp; since light rain also fell Thursday both in the morning and evening, and again Friday evening, the fire only smoldered at first. On Sunday though, the winds rose and the fire got going. That Monday was a town day, so Gary stopped at the ranch on his way out to take a shower and warn the ranch foreman about the fire. Not being able to find the foreman around the ranch buildings, Gary had to leave him a note to report the fire. Jean, on duty at the observation point alone that day, watched the smoke column rising in the distance and contemplated what she would do if the wind rose and drove the fire toward her location. The smoke was a cause for alarm for several reasons, not least because she was then alone at the site and without a vehicular means of escape, Gary having gone to town. A town trip from this site took a lot of time, starting with a stop at the guest building on the ranch for a shower. Gary then drove to town to get mail, do laundry, obtain a few supplies, to call The Peregrine Fund to report the status of our hack site, and call home to report in with family members. This was the site with a rough, six-mile access route first along a gravel road, then an old rail bed with three bridges and two tunnels, and finally a difficult 4WD trail. And the road from the highway into the ranch buildings was no easy drive either.

Gary would ordinarily also stop again at the ranch buildings on his way back from town to pick up a supply of quail, ice and water, and to report to the ranch foreman. On that Monday, however, on his way out of the ranch Gary met one of The Peregrine Fund Specialists bringing more quail to restock the freezer and the Specialist offered to bring quail and ice to Jean in camp and visit awhile with Jean to find out how the falcons were doing. Two consecutive releases were conducted eleven days apart at this site in 1994, giving us a total of eleven young falcons to try to keep track of. Gary was in fact gone from the hack site from 10:40 AM to 5:37 PM, very nearly seven hours. With the difficult access to this site and no water nearer than about three miles-travel over very rough ground, into which she might jump in hopes of surviving, Jean was sitting at the spotting scope watching falcons and pondering what if anything she could do to try to survive if the fire grew larger and came toward her, when she heard an approaching vehicle. This was the Specialist from The Peregrine Fund, who marveled that Jean was just calmly sitting alone watching falcons with a fire in the neighborhood and no way out for her. The next day the ranch foreman gathered a crew and they put out the fire.

## Distance Creates Privacy, Willow Creek Reservoir, 1996

*From the Journals: Willow Creek Reservoir – Gary*
*28 July 1996 – It's a quiet Sunday morn, sunny, calm, warm.*
*Gonna be a hot one. The gals with whom we temporarily share*
*this site, are sitting in the shade of their tent camper, supplied*
*by the Forest Service, one at each end and so are not currently*
*conversing, each lost in their own thoughts, or reading, or*
*studying for they are bound back to college. The domestic sheep*
*are lying out on the south hills, beyond the tower we watch each*
*day, chewing their cud or doing what sheep do when they are*
*lying about. The cattle are lying south of camp, between us and*
*the tower, and just acting like contented cows. The falcons are*
*away from the tower, probably sitting on a rock on a hill or in*
*some shaded boulder corner—their little brains contemplating*
*very little. Jean is off on a long slow sauntering bird walk along*
*the outflow of the dam. I've been sitting in our trailer here*
*reading Waller's book, "Border Music," having prepared the*
*breakfast cornbread earlier, washed the dishes, and completed*
*my exercises including the weights. And I rose to look out our*
*trailer door, to stare upon the lone tower in the distance. And I*
*felt this quiet comfort of a slow morning, drenched in the*
*sunlight of a warm day, the dull buzz of insects and the*
*somnolent slide of the breeze across the prairie. It's a quiet*
*Sunday morn.*

*Out here in these burgeoning prairies, these vast open spaces of*
*rolling hills and valleys and the flatland in between, covered*
*only in short grass and occasional rocks, under Montana's big*
*sky, it is distance that grants your privacy, not shelter, not trees.*
*One walks along on a hike or ventures out from camp to take a*
*pee—you glance at the terrain about, see nothing untoward,*
*and slide your zipper down and water the grass. Living within*
*the campsite is the same, it is barren and open, not enough*

*shelter even to hide and place a latrine. But the distance and*
*vastness creates the security for a comfortable camp, a ring of*
*domain we call our own, time for a response should our*
*perimeter be violated by trespassers. The distance and vastness,*
*once you understand what it can grant, offer their own comfort.*
*You accept the natural world around you or you are forsaken to*
*a lower level of reduced options. It's very nice in its own way.*

## Short-grass Prairie, Willow Creek Reservoir, 1996

*From the Journals: Willow Creek Reservoir – Gary*
*31 July 1996 – Here at Willow Creek, out in the midst of a*
*short-grass prairie, no trees, no shade, hardly any dominant*
*features except for the endless terrain, my chief impression is*
*one of vastness and a feeling for why they call it Big Sky*
*Country. Our initial response to the apparent starkness when*
*we visited last year has mellowed to a comfortable feeling of*
*silence and even privacy. It's just that here, instead of privacy*
*being granted by coulees and hollows and hills and bushes and*
*trees and brush and the abundance of all that is green in*
*Wisconsin, here privacy is granted by distance, by bigness, by*
*an openness that creates its own barrier to invasion.*

The Willow Creek Reservoir hack site was set in the north
central Montana portion of the northern short-grass prairie
ecosystem. Although the tower was located near a large
reservoir, that body of water was not visible until one topped a
slight rise on the access road to our camp and release tower. The
view-scape where we spent our days and nights consisted of
miles and miles of gently rolling terrain, an occasional seasonal
water course, and the prairie, largely short and sparse grass,
very few trees or brush. There was nowhere to hide, no way to
subvert prying eyes. If a pickup truck or a tractor or a cowman
riding his horse to check on his cattle approached from any

direction they could see us from over a mile away. And we could see them. But because of where we were and how the land was used, after a few weeks on site, we knew that 99 percent of the time we would be by ourselves, would not be surprised, and found that distance protected us, and protected the privacy we valued. Lifeforms that lived in this place, birds, mammals—us included—and plants had adapted to the openness and the openness gave the privacy appropriate to their lives and lifestyle.

It is called short-grass prairie for a reason, and the implication is true, for the name differentiates it from another grass zone, that of the tall-grass prairie which lies east and south, toward the Midwestern parts of the nation where more moisture and a more temperate climate over better soils promote faster growth and the response of the species suited to the those conditions. At Willow Creek the grasses were seldom over a foot in height and had been tempered by harsh winters, less rain, winds unfettered by obstructions, periods of drought and a soil structure lacking in humus. Blue grama and other grama grasses, buffalo grass, grease grass, various other bunch grasses, and the occasional prickly pear cactus grew where bison once trod. Over eons the bison helped mold these grasses to tolerate close grazing even though they were growing on soils made up of a hard, dense conglomeration of rocks, sand, gravel, and dry dirt. Cattle and sheep grazed there, substituting for the bison's role in nutrient conversion. Where the grasses were thin and the soil dusty and not compacted, the prairie wind blew the grass fronds about and the leaf tips drew visible arcs on the ground surface.

The grasses around us were all thin and wiry and, as we were there in August, were mostly varied shades of brown, tan, and yellow, the green having gradually disappeared as the season advanced from spring to summer to late summer. These grasses did not have wide blades or the depth or density that invites a walker to lie down, as grasses in Wisconsin do. In the Willow Creek Reservoir area of Montana in August, 1996, the grasses were more like bristles—stiff, brittle, scratchy, their seeds—like those of needle and thread grass types, reached out to stick you, grab on to your clothes for the ride, and to worm their sharp points into your skin. No soft, luxuriant, green blades to recline on and look skyward. No—too rough, too humpy, too sharp, too prickly and coarse. But the grasses lived well and survived year after year, had survived for centuries.

Yet, the survival of short-grass prairie grasses is not without challenges and set-backs. One day that August the outdoor temperature was 95 degrees, a hot, hot, dry day, sunny, very little breeze. It was amazing to recognize what the lack of an extra 3000 to 4000 feet of atmosphere over your heads could feel like at the moderate elevation of Willow Creek. The sun has such radiant heating power when it need not blaze through another few thousand feet of air like it does at lower elevations. Dark metal objects left lying in the sun can literally get too hot to touch. A dark T-shirt or blue jeans absorbs so much heat you want to trade it in immediately for lighter colored clothing or to shed layers. We humans can flee or seek shade or change our clothes. But the grass is rooted in place, sending its roots slowly toward what little moisture it can find. And the blades are thin and wiry to reduce the loss of leaf moisture to the sun and the winds.

Along with the bison, wind and fire also contributed to the centuries of sculpting of the short-grass prairie surrounding us at Willow Creek. One day we counted four small prairie fires within a 20-mile radius of where we sat observing our falcons, the fire sites made visible sometimes by flames as much as six miles away, but normally by distant smoke forming flat gray clouds drifting slowly through the sky. In the driest, hottest portions of summer the already dried-out grasses are like tinder and a cigarette tossed carelessly and thoughtlessly from a moving vehicle can set it ablaze. In other instances the lightning strikes of a late summer thunderstorm can start fires in spite of rain bands which may be moving through.

One exceptionally windy week we witnessed a Double-crested Cormorant, normally a powerful and speedy flier, being thrown into the grasses a few feet below him as he sought better flying conditions a few yards over the prairie. The winds were gusty, roaring constantly 35 to 45 miles an hour and the cormorant misjudged his capabilities. Momentarily stunned the cormorant righted himself, took a few steps on his stubby, poorly-positioned-for-walking legs, legs intended largely to advance his swimming skills, spread his wings and the variable wind lifted him aloft where he thought better of his venture and returned to the lake about a mile to the northwest.

During that same week of the cormorant's embarrassing mishap, we too were suffering from the constant blow which the weather system had delivered. Seemingly day after day our relatively heavy camping trailer was swaying in the breeze, rocking us to sleep, wiggling the liquids in our cups as we sat for a meal. Even though the measured temperature was a relatively mild 60 degrees, the high winds managed to strip your bodies of available heat as we sat still outdoors attempting to continue the monitoring of our falcons. At our observation point the shade tarp over our heads would flex and snap and shake while the whole framework and guy lines would shudder in tension and release. As we walked to get a meal or go to the latrine or stretch our legs, we found ourselves leaning against the wind with each step searching for a secure foothold. The wind dried out our eyes and the howling in our ears began to be painful. We could shut out some of the wind by pulling up and cinching tight the hoods that we always had on some portion of our clothing layers but then we were benumbed by the sense of blinders mounted on our faces, reducing our peripheral vision, and then the wind billowing out our hoods like balloons, our ears nonetheless thankful for any suppression of the pressure pounding on our eardrums. At times like that we understood better why the grass blades were short, wiry, and thin. And the old time stories of early settler women going mad in their homes set in the midst of such conditions and not being able to escape began to make more sense.

Having ourselves been sculpted by our education, upbringing, the environmental surroundings of our youths, by nature and nurture, our conversation would periodically turn to philosophical issues, and we have explored a few of those personal revelations in these pages. Perhaps the direction of our thoughts in this prairie setting was influenced by the incessant pounding of the wind and the consideration of the madness that could be induced by situations one cannot escape. During one deep, philosophical discussion which we had during this time period regarding life, living, death, and the very good people who go through all of this with us, and the assholes who also accompany us, we conjectured a brief truism and philosophy regarding the big picture and continual leveling going on about us: to wit, "You come in naked and you go out dead." Well, we did not claim we were going to reveal a philosophy long and complicated. And the dark humor brought out a fit of laughter in each of us to end the day as we finished writing up our journals that evening.

## Hack Site Snake Experiences

As we established our camp at the Holter Lake site we had been
warned by the local BLM sponsor that rattlesnakes were known
to be in the area, and The Peregrine Fund had issued us one
snake bite kit. The kit was an extraction-type device, designed
to apply vacuum pressure to the fang puncture and pull out the
venom that might have been injected. We had been camped at
Holter, three miles from our truck, for only two days and had
hiked to the hack box only three times, when on the third hike
Gary was struck by a large snake. We were walking down the
incline of the old cattle trail returning to camp and had been
mindlessly kicking off the occasional rock to clear the trail for
many future hikes when, Thwack! Gary's boot was hit from
behind and he jumped a bit from the unknown cause. Jean, who
had been following him in single file, clearly saw the short
event unfolding and could not help but utter a scream. She was
quite startled. As was Gary as he spun around and took in what
had happened within the past very few seconds. Each of us
quickly backed away out of danger to assess the facts. The
snake had struck Gary on the heel of his boot, was over four
feet long, had a head larger than the neck behind, triangular?,
well maybe, rattled its tail loudly, but the rattling was a result of
vigorous shaking and striking tall dry grass, we could not see
any actual rattles, but instead the tail tapered to a smooth,
narrow point.

We were both shaken but learned from this early interaction
with a creature we had not seen so near us before it struck. Back
at camp we questioned how to avoid future surprises from
reptiles hidden in the tall grasses and brush through which we
would be hiking each day. This snake was a Gophersnake,
referred to alternately in some locales as a Bullsnake, and the
species is known to be defensive and to mimic the actions of a

rattlesnake. What if it had been a rattlesnake? And what if it had stuck Gary's leg just six inches higher, above the leather boot? We vowed to carry our snake bite kit everywhere we went and to hike together more frequently than we might have in a less rattlesnake-prone area. The falcons were still locked into their hack box acclimating to their new life in the outdoors, so we made a quick, unscheduled drive down to Helena, Montana, to buy a second snake bite kit from a camp-equipment store so that we could each carry one at all times. We also bought a long, light-weight mop handle from a hardware store with which the lead person could sweep the tall grasses side to side in front of us as we hiked and to provide an advance target four feet in front of us for snakes to strike instead of human flesh. Our "snake sticks" were also used each time we returned to camp after having been absent for the day while we were observing our falcons at the observation site located about a mile from camp. For this application we would sweep our sticks under the fabric of our tent near the door through which we crawled into the tent so as to be certain no rattler had taken up residence in the shade and seclusion available under our tent floor. As advocates of wildlife and as participants in re-establishing a species, it was our goal each summer to learn to live with wildlife, not to kill it.

As the need persisted and as the summer wore on, one of our hobbies to while away between-falcon lulls in our observation time was the carving of additional "natural" snake sticks, the purchased mop handle lacking a certain suave flair and aesthetic appeal. Slender, long, delicately curvaceous, poles from local chokecherry, Western red cedar, and Juneberry were carefully chosen by each of us and taken to the observation site where we would carve off the bark, and smooth down any bumps, branch stubs, or imperfections, and new hiking sticks, known at Holter as "snake sticks" were created by each of us. Some of these hiking sticks, including the mop handle, are still available for our use at our farm decades after they were originally crafted. As the summer wore on our snake sticks proved their utility, helping us find, avoid, and observe a half-dozen instances of startling, close interactions with confirmed rattlesnakes while we were hiking or sitting quietly observing our falcons, each time giving us some level of cautious fright, as we invaded and occupied what was naturally their habitat.

We now routinely and without fail carry snake bite kits with us when we are hiking in western states in habitats known to hold rattlesnakes. Although rattlesnake bites happen infrequently to outdoor visitors and very rarely cause death in the United States, why gamble when these kits are so small and convenient to carry? We no longer questioned the practicality or efficacy of the kits after one of the Release Specialists shared his personal experiences—he had been struck by rattlesnakes TWICE already in his reintroduction work. He described one of these occasions to us: he was alone in the back country of Wyoming dealing with a Peregrine reintroduction problem when he was struck and bitten in his thigh by a rattlesnake. Fortunately he had just received a snake bite kit from his father a week previously as a gift and was near the kit in his truck. He immediately ripped into the contents, quickly reviewed the instructions, and jabbed it onto his wound, where it remained firmly affixed to his leg, held there by the suction power of the device. Then he hobbled quickly to his truck with a six-inch plastic extractor stuck onto his leg, climbed in, and drove 70 miles to the nearest hospital in Cody, Wyoming, where he received a prompt anti-venom shot.

At another site where we encountered a number of our most-feared neighbors in these outdoors which we nonetheless loved, we once had to side-step five of those venomous rattlesnakes in one day, imitating a rapid foot raising, leg jerking, breathless dance of uncontrolled emotion each time. Two of them were on the large size for the Northern Rockies, ranging to the 4-foot category in length. Most humans are anciently preconditioned to respond to snakes with rapid avoidance and fear and we were not exceptions.

In spite of our ability to read and occupy ourselves at the hack sites when there are no falcons in the area to observe we, or certainly Gary, could get a little bored during these assignments where duty and responsibility dictated our priorities. Sometimes it was the repetition, sometimes it was the fault of the Peregrines for staying away from the hack box so long. Well, boredom was sure BLOWN AWAY one early evening! Jean had started rehydrating our supper but we were both back to sitting quietly in folding camp chairs under our observation shade-tarp and trying to identify our evening falcons. Then, about six feet away and to his left, Gary heard or sensed or saw with his peripheral vision a moving something-or-other. As Gary stood immediately up and yelled a quick burst of "Aiieee!" Jean knew right away it was something serious, and looked to where Gary pointed. RATTLER! Big one! Headed to our tent and camp kitchen area and at that point being six to eight feet from each of those.

Our mouse-proof aluminum kitchen supplies box was set on several wooden 2x2s to elevate it above the ground slightly and was located under our rain and shade tarp. Each day both of us would kneel down in front of that cupboard repeatedly as we got ready for our meals and as soon as we saw that snake in camp we recognized the potential danger. This snake could easily lie hidden under our tent floor or under this kitchen box, the raised box presenting a perfect lair for the snake to await his next meal of a mouse or vole common in the grassy area, or of a chipmunk which our camp attracted. Our vivid imaginations easily pictured the snake striking either of our fleshy thighs right above the knee as we knelt there in preparation for our next meal.

It had been our standard policy each summer, to not bother a rattlesnake, not kill a rattlesnake, if they did not bother us. Bad Karma and all, and we did not want the Universe pointing an accusatory finger involving retribution at us. Or at least that was how the guilt factor felt. And for literally well over a dozen times throughout our Peregrine assignments, our policy held and the rattlers went on living their lives after each encounter. But this time we hurriedly exchanged brief comments, quickly reviewed the propriety of killing this one, and easily concluded this particular rattler had to go. This was too close to where we lived and worked, too frightening, we just could not have a rattler where we knelt and sat and crawled around on the ground each day.

Gary told Jean, "Watch him!" and ran to the truck to fetch and load a small rifle we carried with us to use in the rare possibility of a situation such as this. When Gary returned Jean was bravely keeping the rattler, now alert and dangerous, in a holding pattern with two of her snake sticks, one in each hand, while the rattler coiled, slithered, and stared in defiance, his tongue probing forth to sense this new enemy. Gary shot the snake. Repeatedly, in the head and neck area. We were a little sad and regretful but also relieved. And nervous, shaky, and yet anxious from the huge rush of adrenalin while dealing with the issue. Whew! Once Gary calmed down he prescribed two ounces of straight whiskey for his nerves, applied internally. Witnessing the aftermath response of the reptilian nervous system only added to our dismay and mixed emotions—the snake continued to writhe and shake its eleven rattles for a full half hour after being shot. Even dead the snake sure did not act dead. We promised each other to remember how lucky we were to have these jobs to enjoy the next time we felt bored or restless while sitting there waiting for a falcon to observe. Next time we were feeling bored we promised each other to just enjoy it.

## Paddling with Beavers, Saying Good-bye to Ground Squirrels, Green River, 1993

*From the Journals: Green River – Gary*
*17 June 1993 – Yesterday we saw a large beaver, his bright brown fur rippling fluidly, swimming in the river, exploring the bends, and occasionally pulling his ponderous body out onto the banks to sample the succulent plants. This morning I looked out our window and saw him in mid-current, going downstream, propelled rapidly by this swift stream and the movements of his tail, and passing quickly out of view. The beaver was grinning widely and had a look of joyousness about him.*

At our Green River site we used a canoe daily to get from our camp on one side of the river to the Peregrine tower on the other side. One day we had paddled across the river to the other side in order to get closer to a resting falcon hoping we could clearly observe the leg band and identify which falcon we were watching. Having confirmed it was Green, we continued downstream to a small island and circled it through a narrow channel to return upstream to our camp. As we emerged back into the main channel, we spotted a beaver also swimming upstream in the same direction we were now going. We put on a short burst of speed to pull alongside it about a paddle length away to observe the beaver in its natural element, anticipating it

would quickly dive and leave us behind where we could not
follow.

In our previous experiences with beaver while walking along
the bank of the Green River, "Slap!" would go the beaver's tail
upon the water and down the beaver would go as soon as we
were spotted. But in this instance, the beaver did not have the
same fear or awareness of a watercraft floating nearby that it
would have had for a person walking upright on the bank of this
river. And so it continued to swim upstream, ignoring us as best
as it could, and allowing us to witness his strength, grace, and
forbearance as he continued his goal-oriented morning mission.
The beaver just kept swimming on the surface even though
Gary began to talk to it, bidding it "Hello" and asking if we
could visit. Finally having had enough of this objectionable
human behavior the beaver slapped his tail on the water with a
satisfying, "Plop!" and dove under the surface. But he continued
swimming upstream about one to two feet underwater where, in
this clear mountain stream, we could still observe his actions
easily.

We continued to paddle as smoothly and silently as we could
while still keeping pace with the now submerged beaver. He
became a large brown furry fish, tiny bubbles escaping from the
hairs of his pelt making him appear to glisten, as his silent flat
rudder/undulating, propulsive tail provided speed we could
barely match. With the beaver and ourselves moving upstream
at the same pace the experience was somewhat like seeing a
silent movie accompanying us, watching an image of a
swimming beaver on an underwater screen. Seeing these other
species in their natural setting was always a joy of the outdoor
life which our job assignments provided us. Unusual for
wildlife interactions like these we tired of the event before the
beaver did, or perhaps the paddles at the end of our arms were

no match for the paddle the beaver always carried with him at the end of his body. After paddling close to the overhanging bank with the beaver, we began to pull out back to the main channel and the beaver surfaced again. His wet, pock-marked fur was saturated with water, portions running generously off the tips of his above-water hairs. It was like he did not mind at all our paddling the Green River together with him.

Some days are richer than others. This was to be one of those days. When we returned to camp we were walking down the field trail to dump the quail remnants left over from yesterday's Peregrine feeding when we spotted a Richardson's ground squirrel in the middle of the trail fully intent on his own important mission in life—that of survival.

In early summer our Green River site had an abundance of busy, active, hustling ground squirrels. Several could always be spotted at the same instant during daylight hours and we have one photo of our camp site where 17 of the corpulent rascals are shown in one picture frame gathering their stores for the coming season. In mid-August we humans think the season is only half done and there are many days remaining before we need to think about snow shovels and warm clothes. At mid-summer in mid-August in the high mountain country of Wyoming, Richardson's ground squirrels are done with summer and returning to underground burrows because evolution has taught them winter is coming and now is the time to retreat. Each recent day we had seen fewer and fewer of their species until it seemed this chubby squirrel might be the last of his kind still above ground. As if to prove the point, oblivious of his nearby human observers, he was forcing himself down an opening, nearly too small for him. His head and front legs were in the burrow opening, his butt and tail nearly upright in the air, and his little hind legs were vigorously trying to shove his body through the opening. Pushing and squirming and wriggling while Gary snapped pictures of this nearly ridiculous sight, the squirrel was at long last successful and disappeared from sight. A short time later we returned to the same burrow location and found it plugged from underneath with a small mound of dirt blocking the entrance. Staring at the mound and listening carefully we thought we heard a faint murmur from underground, "Now I am ready for winter." But maybe we just imagined that. Regardless, he was the last ground squirrel we saw that summer along the Green.

## The August Singularity, CSKT Tower, 1992 and Bar None Ranch, 1994

The August Singularity is a weather phenomenon long known mostly as local lore among older, more experienced forest fire fighters and older long-term residents in the northern Rocky Mountains of western Montana and Idaho. It is an event that occurs in a highly repetitive pattern nearly every year around the third week of August and is characterized by a rather quick and notable change in weather patterns marked by pressure changes, wind directional and speed shifts, and falling temperatures. Old-time fire-chiefs use the event as a predictor or marker to aid in the planned control of wild fires because wildfires were easier to control at the anticipated lower atmospheric temperatures. Local farmers and ranchers, made wise through experience, noted its likelihood on their calendars and avoided certain field activities if possible, due to the possibility of a noteworthy change in the weather.

University researchers Peter T. Soule and Paul A. Knapp published their analysis of the August Singularity in the *Journal of Applied Meteorology and Climatology* in June of 2008. Their goal had been to determine if this locally-known event could be factually confirmed as occurring within a fixed pattern that could not be explained by random chance. Soule and Knapp studied historical weather data from various reporting centers in the northern Rockies and confirmed chance alone does not explain the existence of measurable weather changes occurring within a 24 to 26 August Singularity period.

During two of the years we were hacking Peregrines in the northern Rockies region with a history of the August Singularity, we had the interesting experience of living within and learning about this weather phenomenon from local news outlets and personal experience.

In August of 1992 while assigned to the CSKT Tower hack site we had recorded daytime high temperatures of 100 degrees on 4 August, 92 degrees on the following day, 95 on 18 August, 96 degrees on 19 August. For the four-week period previous to 22 August we had had no measurable rain and dust coated our clothes, outdoor equipment, the top of our truck, and crept constantly into the camping trailer, necessitating a quick mop of our countertop before using it for meal preparation. Sometimes during this period as we were sitting outdoors observing our falcons and grabbing for another cooling drink of water, our tongue would touch our lips preparatory to lifting our insulated mugs of ice water (hurrah for the camper provided for our use and its propane-powered refrigerator!) and we could taste the countryside's dust where it had settled on our mouths. In the absence of breezes or wind in early morning or late day, we could still see the dust hanging low to the ground illuminated like a type of brown fog, myriads of motes lit by the angular rays of the sun. But, right on schedule, in the third week of August our outdoor world changed dramatically.

On 22 August, within several days of Soule and Knapp's documented research, following a night with flashes of lightning and the booming of thunder, we awoke to find over an inch of rain had collected in a flat water pan we kept outside near the trailer. After a period spent enduring high temperatures in the 90's and one day of 100 degrees, on the 22nd we recorded a high for the day of only 42 degrees. Rapid change indeed! Our bodies could hardly cope as we added layer upon layer of warm clothes which replaced the shorts and T-shirts we had been wearing. A strong wind came out of the north and with the rain and low-hanging clouds and fog, now made up of moisture instead of dust, the perimeter of our vision shrank down to perhaps half a mile horizontally, several hundred feet vertically. After the rain, wet, heavy, sticky snow began coating our camper and truck with white frosting and we wondered what the mountains would look like and when we could see them again.

Neither of us was looking forward to climbing the tower and placing out quail for our falcons, knowing the tower platform would have a coating of snow on it—a condition we had not yet experienced while being 30 feet above the ground without guard rails. Within our habit of trading off of the daily feeding assignment it was Jean's turn to go up, but this morning Gary accompanied her to the tower and watched anxiously from below lending verbal encouragement and precautionary statements when he thought he could get away with it. With snow concealing some of the remnants left over from the previous day's feeding by the Peregrines, the serpentine quail guts left over popped like the bubble wrap used in protective packaging as Jean inadvertently stepped on some of them. We both breathed a small sigh of relief when Jean was back on the ground and we trod through the wet foliage and newly mudded field back to our trailer.

Two days later the daily high temperature had still not made it out of the 40's but the clouds, rain, snow and fog had gradually been worn down and away by shifting winds and the sun began to shine on our hack site again. It was a brand new look to our formerly hot and dusty world. The Mission Mountains to the east wore a dazzle-bright, white shine of new snow extending all the way down to the foothills. Even the nearer and lower foothills of the National Bison Range down at Moise had a new coat of snow. The glare from the new snow almost hurt our eyes but it was so pristine we could not help but gaze at the change of scenery. What was once a range of mountains with a little melting snow left on top had been transformed to a winter scene as we admired it from the contrast of our late summer valley bottom of browns and greens. At that point our August Singularity at CSKT Tower was a singular experience for us.

But we were to experience it once more. August of 1993 found us in Wyoming along the banks of the Green River, southeast of the Jackson, Wyoming area and too far south to be within the domain of the climatological event known as the August Singularity. In August of 1994, however, we were working with Peregrines on the Bar None Ranch and according to local news literature, that area too experiences the Singularity and referenced it as most likely occurring within a 22 August to 4 September time frame. Although located 200 miles southeast of the CSKT hack site, the Bar None Ranch was still far enough north and west in the Rocky Mountains of Montana to be the recipient of weather events similar to those we had seen at CSKT Tower. The area of the nearby Big Belt Mountains had also been recognized locally as often having a marked transition of summer to autumn, a wet rain front moving through, and/or a cold snap during late August or early September.

In the summer of 1994, the fire watch areas of the western states in the Rocky Mountains experienced numerous outbreaks of forest fires, some of them quite large. In late July and August, while at the Bar None Ranch we experienced the typical hot and dry weather with temperatures up into the high 80's, which played a role in the fire outbreaks but, as we were east of most of the large fires, the consequences of the fires that we ourselves noticed most were the vivid sunsets. The setting sun often cast its light through the atmospheric smoke particles released from the large fires and colored the sky west of us in varying hues of red and orange. The lower the sun the more intense the color until at the end of day the sun slipped below the horizon and with it the late-day color show ended.

On 22 August 1994 at the Bar None Ranch the clouds thickened, the storm moved in, rain commenced and by 1800 (6:00 PM) the temperature was down to 52 degrees. The following morning we awoke to frost on many surfaces and grass spears frozen solid and immobile. By evening that day we could sense that we were within a different type of day, a day that forecast autumn's arrival. Just as the elk can tell when to come down off the mountain in advance of a harsh winter storm, just as the Mule Deer of the Gros Ventre and Wyoming Ranges know when to migrate, just as the swallows, nighthawks and swifts had gathered over the Bar None Ranch cliff and begun to migrate a week earlier, so too could we tell change was afoot. The air was cleansed by the cool rain, smoke particles washed out. The canyon breezes seemed less hot, the rocky canyon walls were cooler, less radiant heat emanated from them, all melding to be precursors of cooler days. What we experienced was summer's reversal, the first day of change past summer's peak. Then we knew, then we could tell ..... Fall was coming. We had again personally witnessed the August Singularity.

## C. PERSONAL STORIES

### Gary Loses his Glasses, Grave Point, 1991

One particular day in the relaxed observation period at Grave Point in 1991 we had a flurry of falcon activity at midday, and by early afternoon had seen each of our remaining young falcons plus both of the regularly visiting Sub-adults, all them eating at the tower or carrying a quail away to eat elsewhere. We therefore declared a break for ourselves and, with cameras, water bottles, snacks and other hiking supplies in our daypacks, set off for a long hike together, a rare opportunity. It was sunny, but not especially hot, so a good day for it. We were determined to reach the far west ridge, the goal of Jean's longest hike the previous year. It was a long and tiring hike, total distance estimated at six miles with a couple thousand feet of altitude change, which change had to be done in four increments (and then some, as you will see below), since we started at a high point (camp), descended into a lower "saddle" area, climbed to the high west ridge, and then reversed this process on the way back. From the high ridge of our goal we enjoyed spectacular views of the Snake River in Hells Canyon and the mountainous eastern edge of Oregon on the other side. At one point in the saddle on the way back, Gary stopped to photograph some interesting plant seed-heads, laying his sunglasses on the ground to focus the camera and walking away afterward and up a steep slope before missing the glasses.

*From the Journals: Grave Point – Jean*
*27 July 1991 – To compound the problem of the forgotten glasses, I pushed my tired legs into a further gain uphill toward camp while Gary went back down to search for his glasses alone. Alas, he could not find them and wanted to leave the search until another day, coming part way up to me to say so.*

*This delay seemed to me a risky addition to the problem so I walked back down to him to help search. Together we continued further downslope to the area where he had taken the photo, and I found the glasses. When we finally got back to camp, after more than five hours, my shower water had lost most of its solar gain, but Gary started supper and I took my chilly shower anyway. Gary also mixed a batch of powdered Gatorade with water; after supper and Gatorade we were feeling better. In addition to the mileage of our long, strenuous hike, I had taken a 3-mile hike in the morning while Gary was at the O.P. successfully adding several species to our bird list, while Gary had hiked up to the tower to put out quail that morning and in the evening had to go up to the tower again to remove the quail remnants. After the latter walk, he too cleaned up. We finally crawled into the tent, tired and late, but pleased and proud of our longest Grave Point hike even if some of the distances covered had to do with back-tracking to look for lost glasses.*

Showers and Intimacy, Bar None Ranch, 1994

At each hack site, the sponsoring agency, or an affiliated agency located in the vicinity, would provide an option for Hack Site Attendants to periodically clean up with a refreshing pressurized hot shower facility. In no instance did we ever have such an option immediately adjacent to our campsite. If we wanted a hot shower with a simple twist of the wrist from hot and cold water faucets, it generally involved an absence from the hack site of four to six hours and a round-trip drive of 16 to 52 miles, depending on the site. The worst site for bodily cleanliness was Holter Lake, because we first had to hike three miles out to the truck and drive eight miles to the BLM campground where we could take showers, then reverse the process, drive eight miles again, and walk the three miles to camp, arriving back all hot, sweaty and dusty, having mostly negated the benefit of the shower. The most convenient site was the Bar None Ranch where we could drive from our camp to a pressurized shower, hot and cold water instantly available, inside of an old ranch, one-room school house that had been converted to a guest house. Even at the Bar None Ranch this effort still involved a rugged two-hour, round trip drive of 12 miles on a trail that could be safely driven only in dry weather, driven only very slowly and with a 4-wheel drive vehicle.

Given the time and distance limitations, our preferred and most commonly used method for bodily cleanliness was the simple, rudimentary method of water heated over a camp stove and applied from a small wash basin with a washcloth. A more satisfactory but less-used method was a special bag made of heavy plastic, clear on the top side to let in solar rays and black on the bottom side to absorb those rays, converting them to heat in the water. This solar shower bag was fitted with a shut-off valve and a spray head; when filled with water, placed in sunlight to heat and later hung from a convenient tree branch at the three sites where we lived in tents and under tarps, it made a decent shower possible. Due to walking distances, difficulty in obtaining adequate water supplies, site complexity, and cool weather we spanned six and one-half weeks without a shower while camped at Holter Lake, making do with those washcloth wash-ups. At Holter ALL water used at the site was either delivered three miles via boat across the lake (five times in seven weeks), then carried, 40-48 pounds per jug, two-thirds mile uphill to camp, or brought in by truck to our parking spot on the adjacent ranch, then backpacked three miles from the truck to camp. This meant we were rather stingy with its use, unless we were lucky enough to catch a bit of rain water running off the tarp system. In that case, we used some of the rain water to wash out socks and underwear; these could be hung to dry under the kitchen tarp and we might be able to skip doing laundry on the next town trip. (Laundry at the nearest, tiny town was an iffy project—there were only two washing machines in that little laundromat, they might be busy when we got there, and we could not stay away from our falcon duties longer to wait for a turn.) At five of the camps, we lived in a 15-foot camper trailer, supplied by the sponsor at one site in 1992, or thereafter in our own camper we brought from home to the four sites that were trailer-accessible out of the last five. The camping trailers each had a small waterproof shower stall with hanging plastic curtains. But even though we sometimes had a trailer, never were any of them hooked up to a pressurized water line and in each case, we had to get our water supplies from somewhere else and bring the water to camp in those big five or six-gallon jugs. We would still heat the small quantities of water needed for a shower either in the sun or on a camp stove, and bathe with the solar shower bag or a bucket hung in the shower stall, water flow supplied by gravity and controlled with a simple shut-off valve.

We used solar shower bags to heat water for showers, or hair, or even for dish-washing. The first year, Jean's solar shower bag sprang a leak early in the summer. Thereafter, she heated water via the power of the sun in a translucent plastic ice cream bucket with lid, and when that proved slightly inadequate for a shower including washing her long hair, additional water was set out in the sun to heat in a soot-blackened (from campfires in previous years of camping) camp "boiler" placed with the ice cream bucket in a patch of sun early in the day. This skill, to be able to get body and hair soaped, scrubbed and rinsed once a week in five quarts of sun-heated water, was a matter of pride and a significant savings of water.

At such remote camp sites, surrounded by a broad sweep of privacy wrought by distance from normal civilization, our sexual inclinations would periodically manifest themselves. After all, what is a loving couple to do besides eat, read, and sleep inside of a small tent or camper when driven there by darkness or by rain or lightning, preventing us from our obligatory falcon observations? We kidded one another about the high mountain air, the elevation, the change in ozone concentration and the negative ions after one particularly rousing storm at Grave Point, which set a minor precedent for activities during several ensuing thunderstorms over the Peregrine summers.

In the 1990's skin cancer was not yet of much concern and so on a warm day we occasionally might expose more of our bodies than normal in the wilderness settings, tanning our then more youthful selves in places that did not normally receive exposure to the sun. If such action proved to be a tease, who were we to deny a possible result? Clean bodies, fresh from a recent shower, could sometimes cause another triggering of the mood, given the rarity of full body bathing. At the Bar None Ranch we had driven out for more frozen quail for our falcons and had each enjoyed showers in the guest house. Later that same day, we were able to identify and log in each of the falcons then still on site, thereby meeting a prime goal for each day's viewing. The sun had already set behind our hack box cliff, and although our mountain valley was beginning to shade over and darken, it was still light outside. Nonetheless, we retired to our sleeping pads in the tent and had just commenced in exploring each other's intimacy and level of sensual arousal when we both heard the faint putt-putt-putt growling grind of a diesel engine slowly forging up the hill in back of our camp and we knew it next would be descending into our valley. Jumping up together, instantly alert, without need for speaking or organizing a plan, we each simultaneously threw on the rest of our clothes, grabbed our boots, quickly tied them, ripped open the tailgate, leaped into the back end of the truck, grabbed our binoculars, spotting scopes, and camp chairs, set them up, and were "calmly" seated at our observation site near camp viewing the cliff when the white three-quarter ton truck pulled into our camp.

Turning around, we warmly greeted visitors, rare at this site: the ranch foreman, his wife, his wife's sister, her husband, and their young child. The latter three were visiting the ranch, had heard about our project, and wanted to personally experience the venture—we had become a sort of tourist stop! In the dimming light we were still able to show them a falcon or two through our powerful scope, explain what was happening at this site, and why it had been chosen. The manager and his wife reclined on the grass under our tarp, we shared our chairs, and we seven spent a delightful few hours exchanging stories of lives spent on different paths. They were excellent students, eager to learn about the falcons and our role in their return to this wilderness. They were friendly, and it felt good to share a special quiet evening with them in our mountainous outdoor home.

Our guests left, the growl-grind of their truck receding into the darkness, and the valley became ours again. The stars shone brightly as quiet returned and the night insects buzzed a low murmur. We put our observing equipment back into the truck, again, got ready for bed, again, and crawled into the tent, again. Jean was grinning as Gary flopped onto his pad and said, "Lessee, where were we?"

*Phase Five, Making Hay:  Figures 27 and 28*

*Figure 27:  Gary with sickle-bar mower*

*Figure 28:  Jean with side-delivery  rake*

## Making Hay, Green River, 1993

The Green River site was on Bureau of Land Management (BLM) acres straddling the Green River, with the hack tower on the one side of the river, and our camp on the other, necessitating the use of a canoe twice a day as we crossed the river between camp and the tower in our duties to the falcons. The BLM property was surrounded by private ranchlands, which we crossed by permission, using the private ranch access road several miles from the highway, to reach the hack site, as well as the private bridge over the river. The whole area was encircled by foothills and distant mountains, but our immediate view was of the river, sagebrush grasslands, and the ranch's meadow hayfields. That year, snow melt and spring rains had been generous and the meadows were lushly green, but the haying had been delayed by wet conditions and our arrival in mid-July found the ranch foreman concerned about being behind schedule and short of help. We had been introduced to the ranch owner, his family, and the foreman on the day of our arrival at the site.

That was a busy day, starting with meeting the Release Specialist at the Wyoming Game & Fish compound in town, where we had been allowed to park our camper after arriving the previous day and making contacts at Game & Fish and BLM offices, and where we had thus camped overnight. After the Release Specialist arrived with the falcons and made all the necessary contacts in town, including unloading the freezer of quail, and arranging a canoe and paddles for our use, a caravan of vehicles drove out to the site—The Peregrine Fund truck, a BLM vehicle with representatives of that sponsoring agency, our truck with our 14-foot camper trailer in tow. The next step involved making contact with the ranch owners and the foreman. Most importantly that day, the young falcons for this site were installed in their tower hack box overlooking the Green River, the sagebrush grasslands across the river, and the mountains beyond. In the introductory conversations with the ranch owner, it was decided placing the quail freezer in a ranch outbuilding would be much more convenient for us and this necessitated a return to town to bring the freezer to the ranch. Before the Release Specialist left, we were shown approximately where to park our camper, but the work of placing the camper, leveling it and so forth had to wait until late afternoon after all the other people had left, and after a BLM canoe and paddles had been delivered. Only then could we finally begin the work of setting up our camp, starting to dig a latrine and gathering rocks to support a seat for it. We had also to make yet another trip to town in the evening to make use of a pay phone we had located the day before, to call Jean's mom and one of our daughters with the details of our arrival and our new summer address.

The biggest job remaining was to organize the camper; for the long trip out from Wisconsin, most of our supplies were stored in boxes and crates carefully arranged all over the floor of the camper for safe traveling. Foods needed to be unpacked into the homemade cupboards, clothes into the tiny closet and into baskets on the shelves, and all the rest. The large wooden platform/step had traveled upside down on the floor to hold five-gallon jugs of water and keep them upright and contained during the trip; it needed to be unloaded and the platform set out in front of the door for easier access in and out of the camper. We worked hard on this, ate supper late, worked more, went to bed late, slept hard. The next day we finished digging the latrine and rigged our camouflage net as a privacy screen for it, and continued to unpack and organize in the camper, stowing some of our supplies in the back of the pickup to make more room in the camper. We took a break only to canoe across the river to feed the falcons and observe their behavior.

After release of the falcons a few days later, we settled in to the intense observation period, into the usual issues of worrying about missing falcons, rejoicing when returns occurred, searching for a missing individual, putting out quail on the tower at the beginning of each day, cleaning off quail remnants at the end of the day, making twice-weekly phone reports to Boise, and camp life.

Around us the activities of the ranch were taking place, including mowing of the first meadow patches for hay. Because of the high altitude and consequent long and snowy winters, cattle were not kept year round at this ranch, but brought in for summer grazing only. We saw some in our vicinity, horses too, but most of the cattle seemed to be on distant, upper pastures while we were there. The meadow-hayfields were basically flat but irregularly shaped, bordered by the river and crossed by a meandering stream and some small, narrow irrigation ditches. Very soon after we met the ranch foreman, we learned that he and his wife were from Wisconsin too and about our age. Upon hearing we had grown up on Iowa farms and farmed our own small place in Wisconsin for 20 years, the foreman wanted to know if we would help with the haying on the ranch while we were there.

This was certainly a surprise request, and we explained that we definitely would not have any spare time during the intensive observation weeks and only after that if our Peregrine boss agreed and if the foreman could make use of us one at a time while the other remained on falcon duty. Being farm kids, we knew that haying does not start very early in the day, nor continue late because the dew must dry off in the morning and haying must end when the dew just begins to come on again later in the day. Any damp weather would also prevent haying, so this would mean our help would be needed only in the middle hours of the day, and not every day. Still, the idea of helping to make hay on a Wyoming ranch was intriguing.

The ranch had two smaller tractors fitted with sickle-bar mowers, another small tractor hitched to a side-delivery rake, and a larger tractor to pull the baler or an automatic hay-bale stacker, a device with which we had no experience. Gary had mowing experience and both of us could rake the cut hay into windrows for baling after it had partially dried. At home Jean had driven our not-nearly-so-large tractor and baler, also pulling a flat-rack wagon; Gary rode on the flat rack to grab the bales from the baler chute and stack them in neat rows five layers high with the bales running one direction on the bottom layer and in alternating directions each layer thereafter. A bale-stacker eliminates the need for a person to stand on a moving wagon behind the baler to catch and stack the bales. Instead, the stacker gathers the bales from the ground into a specialized wagon where it arranges them in neat layers that can be efficiently unloaded at a hay storage location.

In the interest of maintaining good relations with the ranch people who were proving so friendly and helpful to the Peregrine reintroduction effort (permitting access on their private road, allowing us access to their shop building to fill our water jugs, receive our mail, plug in the quail freezer, and even to use the shop phone extension in case of emergency), it was felt by all concerned that helping with the haying when it did not interfere with our Peregrine duties was a good idea and our Peregrine boss gave his permission.

And so it came about, that some afternoons after our intense observation weeks, taking it in turns, one of us remained on falcon-watching duty, and the other participated in the interesting experience of haying the meadows of a large Wyoming ranch surrounded by glorious mountain views. In total we helped with the haying on eleven days, even both working a few days at the very end of our seven week period since our young falcons had dispersed from the hack site area a few days early and our Peregrine boss released us from observations. Of the various tasks involved in making hay, both of us mowed—the foreman taught Jean how—usually it was Jean who did the job of raking the mown hay into windrows the baler would be able to pick up, only Gary drove the tractor towing the baler and catch-wagon. At the end of our stay, we were given a joint check for $914, a nice bonus for that fieldwork season.

*From the Journals: Green River – Jean*
*1 August 1993 – The haying season on the ranch started yesterday with two tractors mowing. The ranch foreman's wife, whom we met soon after we arrived here, and who invited us to their home for dinner a couple evenings, also helps during the haying season. She told us there are two things she does not do while driving a tractor in the hay meadows: she does not drive through water (wet patches of the field with a few inches of standing water), and she does not mow over baby birds. Today I saw the mowers stop their tractors several times and rescue baby birds from their mower's path.*

On one of Jean's mowing days, it happened—she was mowing along next to the creek and suddenly found herself driving into a large, albeit fairly shallow, puddle of water, hidden by the tall grasses until she was into it. Remembering the injunction against driving through water, she stopped at once and pulled the lever to lift the mower's sickle-bar out of the water. The foreman was also mowing that day in another nearby patch, noticed Jean had stopped and came to find out why. He discovered beavers had dammed the stream just there and raised the water level until it flooded a low spot in the meadow. Jean also watched for baby birds while raking; one day she saw a baby bird so suddenly in her path that she could only swerve a bit quickly so that the bird's position was in the space between the front tires and between the rear tires of the tractor, and since it was sitting in a small depression, it also safely missed being speared by the rake tines passing overhead. Whew!

*From the Journals: Green River – Gary*
*30 August 1993 – When the foreman broke up the small beaver dam that was flooding the field, he found a beautiful small obsidian arrowhead in the clean gravel, shining from the sluicing action of the water, and gave it to Jean. It is complete and very nice!*

Wildlife Watching, all sites, every summer

Before taking up fieldwork, we had occasionally read bits about the patient, persistent work of wildlife researchers and photographers; it made sense to us that if you spent more time—quiet time—in a wild place, you would see more wildlife. Despite this we were quite unprepared for the wonderful variety of wildlife we would see in the different places we worked and for the fascinating wildlife behaviors we would be privileged to witness. Since we were in the wilderness, moved little and spoke only very quietly, and sat this way for many hours, basically all the daylight hours for weeks at a time (near mid-summer for example, the period spent on observation duty by one or both attendants was sometimes as long as 15.5 hours in a day), there was a lot of opportunity for wildlife, as well as our young falcons, to be in range of our view. We also found wildlife as we walked quietly from camp or observation point to the hack box to put out quail early in the morning, or to remove quail remnants in the evening. At Grave Point and Holter Lake, we also walked long distances from camp to the place where our truck was parked, and we saw wildlife too on the backcountry roads we drove at most sites.

We discovered this wealth of opportunity to watch wildlife very early in our career as Hack Site Attendants. When Jean was at Grave Point in 1990 with CJ, she found Blue Grouse hens with chicks, came close to a coyote while hiking, found a Rubber Boa (snake) in the trail, watched sparrows feed toward her in the grass to within eight feet, saw Ruffed Grouse and Mountain Quail hens with chicks, the latter *"making the loveliest sounds calling their babies."*

Working again at Grave Point the next year, but with Gary this time, yet more variety of wildlife was noted and enjoyed. While Gary was in town one day, a Chukar hen and her eleven chicks walked right past Jean in her short-legged camp chair. One evening on her way up to clean quail remnants off the tower Jean encountered two elk bulls with big antler spreads—they were glorious, but intimidating at only 50 yards distance. They found her presence alarming too, raised their noses to lay their antlers along their backs, and bounded away.

*From the Journals: Bar None Ranch – Gary*
*10 August 1994 – Last Monday I met a bull elk at the switchback roads. He was plodding down, I was plodding up, we both froze and stared at one another. I soon tired of the contest and purposely spooked him off. For a big critter he sure did go off through the brush quietly. How do they do that!? Looking at him again on the road, now 85 yards away, he*

*looked huge with those big antlers reaching so tall into the air over his back, six points on each side.*

Making the long drive alone from Wisconsin to Idaho, Jean did both visiting and birding at various stops along the way. While stopped at South Boysen State Park roadside area in Wyoming for lunch one day, she saw and identified her first ("Life") Clark's Grebe. At the same place she watched a Loggerhead Shrike hunting in the trees and openings. This bird is not much larger than an American Robin and has no relationship to raptors, yet it is an efficient predator. After capturing a rather large (relative to the size of the bird) lizard, the shrike carried the lizard into a Russian olive tree and struggled to impale the lizard on one of the tree's thorns. Shrikes are known to store prey on thorns, or even on barbs of a barbed wire fence, for future consumption, but in this case the shrike pulled the lizard back off the thorn and flew away with it.

*From the Journals: Grave Point – Jean*
*18 Jun 1991 – Maybe the thorn was a way to deal a fatal blow to prey, which the shrike's small beak hook and feet lacking the sharp talons of a raptor could not deliver. I noticed the shrike carry a series of prey always along the same flight line, observed its disappearance into the same tree each time and prompt reappearance. I checked the tree and found a nest, got my camera and took several photos of the nest with seven well-grown shrike nestlings.*

*From the Journals: Grave Point – Jean*
*7 July 1991 – Four days ago during my evening walk down to the truck to bring water up to camp, I saw two big toads. Tonight we went together for a toad walk down the road from camp as it got dark. Though we went as far as the tiny spring, it was a totally toad-less venture.*

A variety of small animals made use of the structure of the Grave Point tower, including house mice, deer mice, least chipmunks, yellow pine chipmunks, and golden-mantled ground squirrels. American toads were seen in their pits in the mud near tiny seeps.

*From the Journals: Grave Point – Jean*
*3 July 1991 – This afternoon I noticed fresh dirt being pushed out of the Northern pocket gopher mound nearby; sneaking up on it, I got a glimpse of the gopher, but not a really good look, and resolved to try to photograph this underground creature.*

After several days of trying, Jean got a photo of the dark brown gopher's face, nose damp from shoving soil out of the hole ahead of itself. The gophers made two kinds of holes; one they used as an opening through which to shove dirt from newly-excavated tunnels, forming a large mound above ground, and the other for bringing food down into their tunnels from above. Balsamroot plants with their large, grayish-green leaves and long-stalked golden, sunflower-like blooms were common on our hillside at Grave Point and used as food by the gophers. At first it was a bit eerie to notice a Balsamroot stem, its drying flower head in process of seed-production, start to wiggle before us and then slowly seem to disappear from the bottom up, but soon we realized the stem and flower were being pulled down by a gopher into a small, inconspicuous opening at ground surface.

*From the Journals: Grave Point – Jean*
*1 July 1991 – A clicking sound, followed to a pine—two cicadas on a branch with intricate wing-cell design—I sit and discover for myself what Phillip Wylie, in his book "The Magic Animal," says about one square foot of grass. In so small a space, I*

269

*observe a beetle on a golden flower through reversed binocular lenses, a ladybird beetle rides on a wind-waved stem of grass, tiny sun-pink flowers turn blue when shaded by my presence, a clear-wing moth gathers nectar, four seeds already form in each 4-carpeled ovary of the waterleaf's fuzzy fruit ball, hummingbirds visit red flowers, bumblebees prefer the larkspurs' rich purple, no human design this, but ours to cherish and preserve. Or destroy, but in its destruction we destroy ourselves.*

Driving across Wyoming to our job at Holter Lake, we witnessed a Pronghorn doe giving birth to twins beside the backroad we were traveling as we explored our way west. Soon after arriving on site, we encountered a mule deer doe and fawn on our way up to the hack box; in their surprise they ran from us in opposite directions so we stood in place until mother and child reunited. The day before a Blue Grouse hen and her four chicks waited to flush until we had almost stepped on them. Sitting for hours at the mountainside observation point noting falcon activities, we also watched ant lions dig their ant traps, and ants falling therein and trying to climb out before the "lion" got them. There were mountain goats in the area, and we saw a grizzly trying to climb a fence along Interstate 15 the day we went to Helena for antibiotics, lumber, a mop handle to use as a snake stick, and a snake-bite kit. Also at Holter we heard the strange sound elks make, and were greeted by an Osprey pair when we hiked past their nest above the three-mile trail between camp and the place we had to leave our truck. We always returned the Ospreys greeting, feeling as though we should ask their permission or apologize for disturbing them as we went by. Between the Osprey nest and the truck's parking spot there was yet another wildlife treat—a prairie dog town to walk through. After the prairie dogs, it was not much farther to our truck, parked in a bit of shade under some pines by an old cattle or sheep shed. Just as we sought shade for ourselves and our truck, so did the mule deer and we often found several of them spending the heat of the day resting and making that old shed look like it contained *"a forest of ears and antlers."*

At CSKT Tower, as we walked our exercise loop around the outer edge of the 80 acres of grassland, we often saw Short-eared Owls perched on the piles of rocks along the fence, as many as 13 of the owls at once. We watched several weasels cavorting (they do not seem to just walk along) in the grasses near our trailer. We could often hear and see voles chewing their way in the grasses beside our lawn chairs—no wonder we saw so many owls and hawks at that place! Another day a Brewer's Sparrow came in under our shade tarp, landing on our little table, within three feet of us. After a rest, the sparrow took flight and next landed on our truck and then on top of the shade tarp before departing.

At Green River we saw a family of Sandhill Cranes, and worried about living in proximity to a bull moose, a cow and her calf. A Trumpeter Swan, wearing a neckband was seen in the area, its identification code read and reported. Several times Gary had to avoid skunks and badgers that frequented the tower area, possibly scavenging for quail bits dropped from the tower by our falcons. Otters frolicked in the river by our camp and beavers swam by.

We had had mice in the truck at Holter Lake and had them again at Wood Lake, less-than-pleasant wildlife encounters. With the latter small lake near camp, we enjoyed seeing ducks and ducklings, muskrats and beaver. There were mountain cottontails and snowshoe hares to watch, several kinds of rodents including a new-to-us species of chipmunk. It was our first site with bighorn sheep and their climbing abilities on the cliff in front of us were a delight. We also enjoyed Columbian ground squirrel-watching, right up until we caught somebody shooting at them beside camp—after that we worried about the squirrels and watched for shooters.

CSKT Cliff was most notable for 16 bear sightings, even though the site failed and we were only there nineteen days. Most memorable of these were the day a bear was seen by the hack box, the day Jean came upon a bear and cubs that were harvesting a berry bush between her and camp, and the day we returned to the camper to find a bear had attacked it and some of our gear.

Willow Creek provided excellent bird-watching at a little seep, at the nearby reservoir where migrating shorebirds accumulated late in the summer, and along the creek below the dam that held the lake. Birds in that area tended to concentrate at these water sources and Jean concentrated her efforts in those areas to improve the bird list started by the previous attendants.

While hearing Great Horned Owls at night caused us to worry since these big owls were known to seize young Peregrines at night, especially before they learned to find hidden places to roost, we very much enjoyed other, smaller and less-threatening owls. Jean once saw the very small Northern Saw-whet Owl sitting in a horizontal position on a branch and giving its whistle-like hoots. We loved the moth-like, irregular flight of Short-eared Owls; they exhibited little concern about our presence in their territory and flew quite close to us.

*From the Journals: Grave Point – Jean*
*8 July 1991 – After supper we went up to the tower to begin preparations for going into the tower to try to identify our visiting Subadults. It was getting quite dark when we got off the*

*tower and started back to camp. During our walk down the hill,
a Common Nighthawk and a Short-eared Owl, flying together
low over the grass, circled around us and we stopped and
turned their circle with them to cherish their closeness and their
beautiful, erratic, moth-like flight.*

There were ten species of raptors at our various hack sites, ten
that is, besides the four species of falcons described in Phase
Four earlier in this book. Several times we saw one of these
raptors attempt attacks on our young falcons, once tragically.
From the earliest days after their release from the hack box, the
young Peregrines would give their "cacking" territorial defense
call when another raptor was in the sky nearby, making it clear
they instinctively knew these were threatening birds, or at least
competitors for prey. We saw these raptors usually going about
their "business" of hunting, such as the omnipresent Northern
Harriers that hunted over the grasslands around us at CSKT
Tower, but we also watched them caring for their newly fledged
young, as the Northern Goshawks did at Bar None Ranch, and
Red-tailed Hawks at more than one site. We saw an American
Kestrel catch and devour grasshoppers as we were watching our
falcons at Grave Point, and another kestrel landing on Cliff
Swallow nests and trying to catch the swallows under the eaves
of the barn on the ranch at Green River. A Ferruginous Hawk
soared over our shade tarp at CSKT tower with one leg dangling
straight down, probably injured. Another Goshawk, another
year soared above us with a small branch of a tree stuck in the
feathers of one wing—no doubt acquired during a chase through
trees after a smaller bird it sought to eat.

Jean started birding at age ten or eleven when her mother gave
her her first bird book, a little *Golden Nature Guide to Birds*.
Spending many weeks for seven summers in these western
states gave her much birding pleasure; preparing the birds lists

for Peregrine Fund reports was more fun than work. During nine hack site jobs, in eight different locations, a few weeks in each of seven summers, in three states (not counting the trips to and from Wisconsin) she saw 175 species of birds. Eight of these were "Life Birds," seen for the first time in her life at the various hack sites we worked. (Four other Lifers were seen en route to hacking jobs.)

*Phase Six, Final Week: Figures 29 and 30*

*Figure 29: Gary in fire tower observing through peephole*

*Figure 30: Juvenile feeding, as seen from inside tower*

# PHASE SIX – FINAL WEEK ON SITE AND CLOSING: week seven

## A. INTRODUCTION TO ACTIVITIES DURING FINAL WEEK ON SITE: closing the site

*From the Journals: Grave Point – Jean*
*29 July 1990 – In the tent for the night: the pine trees are doing their non-sticky, tiny drippings, like blessings dripping down on me a moment at a time. I feel very lucky being here, yet also as though I earned my way here in 46 years. It feels so good to be doing this job, in such a place. I look out at pines through my wide-open, screened tent window, black lace against the last light of dusk in the sky. On my one mile hike to clean the tower and 1.4-mile hike to the truck for water tonight, my legs felt strong, my breath came easily, my body loved the movement and my mind smiled at the rhythms.*

By the last week of each hack site job, the Peregrines were being seen much less often at the hack box. They were flying very well, roosting away from the hack box, often hunting and undoubtedly succeeding in catching at least some of their own food and capable of full independence by this time. Although we were never fortunate enough to witness an actual "kill" by one of our Peregrines, we often saw them attempt to catch prey. To encourage the falcons to finally disperse away from the hack site, we were instructed to put out quail for them only every other day during the final week. Sometimes this was painful for us to observe. An individual falcon might have been away from the hack box for several days and then show up hungry on the first day we skipped feeding. We would have to watch the sometimes lengthy search for a quail by that falcon that day. That individual might return the next day and try again, but often they just left the area and we never saw them again.

During this final week, we had a great deal to do in preparation for closing the site on the last day of feeding. We usually began taking things we no longer needed, foods that we would not have time to eat, and bits of our camp setup back to our truck. By now we would have been working on at least some of the sections of the required reports. We also made lists of equipment or modifications "for next year."

## B. STORIES FROM THE FINAL WEEK ON SITE

### Hells Canyon Fire, Grave Point, 1991

If one lives near or within the grasslands or forested areas of the American West, wild fires are a potential reality. Sometimes a rising column of smoke, or local sirens, or newscasts on radio or television provide prior knowledge of the lurking dangers of flames running loose through the environment. Or, in our case, one might be suddenly jarred to awareness by a large four-engine propeller plane roaring a scant few hundred feet above our tent and us thinking, "Now, what the hell is that about?!" given that for the previous six weeks on site the immediate airspace above our tent had never held any airplane, let alone a four-engine giant, anywhere near that low.

On 5 August 1991 at Grave Point we were in our final week of activity at the site and had carried several loads of camping and Peregrine Fund equipment to our truck parked two-thirds mile downhill from our camp site. We were close enough to the end of the assignment, within a few days, that we could reasonably predict items we would not need at camp anymore that summer: the large quail cooler, exercise weights, heavy-weight clothing, extra food, and books we had finished reading. As we were returning to camp from our last trip to the truck it began to cloud up and look rainy so we moved remaining exposed items left over from our sorting back under the tarp of our outdoor kitchen area. We ate our supper of tuna and alfalfa-sprout sandwiches under the tarp and as some rain started to gently patter on the roof we could hear distant thunder and retreated to the cozy confines of the adjoining tent. We had just snuggled into a relaxed, reclined position, propped up by our piled sleeping bags and pillows, and had commenced reading from our latest books when the noisome roar of four big airplane engines erupted above us.

The plane had come from the north, was on our side, the Idaho side, of Hells Canyon of the Snake River, and because the plane was flying close to treetop height at that point we did not hear it coming until it cleared the top of the mountain, a few hundred yards to the north of our tent site, on which Grave Point tower stood. The mountain had acted as an auditory shield until the plane was directly overhead.

We immediately pulled on our boots, grabbed light jackets and our binoculars, piled out of our tent and jogged to some higher, open ground to get a better look at what was going on. As soon as we had heard that plane we were immediately thinking, "Forest fire??!?," and given we were within a forest knew we wanted to collect additional facts. Plus, get a good look at the noisy giant and confirm our speculation. To do this, we had jogged over to what we called "Weather Hill." Weather Hill was an exposed point west of our more sheltered tent site where we could better see the western skies and get a sense of weather conditions and what kind of weather might be approaching us from over there in Oregon. We had used it frequently throughout that summer in order to do a better job of planning our priorities for the day. Once we had arrived at the Weather Hill, we heard and then could see the big plane coming around again, circling the Hells Canyon area, and we could see a column of smoke rising up from the canyon to the south of us and far enough away that we could breathe easier for our own safety and could turn instead to just watching an aeronautical fire-fighting show.

Beginning to pant from the excitement and exertion we climbed higher up our steep Grave Point Mountain to get an expansive view of the canyon bottom, the Oregon side, and the sky above. From there we could see the flames creeping across a dry grassy area of the Oregon side of the canyon, not on top of the canyon but on the angular walls, and could tell this was not a forest fire but instead an expanding grass fire crawling across steep ground too dry and exposed to the sun to grow trees. And too steep and remote to have any type of trails or roads accessible to any kind of wheeled vehicle. Hence, it was obvious an air strike had been called in to prevent the spread of the fire should any winds come up in the night, for there were trees at risk above, on top of the canyon walls. A large area had already been blackened on the canyon side opposite from our position on the Idaho side.

There were three large four-engine firefighting planes and one light duty single-engine guide plane. All the large planes carried fire retardant to drop; our favorite was the one we called "Big Red." Its belly had been modified and widened to allow it to carry more retardant, and its fuselage was encircled by three broad painted stripes: red at the front, white in the mid-section, and red at the tail. Very easy to see and follow. The three large planes would circle overhead and then one at a time, with the small plane flying ahead to guide it to the drop zone, each large plane would fly down inside the canyon instead of over it, cross over the intervening ridges, cope with shifting air currents in the canyon, and drop its red filmy, wispy fire retardant at the leading edge of the flames and then quickly pull up and away. Each large plane was able to make three passes to drop retardant before they were apparently empty of their supplies. By this time it was nearly dark anyway and as the planes receded into the distance, returning to their base wherever that was, most likely over 100 miles away, we returned to our tent, our minds filled with dramatic images until sleep could finally turn them to restless dreams.

The following morning we followed through on our plans to do a little sight-seeing in the area before closing camp and leaving the next day. We drove north and west to Pittsburgh Landing, Idaho, descending 4470 feet into Hells Canyon via numerous switchbacks of the dusty gravel road needed to get to that point of the canyon which offered fantastic views of the canyon depth and a boat landing for the many tourists and boat tours operating on the Snake River. At the landing we could clearly see the extent of the grass fire from the day before. While enjoying our visit to the famous landing as "normal tourists" instead of "Peregrine hackers" with a little free time available, we took a short bird walk through a wooded ravine, explored the campground available there, and looked at the boat dock facilities geared up to accommodate float trips on the river along with jet boat tours of the canyon which depart from Lewiston and Cambridge, Idaho. While there, because of what we had experienced the night before, we kept looking at the expanse of black disfiguring the opposite canyon wall. And yes, there it was, around 9:30 AM, at first a slight curl of white which might be dismissed as a temporary illusion of the morning sun rays. But there it was again and it developed into a rising column of smoke, gradually increasing until we could see flames big enough at the base of the smoke to know the grass fire was not yet completely out.

Clearly the Forest Service was alert to this possibility and had planned a routine follow-up patrol, because not long after the smoke appeared a single helicopter came from the north and flew low over the site to check on the status of the fire. Later the helicopter was followed by a large four-engine plane following the same course over the now confirmed re-ignition of the fire from the day before and we concluded it must be time for another strike by high-technology resources available to concerned agencies responsible for protecting the region.

About an hour later, after we had returned to our assignment up on Grave Point and were monitoring activity at the fire area with our binoculars and camera from an open viewing position nearer to the mountaintop, we saw a two-engine propeller plane circling and circling over the burn area. Again we wondered, "What is going on?" Suddenly parachutes appeared! At medium height over the drop zone, three parachutists with round steering chutes jumped out to deal with the escaping flames threatening the nearby environment. A second pass of the plane over the burn area—three more parachutists with round steering chutes. A third pass, but higher this time—two parachutists with larger para-wing, highly-steerable chutes jumped from the plane and glided to earth. A fourth pass—two more para-wing parachutists. A fifth pass—an additional two para-wing parachutists. A total of twelve smoke jumpers had come to put an end to this wandering burn. All twelve jumpers steered accurately and landed within 50 yards of one another. But the plane and planned drop were not done yet. A sixth pass with the plane flying very low that time—a large cargo box fell from the plane suspended under four round parachutes which just barely opened fully before the box came to ground. A seventh pass—a second cargo box descended to the drop zone suspended under three round parachutes. After the eighth pass of the two engine plane a final cargo box under three round parachutes descended into the drop zone and the plane left the area. The smoke jumpers were at their assignment along with all the equipment, food, and resources needed for the next several days of difficult, strenuous work.

It was an amazing, impressive display, of both the planning and execution phases. The para-wing jumpers glided a long distance and at times seemed as though they were dropping as they purposely collapsed their chutes momentarily and twirled down to lose altitude before gliding again. Those fellows knew their stuff! The gear drops were naturally a little bit more scattered but still very well calculated to land convenient to the jumpers. Their job task looked very risky, and indeed history confirms that it is, but we were told they love their job. Having lived, worked, and carried heavy backpacks ourselves on our mountain and having experienced the sun and heat of the canyon, we could empathize with those smoke jumpers and know from the fiber of our being the hard, hard work they would engage in for a short intense one or two days to battle the remaining flames while traversing over rugged, steep canyon faces and carrying heavy, cumbersome gear.

The following morning, our last day at Grave Point, we grabbed our binoculars for one more look at the smoke jumpers. The flames were all out, no more smoke curls in sight, and instead we looked down from our lofty perch on the opposite side of the canyon onto a small, pleasant camp site which the smoke jumpers had set up on a semi-flat swale slightly above and behind the burned area. We could see several small tents, a lot of scattered gear lying about, and several of the smoke jumpers were walking about doing what smoke jumpers do after a successful mission. It was a calm sunny morning and with their responsibilities at this location fulfilled we could now rather envy them their morning in a brand new unique camp site, the beautiful canyon and river below them, as they had the satisfaction of a job well and quickly done, and could relax and enjoy the view a few hours, while chowing down their breakfast and liquids. And awaiting transport out of the canyon, which we guessed was to be by boat.

## Migration of Peregrines and Prey

As the released Peregrines gained competence in hunting for themselves, they were next faced with the problem of approaching fall and winter seasons. Many of the avian species that were potential prey would soon be gone to places to the south, sometimes very far south, where they could find food and warmer temperatures for the winter. Signs of fall bird migration began to appear especially early in our higher altitude sites such as Green River, and in the late-season sites we worked, CSKT Tower and Bar None Ranch. Our young falcons dispersed a bit early at Green River, but we could only report that we were no longer seeing them. We also kept track of how many quail we put out on the tower in the mornings, and how many were left at the end of the day, giving us a way to tell if any Peregrines had been to the tower that we missed seeing. For example, if we put out six quail one morning, observed a Prairie Falcon come and eat one, and found five quail left on the hack box at the end of the day, we could reasonably conclude that no Peregrines came that day, or if they paid a visit we did not observe, then they were not hungry. If absence of individual falcons that had reached the three week "independent" status continued to the end of the hack site period, they were considered to have dispersed. Dispersal meant the Peregrine was no longer in the general hack site area, not necessarily that it had begun actual migration—movement serious distances toward an area with a good prey base where a Peregrine Falcon could spend the winter.

Without attaching radio transmitters, a technique that had been used with some released falcons in earlier years of the reintroduction project, there was little chance to find out where a released Peregrine spent its winters, nor what route it used to reach its wintering location. Such radio transmitter studies have been made. Other researchers have set up trapping stations on known migration routes, and when a banded, released Peregrine is captured, information about place and date of capture is reported to the USGS Bird Banding Lab and to The Peregrine Fund. Another other way the fate of a released Peregrine can be learned after dispersal is if it appears at a hack site in future years and is identified, just as two subadults and one adult were identified by us when they visited our hack sites. These identifications were our only contribution to data on the fate of released Peregrines after they dispersed from their hack sites.

Sponsoring agencies carried out their own surveys to assess the Peregrine Falcon population in the lands under their jurisdiction, from the time the Peregrine population decline was noticed and through the reintroduction process. As their population increased, Peregrines were again seen establishing nesting territories in the spring at various cliff sites. After reaching two or more years of age, some released Peregrines chose to claim a hack box as a nesting site. In 1991 on her solo drive from Wisconsin to Boise, where she would meet Gary at the airport, Jean stopped at Camas National Wildlife Refuge in Idaho where a Peregrine pair was nesting in a hack box on a tower in the marsh. In 1996 on our way to our assignment at CSKT Cliff, we stopped at the CSKT Tower hack site where we had worked in 1992. We had been told that this hack box too had been claimed as a nest site, and we were able to see a Peregrine on the box through our spotting scope from the road. It was a thrill to see such vivid proof of the success of the reintroduction project to which so many individuals and groups had contributed. The bird on that hack box might even have been one of ours, but we dared not disturb it by approaching close enough to try to see and read any leg bands.

We did, however, record when we noticed evidence of avian migration activities since this information—the disappearance of suitable prey—was relevant to the departure of our young Peregrines after they were independent. On 2 August 1991 at Grave Point Jean observed a flight of Common Nighthawks. At CSKT Tower we noted that ducks, geese and cormorants were gathering in flocks after the August Singularity. At Green River the ground squirrels had disappeared underground to hibernate already in mid-August and about the same time the small birds were beginning to leave this valley of long winters.

*From the Journals: Bar None Ranch – Gary*
*30 August 1994 – Further evidence of the changes since the*
*August Singularity event—on the past two nights we have not*
*seen any nighthawks. Prior to that, all during our stay here,*
*many filled the evening skies, then four nights ago they were*
*low and few, flying right through camp and silently about*
*Jean's head, the next night fewer, then—GONE—like turning a*
*switch. Same story for the bats. Let's face it: with 40° F.*
*morning lows and summer's maturation, there are very few*
*flying insects for these birds (and bats) to eat.*

Phase Six, Personal Stories: Figures 31 and 32

Figure 31: Jean prepares a meal at Holter Lake O.P.

Figure 32: Jean on trail to truck at Holter Lake

## C. PERSONAL STORIES

<u>Rural Silence, CSKT Tower, 1992</u>

In the summer of 1992 one of our hack site assignments was the CSKT Tower near Ronan, Montana. Although we were positioned in the middle of several hundred acres of land devoted to the conservation and propagation of both waterfowl and game birds and were surrounded by mountains in the distance, we were still within a largely rural farming and ranching area. Of the eight different sites where we were located, CSKT Tower was the most "public" and many farms and ranches surrounded us. That said, it was still very rural and had a low population density outside of the small town, and reminded us somewhat of the rural farm area in western Iowa where we grew up. However, each area of the country harbors its own uniqueness under the shawl of its existence. Here in these Montana grasslands, under the dome of the broad sky above, over the surface of the geologic past which created the soil structure under us, held in by the rims of the mountain bowl around us, the prairie grasses, yellowing fields, browning pastures all combined and somehow created the hush of an anechoic sound chamber in which we could hear sounds that in other settings would be concealed from our awareness.

*From the Journals: CSKT Tower – Gary*
*26 August 1992 – Compared to many other locations the silence here, when it is quiet and calm, as it often is, amazes us. We know a busy highway is four to five miles east of us. But the rural population is not so much thin as it is quiet. There is some traffic on the gravel roads during the day. But in the late evening or early morn, when the winds are stilled, the silence fills the air. Not a numbing, internal ringing of the ear, listen to your own heart type of silence we had experienced one winter in Big Bend National Park down in Texas. But a warm, serene,*

*wholesome, absorbent type of silence. It just kind of wraps around you like a warm hug and leaves you feeling peaceful and as tranquil as the unmoving air.*

*From the Journals: CSKT Tower – Gary*
*13 August 1992 – On a quiet, sunny, rural morning many different sounds penetrate the still air from both near and far to remind us of our farm and ranch setting: dogs barking, crickets chirping, the scurry of a mouse through the dry grass, an irrigation pump tap-tapping continuously, a combine on its way to another golden field, cars and pickups coursing and stone-throwing their way along gravel roads, geese honking as they wing their way toward a harvested field to glean the remains, the rapid whishing wing-beats of cormorants overhead, a pheasant crowing in the distance, our Peregrine cacking at a nearby Osprey, the bellowing and mooing of range and pasture cattle, a muffled thumping as a hay baler compresses its sweet green intake, a young meadowlark practicing its call, the bizz-buzzing of flies and beetles, rustling of nylon and denim as this is being written—all amidst the ever-blazing, burning, silent glare of the sun as it slowly glides another arc, east mountain range to west mountain range, horizon to horizon.*

Coping With Critters in Camp

Not all of the smaller critters we lived amongst during our Peregrine summers were cute, and not all of the cute ones were always good neighbors. In Grave Point 1990, we had chipmunks trying to get into our food stores. CJ had brought a "chuck box," or camp kitchen, made of plywood and this kept the chipmunks out but wasn't large enough to store all our food supplies. Jean had brought her dehydrated foods in metal cans, those large ones you can buy full of popcorn especially during the holidays, so these food stores too were safe from chipmunks and other small rodents. Nevertheless, we still had problems of food storage, and where could we put our bags of garbage accumulating until a town trip? In exploring the Grave Point site that first week, we checked out two small buildings located near the base of the tower. One was an outhouse—hurrah—but we could only use it during the week while the Peregrines were confined in the hack box, and besides, it was half a mile from camp. The other had thick double walls so we concluded it was a big icebox for the days when the tower was inhabited for months at a time by US Forest Service fire watchers, but more latterly it was being used as a storage shed. We found an active American Robin nest in the outhouse, and Western Bluebirds were nesting in a cavity no doubt originally excavated by some woodpecker species into the space between the inner and outer walls of the icebox/storage shed. For us the latter shed proved to be a treasure trove, for it contained a pickax we used to help dig our latrines in the stony soil, and a big stoutly-constructed garbage can. In both years at Grave Point this garbage can was carried down to camp at the beginning of the season, cleaned out and used as a pantry to store food supplies away from critters, and to temporarily hold sacks of non-smelly garbage until we could take them to the dumpster along the highway the next time we went to town. We carried the garbage can and pickax back to the storage shed at the end of each season.

When we planned for Grave Point in 1991, we needed to have our own replacement for CJ's chuck box. With the threat of gnawing rodents in mind, at home in Wisconsin over the winter Gary designed a kitchen box that would hold our camp cooking kettles, dishes, utensils, salt and pepper and a few other basic camp kitchen items. From Gary's drawings, a metal-worker prepared the camp kitchen in the spring from heavy sheet aluminum—light, yet strong—with a door we could close and latch tightly enough to keep out rodents, if not ants. Friends gave us a folding camp kitchen stand to hold the kitchen above ground for easier access and we were set. We used this camp kitchen every year starting in 1991.

When we purchased a 7x14 foot cargo trailer in late 1991, specially ordered with insulation, three windows and a camper door, Gary built in a bed, tiny closet, kitchen counter with two-burner propane cook surface, bar-size sink with catch bucket underneath, etc. He also made a shelf above that kitchen counter onto which we could clamp the aluminum camp kitchen. We used this trailer at Peregrine camps in 1993, 1995 and 1996 (and for personal camping trips many years thereafter). The sheet metal worker also built a galvanized shower base with drain over which we could hang a shower curtain. We could still heat water in the solar shower bag, but then hang it within this shower "stall" and take our showers inside the trailer—pretty handy especially at Green River where we had little privacy, a lot of mosquitoes, and chilly temperatures.

At Green River in 1993 we also had chipmunks, but we were living in our trailer so they were not able to get at our food supplies. Instead we were able to enjoy them, and would put out the leaf end of a carrot or a leftover pancake very occasionally on top of a fence post for them. Conversely, our Bar None Ranch tent campsite in 1994 was dry, and we had chipmunks trying to get at our small hand-wash basin to gnaw the little soap bar and drink the water. Our large, orange five-gallon insulated plastic water jug with a spigot was sitting near the basin and sometimes a drip formed on the spigot and the chipmunks located this drip. This dripping water was an attraction, but we did not want the chipmunks in our wash basin and especially did not want them drinking from the spigot from which we got our own drinking water. Accordingly, we covered the spigot, saved and cleaned a tuna can, and thereafter kept water in it on a nearby log so the chipmunks could drink and we could watch them.

*From the Journals: Bar None Ranch – Gary*
*3 August 1994 – Early in our stay here I was in the lean-to watching silently as a chipmunk explored and tasted all the new things brought to his neighborhood by our arrival. He scampered, hopped, climbed, and scampered more as his tracks figuratively wove a web covering all our goods. His longest stop was under the spigot of our orange water cooler job where he bent his head up in an arch and from underneath the spout he carefully sucked out and licked whatever trace of moisture that lay there. Not good. Later we sealed off this access from him. He then took to daily drinking water from our soapy water wash basin to reach which he had to climb up a bucket (on which the basin rests), peer into it, hang over the edge, and then, with his little front feet thrust into the water to support his fore-body, he lapped the water up while his hind legs and feet grasped the rim of the basin and his tail whisked sweepingly from side to side while he quenched his thirst.*

At Grave Point we even saw house mice and deer mice on the tower, but they appeared to be just using it for a home, and maybe eating some quail bits opportunistically. Coyotes were enjoyed at this and other sites for their "songs" but they were also a nuisance at Grave Point because they dug up the quail remnants, vegetable trimmings and the like that we tried to dispose of during the first year by burying them. We soon learned to take those organic refuse items along when we went to town and throw them over the edge of the road into the forest away from camp so scavengers could still find them but not near camp. At CSKT Tower we had raccoons, but continuing the practice of scattering the quail remnants along uninhabited roadsides kept these critters away from our camp. Striped skunks were likewise present at several sites but a problem only at Green River as already mentioned.

*From the Journals: Holter Lake – Jean*
*2 July 1992 – Gary discovered the reason the truck smells bad is not his dirty socks under the front seat, but a visit by a mouse-type critter. Evidence included chewed ice cream bar wrapper and garbage sack, and turds on his rubber overshoes. This find caused us to repack vulnerable groceries into large plastic storage tubs in the back (mouse evidence was all in the cab of the truck so far) and to close the driver's side vent in case that was the entry point.*

*6 July 1992 – We've just discovered a deer mouse is living in a cardboard box in the back of the truck with a nest made of shredded paper, shredded towel, some carpet fibers, and upholstery-like stuffing of unknown source. Fortunately, she did not get into any of our food supplies! She had four naked babies in her nest and I dumped her and them out on the ground.*

*9 July 1992 – We bought aluminum foil while we were in town. At the truck before hiking back into camp, Gary stuffed foil in the gaps around the tailgate against deer mouse entry.*

Many, many other species of non-avian wildlife were encountered during our Peregrine summers, most of them interesting, positive encounters. Nevertheless, this discussion of problem species cannot be ended without mention of a few more of the most unpleasant species (besides rattlesnakes, which have already been covered). A few of our sites were within open rangeland and this meant domestic livestock, mostly cattle, were our neighbors. Since a herd of cattle wandering through camp while we were away at an O.P. could be very destructive to our tents, tarps and other gear, this was a serious concern, especially at Grave Point—not to mention again their messy droppings. There the cattle seemed to favor a route down the roadway (which we could not drive because of the locked gate) between their grazing areas and the springs and water tanks that provided their drinking water in the area and this route took them right through our camp. Accordingly, whenever we found cattle in or near camp, we chased them away. In 1991 two Range Inspectors on horseback stopped to talk to us on 30 July and were quite surprised to learn there were still cattle on the allotment, when they were supposed to have been removed by 15 June.

Insects were a nuisance at times each summer, but we had serious difficulties with them in two sites, two years. Grave Point 1991 was more rainy and cooler than it had been in 1990, which perhaps explains the high numbers of a certain kind of small, brown, biting fly that drove us nearly mad some days as we tried to sit still and observe falcons all the daylight hours. In our presentations about Peregrines we show many photos of the wildlife we enjoyed, but always say the most numerous species at Green River was mosquitoes and we have a photo taken near dusk to prove it—in that photo the mosquitoes are a dense, whitish cloud above the river. The chilly nights there helped since this meant the mosquitoes often could not fly during the early morning and evening hours. We sometimes found the mosquitoes there intolerable and observed falcons by setting up a spotting scope inside our trailer aimed at the tower through window glass.

Starting the very first year, we also had problems of ants finding and entering our coolers. We always had two small coolers to use during town trips to transport quail, fresh foods and ice back to camp. In camp we had a very large insulated cooler provided by The Peregrine Fund in which we kept quail, ice and food between town trips. In our tent camps especially, ants found their way into this cooler usually several times each of the summers when the coolers had to sit out on the ground. Fortunately, as an experienced camper, Jean had packed along a small bottle of bleach even the first year, even not knowing about the impending ant problem. Whenever ants were discovered in the cooler, it was time to unload it and wipe it down inside and out with bleach-drenched paper towels to destroy the ants' "follow-me-trails" leading their colony members to the attractions of gradually thawing quail and assorted human foods.

*From the Journals: Grave Point – Jean*
*23 July 1991 – The flies come out around 10:00 or 11:00 AM depending on the temperature, sunshine and winds of the day. After the flies come out and until 5:00 p.m. or so we must wear jeans with the legs tucked into our socks, long-sleeved shirts, and protective headgear—sweatshirt with the hood up or cap with a bandana draped behind it to cover the back and sides of our necks—even a mesh head net under the hooded sweatshirt! What a nuisance! Also, we swat flies furiously at times, killing twenty or more, and it only helps for a few moments. They can bite through clothing, even. Gary has more bites and uses a camphor external analgesic gel product on the itches at night to be able to sleep.*

*From the Journals: CSKT Tower – Gary*
*8 September 1992 – Miller Time! After supper we took a long road hike down to lower Crow Creek Bridge and then came back to our customary miller invasion and counter-assault.*

Miller: any of various moths having powdery wings (Webster's Ninth Collegiate Dictionary).

Late in the summer at CSKT Tower, the black, dusty-winged moths, "millers," became numerous in our tower-dominated, dusty, grassland. It was the moths' nature to hide from daylight in inconvenient places. Gary kept a red bandana hanging under the shade tarp, handy to his need. The miller nuisance became clear one day when he took it down to use; a miller fluttered from the bandana's folds into his face and left a mark from the powder of its wings on his nose. In the increasing light of dawn, moths collected in the narrow space between the edges of the shade tarp and the conduit tubes that formed the framework of our shade shelter. Later, as the tarp flapped in the rising winds of daytime, squished miller bodies fell on our laps, our little table and notebooks. In the evenings it became necessary to hunt them down in the trailer before we went to bed, lest moths flutter in our sleeping faces. The evening miller-hunt became our "Miller Time." In the camping trailer, the moths hid in the folds of the hanging dishtowel or a jacket, amongst cans and packets of food in cupboards, at the edges of air mattresses and bedding, behind trailer curtains, in folded clothing—any crevice that would provide daytime darkness. At dusk they came from their hiding places to flutter against the windows, wanting out into the failing evening light. Miller time.

Family Matters

Being gone weeks at time, summer after summer in this way, inevitably we missed out on things such as the wedding of a son of close friends, and we usually spent our wedding anniversaries quietly by ourselves in some remote location. We weren't there when Janis moved into her first apartment with the help of Jean's sister and brother-in-law, but we did get back in time at the end of a different summer to help Gayle move to a new apartment. When Gayle and Dean told us they were planning to elope, we were in the wilderness watching

Peregrines, and waited eleven days to finally get the news: on a town trip Gary found a letter from Janis saying Gayle and Dean had been married in shorts and T-shirts by a Wyoming judge and had spent the rest of their vacation/wedding trip camping and fishing in the Bighorn Mountains. While in town Gary purchased cold sodas and a big chocolate bar; after he returned to camp and had given Jean the news, we toasted the newlyweds in sodas (with added whiskey for Gary) and ate chocolate.

*From the Journals: Grave Point – Jean*
*5 August 1991 – Waiting for sleep, thinking of Gayle and hoping she can put into her marriage and take from it something like the richness I have found in mine with Gary.*

In another year, at another site, a letter came with the news of a terrible diagnosis for a close family member and Jean struggled with tears and despair at being so far from home, and able to respond only by letter.

For two years in a row, as her father's July birthday approached and she began birthday letters to him, Jean dreamed of him, of the threat of cancer hanging over him, of guilt for being so far away and she tried to visit him and her mom at least on the way west to Peregrine work. And before another July, he was gone.

Each week as we made our town trips, trepidation arose: would everything be okay with our daughters and other family members when we called or read the mail? Would we even be able to reach anyone in the family by phone during a given town trip? What news would there be? We felt this problem each Peregrine assignment, and had to face down our fears and live with them each summer.

Personal Closing Ceremonies

Leaving a hack site job filled with the memories of the falcons released under our care and our experiences there was always wrenching. We tried to ease the feelings of loss each time with simple ceremonies that occurred to us. That first year (1990) C.J. and Jean toasted the falcons and our partnership at the gate after camp had been struck and our trucks were loaded (we toasted with juice not alcohol before driving down the mountain road!) and after camping together in the valley below that night, celebrated further the next day with a guided float trip down the Salmon River.

From the gate that served as the location for vehicle parking at Grave Point (in both 1990 and 1991), each time Jean drove down the mountain for her weekly share of the town trips, she punched the "on button" of the tape deck in her small pickup and listened to one side of an instrumental tape on the way to town, and to the other side of the tape on the way back up to the hack site. This tape was "Heartsounds," piano music by David Lanz, and it was played again the last day as we left Grave Point together. The musical emphasis points in the first song on side one corresponded exactly to the first curves in the narrow, graveled mountain road and the large trees appearing at each curve. The music so well suited the road that for years afterward, playing the tape would raise the scenic images in Jean's mind.

*From the Journals: Grave Point – Gary*
*29 June 1991 – Between getting up at 5:15 and now at 7:30 the red thread bracelet from Janis, made by Janis, that I wore on my left wrist has at last severed and I cannot find it. It served a significant symbolic role in my life and I was glad and proud to have it. To look upon it and use it as a tool or encouragement to*

*do what I have done over the last year, to be what I want to be—different, unique, and yet to have and retain a daughter's love. It almost lasted 13 months, my mystic special number: from 3 June 1990 to 29 June 1991. From Puckerbrush where I tied it on prior to going north, through BWCAW, through the act and decision of leaving The Trane Company, and now to this mountain in Idaho, over 1500 miles west, known as Grave Point, a 5600-foot prominence overlooking both the Salmon and Snake River valleys.*

*Later the same day – When I came off the hill from feeding the falcons this morning I found my Janis-bracelet at the foot of my big chair (where we sit for observing the falcons). I took several photos of it in place and will save it to tie in a tree on the mountain top.*

*From the Journals: Grave Point – Jean*
*7 August 1991 – Just as we will take photos and seeds, a pine cone and memories with us away from this mountain that has been ours for a few weeks, so we wanted to leave behind bits of ourselves: a white crocheted bracelet I made and wore here, a red woven bracelet Janis made and Gary wore; the "Love, Gayle" ending from one of the letters our other daughter sent, and a piece of paper on which Gary wrote: Thank you mountain for all you have given us."* [Note: all our mementoes were of cotton or paper so they would naturally degrade.]

These emotional responses to the end of our hack site experiences came to us each time, in individual varieties, even when a given hack site was less beautiful, or had difficult problems for us to surmount. And sometimes, the emotional responses were to issues beyond the closing of a particular site and the end of that summer's Peregrine adventures. The journals tell these feelings best.

*From the Journals: Holter Lake – Jean*
*24 July 1992 – Up early, even before the alarm, by Towhee*
*wake-up call. I went up to feed the falcons one last time and say*
*good-bye to the hack box, the mountain, the experiences of this*
*place. Gary packed the remnant camp meanwhile. I made my*
*fastest trip up and back ever—46 minutes, so he wasn't ready*
*when I got back. I helped a bit and in 16 minutes more he was*
*ready. We hiked out the three miles to the truck for the last time,*
*saying good-bye to the Ospreys at their nest as we passed on*
*the trail below them, and doubled our previous cottontail rabbit*
*sighting for the area.* [Note: We had 24 hours to restock before
reporting at another hack site—the only time we did two
complete hack site jobs in one summer.]

*From the Journals: CSKT Tower – Gary*
*11 September 1992 – We got up extra early at 4:00 AM per our*
*plan—the full moon was shining through a few clouds—and*
*aimed the pickup headlights at the tower from our trailer site.*
*We walked to the tower and I provided further illumination with*
*a big flashlight while Jean climbed the tower to lay out ten*
*quail for our falcons, their last feeding. I urged extra caution*
*as there was frost this morning and I feared she might slip on*
*the deer steps or the tower platform. Returning to the trailer, we*
*changed out of our falcon-feeding clothes into traveling clothes*
*and left about 5:00 AM to start the long trip home. This one will*
*have to be fast as Jean has a teaching job waiting and the*
*semester has started.*

*Phase Seven, Final Reports:  Figures 33 and 34*

*Figure 33:  Early reports produced via manual typewriter*

*Figure 34:  Later reports prepared with laptop computer*

# PHASE SEVEN – PREPARING THE FINAL REPORTS

## A. INTRODUCTION TO REPORT REQUIREMENTS OF THE PEREGRINE FUND

Included in the packet of information mailed to us by The Peregrine Fund each year upon our acceptance as Hack Site Attendants, was a set of instructions and examples of the format to be used for the reports we were required to write, type and turn in within two weeks of the closing of the hack site. Receipt of the second half of each of our grants hinged on satisfactory and timely completion of two reports. One report, the one with the most rigid and detailed format, would be published by The Peregrine Fund in their annual *Operation Report* for that year. This explains the need for all Hack Site Attendants to conform to a particular format in their reports; all the reports could thus be easily compared not only with other hack site reports within a specific year, but with reports from other hack sites in other years, even sometimes with other reports from the same hack site in different years. These reports contained charts including the names, identification numbers and dates of each of the falcons at three stages in the reintroduction process: installation, release, and patterns of dispersal (last sightings). Other sections of this report for publication included a description of the site, Hack Site Attendants at the site, sponsor(s) of the site, notes about the pre-release behavior of the falcons, observed hunting and roosting behavior, and general evaluation of the falcons, as well as sections describing unusual incidents, and listing acknowledgements.

The other report was not meant for publication but provided useful information for The Peregrine Fund about other aspects of the attendants' experiences at a specific hack site in a specific year. This Internal Report was to include the attendants' evaluation of the site and equipment provided to them, suggestions on how to improve the release program and better assist future attendants, information about people we interacted with and any associated problems. We were also asked to each write a statement as to the value of the experience for us personally. In addition, we were required to provide lists of all birds, mammals and reptiles observed in the release area with indications as to frequency of occurrence for each species, and a list of all visitors to the release site with their addresses and affiliations.

At each hack site, even the very first one, we attendants began to write the first sections of the main report as the early phases of the reintroduction process were completed. For example, we could compose the site description and installation sections after the first week. As the weeks passed, we tried to keep working on the reports so this entire task would not have to be done all at once when the site closed and we wanted to head home. In most cases, we even typed the reports in stages as the weeks went by; only at Holter Lake was this not possible—no one wanted to backpack the manual typewriter three miles from the truck to camp, or try to keep it dry during a boat ride or during the stormy weather of that site. Nor did we have time in camp for typing, or suitable conditions for such an activity at that O.P.

## B. STORIES ABOUT PREPARING REPORTS

### Using a Manual Typewriter in the Wilderness and at a Laundromat

In order to be prepared to produce these required reports, in 1990 Jean included in her gear list her manual, portable typewriter and a supply of typing paper. She also brought an upright folding camp chair and a very small table made of plywood with legs attached by screws to metal plates on the underside, making it possible to disassemble the table for transport. We kept the chair, table and typewriter, as well as our supply of reading material, in the small dome-tent CJ brought to Grave Point and which we christened our "Library." Most of the report-writing was done by hand one section at a time at the O.P., with much consulting of each other and our recorded observations, as each phase of the reintroduction process was completed. The typing, however, was done on fine days in camp with the comfort of table and chair.

The typewriter/chair/table method of turning out reports continued the next year at Grave Point, but this was too much equipment to take in to the Holter Lake site with its much more complex and difficult access logistics. At Holter, we got the report hand-written before the end of our time at the hack site, but then, having had almost all of our equipment, including the 4-person "bedroom" tent, moved out two days before by boat, and spending that night in camp in the former gear tent we had left behind to sleep in the last two nights, we still had the typing to do. To achieve this, we packed yet more of our gear out to the pickup and drove to Wolf Creek to pick up our mail and then go to a laundromat in Cascade, Montana, a somewhat larger town. Finding a big batch of tourists, who were in the area for a family reunion, had tied up all available washers, Jean set her typewriter on one of the tables and began typing. Gary went out to deal with various necessary errands, returned with sodas for each of us and began to proofread some finished pages, went out again to find food for our lunch. Meanwhile, the reunion group finally returned to move their laundry from washers to dryers, so Jean and another woman who had been waiting even longer, could put their laundry in to wash. The family reunion group sat around visiting while the dryers spun, making concentration difficult for our typist. Gary continued to proofread pages as they were completed, moved our cleaned clothes from washers into dryers as they became available, and read. Through all this, Jean typed, typed, typed—for five hours! When both reports were done, and the fauna lists typed as well, we went back to Wolf Creek and ate chicken for supper at the café before hiking back in to sleep in our minimal, remnant camp one last night in order to be able to put out the last batch of quail for the falcons the next morning.

*From the Journals: Holter Lake – Jean*
*23 July 1992 – Eventually the reunion group was finished with the dryers too. When they left they took a lot of towels with them, complaining of how many towels were being used by everyone at the reunion. A little later, a young girl showed up at the laundromat looking for a load of towels that belonged to the beauty shop!*

## Laptop, Converter, and Truck Power Point or Deep Cycle Battery Power

As soon as we could escape the tyranny of a manual typewriter, we did so. In 1993 we purchased our first laptop computer, a small but heavy portable that we continued to use thereafter, along with a small dot-matrix printer, for producing our reports. With a converter, the computer and printer could be plugged into the 12-volt power point of the truck, or into the deep-cycle battery on our camper trailer. At Wood Lake, Jean could type the reports while seated at the picnic table by our camper in the campground, but at Bar None Ranch some of the typing was done with the laptop literally on her lap in the pickup cab, and with the printer on the wooden shelf Gary had built inside the pickup topper just behind the cab—power cables passing through the little windows at the back of the cab and front of the topper. Once the reports were finished each year, we had next to find a town large enough to have an office store or other location where we could photocopy both reports. After the first year, we also made photocopies of each of our observation notebooks in order to be able to keep copies of all this information for ourselves as well as turning in the reports and notebooks to The Peregrine Fund.

Preparing Bird, Mammal, and Reptile Lists

*From the Journals: Grave Point – Jean*
*11 August 1990 – For my last hike, in the last week at this fine place, I left camp at 6:30 AM and hiked the steep-slope cow path west of camp, out and down the tip of CJ's favorite ridge, and along the road to Lower Klapton Creek trailhead. The trail splits into three, and I took the left fork in lieu of any markers. The trail is in very bad condition, and I really had to struggle through the brush and young pines invading it. Suddenly, on a very steep slope, it became a cow path, then a deer trail, then brushy and dangerous. I saw two Blue Grouse and two Ruffed Grouse, one with about eight chicks. When I reached and understood the straight line (a road way) in the trees, I gave up and struggled down to the creek, tiny, lovely. There I found life birds—two Mountain Quail with about 16 chicks. They made the loveliest sounds calling their babies.*
*Though it was only 9:00 AM, I sat on the south slope to eat the lunch I'd packed along and to write this. There is a big smoke on the Oregon side of the canyon and south of us. An aspen or two and a cottonwood dominate this lovely, brushy ravine where the quail are.*

Part of our Internal Report to be submitted to The Peregrine Fund at the conclusion of each hack site job was a required list of all the birds, mammals and reptiles observed in the release area, and these lists were to include indications as to relative frequency of sightings of each species. It was therefore important to keep lists and notes of species seen from the first day until the last at each site. Since Jean had long been an experienced birder and degreed biologist, this task fell mostly to her, although Gary was certainly involved in reporting his sightings to her. To facilitate this part of the job, Jean packed field guides to reptiles, birds and mammals each summer as we loaded the pickup preparatory to setting out on the long drive from home to our assigned hack site location for that summer. Being an inveterate lister, compulsive identifier, and always-biologist, she also packed along field guides for amphibians and plants. Gary leaned less toward identifying, and more toward photographing, the plants and animals he encountered, whenever possible.

More of a joy than a job for Jean, it was easy to make lists of species of animals encountered in release area during daily activities, whether personal or part of the job. Beyond this base of species seen around the hack box, observation point or campsite, it was possible to add more species during our hikes. At Grave Point, for example, we made frequent hikes from camp down to our pickup parked below the gate in order to bring up water in small jugs filled from the big jugs in the truck, and to bring up other supplies. In the later weeks at each site, after the intense observation period, it was possible to take turns taking longer hikes. In these explorations, we could find patches of different habitat types and so add more bird and other animal species to our lists. [Note: Those who are interested can find composite lists of birds, mammals and reptiles seen at our hack sites in Appendix Three of this book.]

*From the Journals: Grave Point – Jean*
*6 August 1991 – Today we drove down to the campground by the river. I walked through a defunct set of ranch buildings and imagined the lives and uses they had served in the past. I also*

*watched birds: American Kestrels, Mourning Doves, Western Kingbirds, Lark Sparrows, Black-billed Magpies, a Lazuli Bunting and, along the creek, a Yellow-breasted Chat that was swallowing a red woody-nightshade berry that looked too big for his beak and throat.*

## C. PERSONAL STORIES

*From the Journals: Grave Point – Jean*
*9 August 1991 – Our first task after arriving in Boise this morning, was to visit a business where we could make copies of both reports and both field notebooks. Driving up to the World Center for Birds of Prey, we registered for a tour, and ate our lunch on the curb in the parking lot while waiting for the tour to start. It was led by a Center volunteer Jean had met at Grave Point last year on the Volunteers' Field Trip. We introduced ourselves as Hack Site Attendants and discovered two others present in the tour group: Chris and Mike from the High Dive, Idaho, site. It was really fun to talk to them and learn how it went for them, etc. They shared the same Release Specialist and had heard about our trouble with owls as we had heard about their snow. They only lost the last snow two days ago and just came out today. It was Mike's third hack site. In addition to snow at High Dive, they had mosquitoes morning and evening, and flies at midday—sounded like the same kind of flies as the ones we had so much trouble with.*

*We turned in the scope and tripod, the reports and field notebooks, and got our checks. No application blanks available, but they said all we probably had to do next year was call Bill and say we want to do it all again!*

*From the Journals: Grave Point – Jean*
*11 August 1991 – After leaving our Boise-area hosts (Jean's*
*cousin and wife) of the last two nights, we drove straight to the*
*airport. After Gary checked in, we sat talking. How strange it is*
*to think he'll be home tonight—what an abrupt change! Equally*
*strange will it be for me to be suddenly alone. I discussed my*
*proposed route with him, wondering if I would have sufficient*
*nerve to do it all alone.*

*Though it's only for a few days, this parting is hard for us as*
*they all are, but in time his flight was called and he walked*
*away to board it in further-faded jeans, chambray western shirt,*
*long hair and beard, and backpack, looking back once to wave.*
*I was watching at the window though I am sure he could not see*
*me; as they wanted to put his pack in the nose cargo, Gary had*
*to open it to take out his journal and book. He is reading*
*"Sojourner," recommended by our Release Specialist.*

*Feeling choked up and teary, I turned away from the window*
*and collected my truck from hock in the airport parking lot. I*
*drove back to the Orchard Street Exit I am most familiar with to*
*get gas for the truck and groceries for my long drive home.*
*[NOTE: I did take the planned route home and it gave me*
*adventures such as a flat tire just as I completed 28 miles of*
*rough gravel road and turned into the campground at Red Rock*
*Lakes National Wildlife Refuge. A hiker doing the Continental*
*Divide Trail, a woman who taught first graders, and her*
*husband, a ranger, offered help in changing the tire and the*
*couple invited the hiker and me to share their steak supper*
*grilled over the campfire. I enjoyed listening while the other*
*three, who had all hiked most of the same major trails, shared*
*stories. I ate my salad but the hiker ate two of the couple's*
*steaks. The next day I drove very carefully and slowly (now*
*lacking a spare tire) the long gravel miles, seeing my Lifer*

*Great Gray Owl hunting along the way, to reach the highway to West Yellowstone where I got the tire fixed. The next day I drove through Yellowstone National Park, birded at the Cody alkali ponds, camped at Horseshoe Bend. I spent a day in the Bighorn Mountains and unrolled my sleeping bag on the ground beside my truck to camp there under the stars, alone, off-road. After a long day of driving, I slept in my truck one night at an Interstate Highway Rest Area, and finally, stayed one night with my mom in Iowa before reaching home five days after Gary.]*

Amtrak, Bar None Ranch, 1994

There were two years when the schedules of Jean's teaching career and our Peregrine jobs conflicted. As the spring 1992 semester ended, Jean's department chairman informed her that he could foresee no teaching contract for her in the biology department for the coming fall semester. Based on that information we committed to working two consecutive hack site jobs for The Peregrine Fund during summer 1992, Holter Lake and then CSKT Tower with only a 24-hour break between the two seven-week jobs. While at the second site, Jean received a letter from her chairman on 20 August, asking her to call him about a fall-only, full-time job opening that had developed for her after all. The chairman wanted Jean to appear in early September for this job, but during the subsequent phone call on 31 August, he was firmly informed that she had a contract first with The Peregrine Fund to complete, and she would take the teaching job only if she could start it two weeks late (missing one week of meetings, and the first week of classes). The chairman arranged other teaching staff to teach the first three "Introduction to Biology" lectures and one lab that she would miss in the first week of classes. We left the CSKT Tower site on 12 September, arrived home on the 13th, and Jean reported to her teaching job on Monday, 14 September, signing her teaching contract on that date.

The second time the schedules of teaching and hack site work conflicted was in summer of 1994, but the circumstances were reversed. That year Jean had already signed (on 8 June) a contract to teach full time for fall semester 1994, well before heading west for Peregrine work. The Bar None Ranch hack site job began with installation of six falcons into the cliff-top hack box on 15 July, but we had arrived on site the day before in order to set up our camp. Release occurred on 21 July and the estimated closing date for that job would have been expected, after a total of seven weeks, on or about 2 September. However, on 25 July we were informed that Bill Heinrich, Operations Manager of The Peregrine Fund, had decided to install a second batch of five more falcons for release from this site, rather than at the originally planned site because circumstances there were found to be unsuitable. Bill Heinrich, trusting our dependability as hack site attendants, drove all the way from Boise to deliver the new batch of young falcons and installed them in the Bar None Ranch hack box on 26 July. This second group of falcons was released on 1 August, giving us a final closing date on or about 12 September, creating the second scheduling problem for us, only this time it was The Peregrine Fund Jean had to inform that she had a prior commitment, a signed contract to teach beginning 29 August 1994. An accommodation was reached wherein Jean would miss "meetings week" at the university, but depart the hack site job early in order to be home for the start of classes. It was agreed between The Peregrine Fund and Gary that he would complete the hack site job, spending the last ten days on site alone.

But how would Jean get home, since we had arrived in Montana together in one vehicle? The compromise included a coach

Amtrak ticket for Jean, a delight for her since she had already traveled by Amtrak several times and enjoyed it, and this train would get her home in less than 24 hours. We fed the Peregrines early on the morning of 31 August and, in between making observations of the falcons, took down the observation tarp, emptied the food tubs, completed most of the work on each of The Peregrine Fund's required reports for the site, packed Jean's bags for her trip home and her half of the camp gear and loaded it all into the truck. At mid-afternoon we drove out to the ranch building site and took showers, then headed north. We stopped for gas in Helena, stopped at a grocery store in Great Falls for food for a tailgate supper, and found an RV park in Conrad, Montana, where we could camp in our truck. The next morning we ate bagels as we drove, stopped to heat water on a camp stove to fill a thermos for Jean's train trip, and found the Amtrak depot in Shelby. Jean's bags were heavy in order to carry home as much as she thought she might need before Gary could get there. After seeing her into the train that morning (1 September), Gary returned to camp and to duty at the hack site.

Jean arrived home the morning of 2 September; Gary closed the site 11 September and arrived home the 16th after visiting friends and daughter Gayle in Wyoming en route. There are two last bits to tell about the end of the Bar None Ranch job however, about critters Gary encountered after Jean went home. In the first few nights of camping after Gary returned from taking Jean to the train, several voles moved in under the ground cloth under our sleeping tent. He put up with their shenanigans for five nights before moving his pad and sleeping bag into the back of the pickup and taking down the tent. Below are his journal comments about this experience, and about a bear sighting too.

*From the Journals: Bar None Ranch – Gary*
*6 September 1994 – Ever since Jean left the little guys have*
*been under my corner of the tent in the dark of the night,*
*chewing, rustling, digging, chittering. What amazes me is that*
*for four nights they have been extremely time-conscious. I am*
*wakened at 11:37 or 11:47 PM and they finally quiet down*
*about an hour later. On the fourth night there was another*
*period of activity around 3:00 or 4:00 AM. Sometimes I feel*
*their bodies passing under my arm or head—and I slap the*
*floor and tell them to "knock it off and be quiet!" Which they*
*do—momentarily—until I am almost sleepy again. Then we*
*repeat the process. ... ... I was hoping to train them or outlast*
*them but they are persistent. On the fifth night they were busy*
*chewing and rustling from around 11:30 PM to 4:00 AM, so*
*I've had enough of them.*

*From the Journals: Bar None Ranch – Gary*
*9 September 1994 – After my hike up to the hack box to put out*
*quail for the falcons, I drove to the ranch building site for a*
*shower and to town for mail, a few supplies, and to call The*
*Peregrine Fund to make another semi-weekly report. On the*
*way back I had a nice short chat with the foreman and his wife*
*and let them know which day I would be leaving. They told me a*
*cow had died a few days before by the tunnel on the old*
*railroad bed on the route between the ranch building site and*
*our camp. The foreman had drug the carcass off the roadway*
*into the ditch. ... The next morning I had the camera all ready*
*for mountain lion, bear, coyotes, anything—but there was*
*nothing. In the evening I flushed a nice-sized (more than 200*
*pounds) brownish-tinged adult bear off the cow carcass. Boy!*
*Did that bear scamper! Alas, the bear was too quick and it was*
*already getting too dark so there is no photo. Only a memory.*

Experienced Campers

We have always been campers. Gary began while he was a Cub
Scout and afterwards camped with his friends during boyhood.
Jean had older cousins, boys who were heavy into camping,
also through scouting, and who would loan some of their gear to
their younger sister. Thus, Jean went camping with this girl
cousin, first on their lawn and, when the two of them were
older, on a large Iowa farm with significant woodlands.

As a young couple, we were impoverished because we were still
finishing college, and camping was the only way to have a
vacation. We delayed our "honeymoon" trip for a year and then
we went camping in Wyoming. Loved it, so we continued to
camp before we had children. We kept camping after our
daughters were born, with a mosquito net over the folding
playpen/crib and a diaper pail in the trunk with the other
camping gear. (Those were the days when cloth diapers were
still the norm and visiting a laundromat every few days a
necessity while on vacation with very young children.)

So fieldwork jobs that required camping were right up our alley.
Toward the end of our Peregrine summers, we tried to tally the
nights spent camping for our fieldwork jobs to that point,
including camping en route to and from Wisconsin and the
various job sites. We came up with an estimate of about 650
nights of camping. And we defined camping as sleeping away
from home in tent or other "structure" without running water or
a flush toilet in the structure with you. [Note: besides our
Peregrine work 1990-1996 in Idaho, Montana and Wyoming,
we had had several other fieldwork jobs in 1990, 1993, 1994 in
Minnesota, Arizona and Colorado, and we would have still
more fieldwork experiences in later years in Texas, Wyoming

and Wisconsin—perhaps yielding enough material for another book of fieldwork adventures.]

This impressive number of camping nights, almost two years total, came in handy in early 1996 when we were winter camping in Wyoming on private property and a native Wyomingite assumed that, as "easterners," we would not know what we were doing and he called the county Sheriff to find our frozen bodies, or to rescue us as the case might be. We were headed for a visit with family in Casper, Wyoming, after the holidays, but intending to camp first in early January in the northeastern corner of the state. When we reached the chosen area it was late in the day so we spent the first night sleeping in our truck in a US Forest Service campsite and organizing our gear. The next day we informed the nearest neighbors of our plans to camp and asked permission to park along the two-track access road a couple hundred yards from their ranch home. Next we donned our snowshoes and loaded our gear-filled backpacks onto two children's plastic sleds we had happened to see along the highway just after entering Wyoming and stopped to scavenge. We hiked almost four miles through the snow, about 12 inches of it, on the minimum-access road and set up our dome tent in a sheltered draw among hawthorn shrubs. We slept comfortably warm, but during the night it snowed eight inches more, bowing in the tent fabric between the poles. Our first task in the morning was to push up on the tent ceiling to dislodge the snow, and then we made breakfast of oatmeal and cocoa with our little backpacking stove.

It was a bright, sunny winter morning and we decided to do some snowshoeing. As we exited the tent though, we heard repeated short bursts from a siren that seemed to be coming from a vehicle nearby. With our hearts speeding up with worry that this might mean bad news from home, we hiked as quickly as we could in the deep snow to try to find the source of the siren. Crossing that private property was a County Deputy's 4WD vehicle, and with the Deputy was the neighbor we had informed of our plans to camp. The first words from the Deputy were, thankfully, not bad news from home, but, "Do you know whose property you are on?" When we explained that we did indeed know, the Deputy gave a look at our rancher neighbor that seemed to say, "You might have told me." We hastened to assure the men that we had nearly two years of camping experience, including other occasions of winter camping, that we had appropriate gear and had set up our tent in a sheltered area. We learned they had not even stopped on the way in to brush the snow off the windows of our parked pickup to see if we were in it, and so had not seen the note we had left on the dash confirming our camping plans. Normally, all "calls" to service that the Sheriff's Department receives in that county are reported in the small local paper, however, this episode was never mentioned. Although we believe that concern for us motivated the rancher to call for help and induced both men to search for us, we also got the strong impression that "Easterners" were not expected to be able to survive in western conditions, especially the West's winter conditions, without help. It remains in our mind an occasion of pride that we disproved that notion, and we owe much of our skill and knowledge to a lifetime of camping and to years of fieldwork experiences.

*Concluding Comments: Figures 35 and 36*

*Figure 35: Osprey above its nest at Holter Lake*

*Figure 36: Prairie Coneflower at Holter Lake*

# CONCLUDING COMMENTS

<u>Revisiting the Hack Site List</u>

Near the beginning of this book we wrote a description of each of the eight hack site locations where we served as attendants for young Peregrines. Now let us revisit each site and add our personal reactions to these sites from a quarter century's perspective.

Grave Point, Idaho – June, July, August 1990 and 1991

Grave Point remains for each of us one of our top favorite sites and the reasons are many. It was for each of us (Jean in 1990, Gary in 1991) our first experience as Hack Site Attendants for Peregrines. The scenery and views were stupendous, and the terrain provided a wide variety of hiking opportunities. We got a great deal of exercise just in daily activities at this site. The wildflowers were exceptional, especially with better spring rainfall in 1991, although that weather condition also seemed to have made biting flies more prevalent and annoying. Rains also allowed more growth in the grasses so that grazing cattle were much more of an annoyance for us as tent-dwellers and hikers; on the positive side, wildlife was more varied too. The released Peregrines did very well at this site and, in 1991, we got to see several visiting Peregrines that had been released in the previous year by The Peregrine Fund.

Holter Lake, Montana – June, July 1992

The geographic details of this location, including distances between camp, observation point, and our truck, plus the efforts required to supply the Peregrines with quail and ourselves with food, water, ice, and to get to town for mail, laundry and other needs made this our most difficult site. Holter Lake was also one of two sites at which we encountered many snakes. The weather here in 1992 was cold and wet often and therefore we also were often cold and wet. There were several storms as well. We definitely did not appreciate the noise of power boats, jet skis and other activities on the lake, especially on the weekends—the shape of the valley with the lake at the bottom seemed to act as a megaphone to magnify the sounds and direct them right up toward our observation position on the mountainside above the lake. We did enjoy the historic Lewis and Clark setting and the wildlife very much—the birdlife was especially varied here to Jean's delight. We did not mind that we had very few visitors here, none of whom strayed in from the general public. While we were at Holter Lake, the difficulties and negatives above kept us from enjoying this site as much as some of the others, but in retrospect we take much pride in the methods we developed to surmount the difficulties, and in our achievements there.

CSKT Tower, Montana – July, August, September 1992

By contrast, we had very many visitors at this site, one of two where we and our camp were quite visible to the public. Although we regarded educating the public by answering questions and letting people have a peek at the falcons through a spotting scope as important and useful to the reintroduction project as a whole, it was sometimes trying to have visitors drop in when we were at an especially busy point in the hacking process, or when we were very tired from our dawn to dusk observation duties or the realities of camp life. In these circumstances we were glad to be provided a camping trailer to live in rather than tents. The distant scenery around CSKT Tower was striking and the double, simultaneous release of two batches of Peregrines from two hack boxes on one tower was challenging. Hiking opportunities were few and uninteresting. A highlight of this site was seeing the rings of Saturn through a 60-power scope.

Green River, Wyoming – July, August 1993

The Green River site was inaccessible to the public because of its access through private ranchland, so we had no contact with the public, but thoroughly enjoyed frequent brief contacts with the ranch foreman as he passed by our camp in the course of his duties, and the continuing friendship we developed with him and his wife. We enjoyed living beside the river and learning something of the early history of the area. Wildlife abounded and enriched our stay. On the down side, this was our coldest site and mosquitoes were very numerous. An unexpected bonus was the opportunity to join in the haying work of a Wyoming ranch, particularly for Jean who learned to mow the tall meadow grasses.

Bar None Ranch, Montana – July, August, September 1994

This too was a quiet site, out of reach of the public, so that we had few visitors. With two batches of falcons released sequentially from the same hack box, this was a lengthy job; because the second release was not originally planned and Jean had a teaching contract for fall, she left a few days early and Gary completed the job alone. Gary was pleased to have the opportunity to meet the ranch owner near the end of the job. Snakes were also numerous at this location. Varied hiking opportunities were available, and the scenery was striking. However, the difficult access road and restrictions imposed when the owners were in residence made our time there seem long and quiet. The opportunity to point The Peregrine Fund's loaned 120-power scope at Jupiter's comet impact sites made for a lasting memory.

Wood Lake, Montana – June, July 1995

At this site we lived comfortably in our own camper for the second time, and because it was parked in a public campground, we had access to pit toilets for the first and only time during our Hack Site Attendant careers. For the first time, two observation positions were necessary and, because those positions were quite far apart, it was here that we developed our method of communicating by a system of signals that proved so useful both here, and again at a later site. At the beginning, other campers often mistook us for "campground hosts" and came to us with tourist-type questions. Instead of answers to their questions (which we usually didn't know), they were educated about Peregrines and the reintroduction project. The access road for our trips to town damaged three tires on our truck that summer. It was fun to watch Bighorn sheep demonstrate their excellent skill in surmounting the hack box cliff.

CSKT Cliff, Montana – July 1996

Although the setting where we parked our camper was pretty, with good views from the cliff, and there was no access to the public, this site was our most negative—all the young Peregrines were killed by predators in the first few days. Though we were not at this site long, we had numerous black bear interactions.

Willow Creek Reservoir, Montana – July, August 1996

After the failure of the CSKT Cliff site, we were re-assigned to finish the last three weeks of this site. The habitat here was short-grass prairie with open views, yet the tower and camp were blocked to the public's view by a low ridge. There was no privacy cover at all—we parked our camper beside a corral and dug our latrine where the pole fences narrowed for the loading chute. Despite our short tenure, we enjoyed good birding here because of the reservoir and Willow Creek.

## The North American Peregrine Falcon Victory Celebration

On 20 August 1999, at a press conference in Boise, Idaho, Secretary of the Interior Bruce Babbitt officially declared the delisting of the Peregrine Falcon from the Endangered Species List. The work to preserve this precious bird as an important component of the environment and to save it from extinction in the North American continent was successful and the Peregrine population was coming back from the brink. Dozens of organizations and thousands of individuals, including the two of us during seven summers, had participated in the recovery. We are thankful and proud of our participation in this momentous achievement.

On 20 and 21 August, 1999, more than a thousand people gathered in Boise, Idaho, for a gala celebration partially hosted by our employer, The Peregrine Fund. It was a commemoration befitting vigorous efforts expended over three and a half decades: there was on open house at the World Center for Birds of Prey, speeches and visits by dignitaries, talks reliving the history by various participants and advocates, a social at the Boise Zoo, a "Peregrine Extravaganza" at Boise State University—all followed by a grand finale "Peregrine Party" at the historic Idaho Penitentiary grounds and adjoining Idaho Botanical Gardens. Many memories were shared and emotions were strong as we attended and rekindled friendships initially originated in the Rocky Mountains of the American West in defense of a two-pound bird, the Peregrine Falcon. We will always remember that weekend of celebration, and our experiences of working with Peregrines alongside many other Peregrine advocates, with both pleasure and gratitude.

## Concern about What We Imposed on Our Family

*From the Journals: CSKT Tower – Gary*
*3 September 1992 – Late this day I had trouble again with thoughts about what we could do if our daughters got into a bad situation while we are so far away. I try to push such thoughts out of my mind. It is a phobia worsening now since we've been gone so long doing two hack site jobs in one summer. I look forward very much to seeing both our girls again—soon now.*

This was one of the hardships of doing fieldwork far from home, something that bothered both of us every summer. It never got any easier. Each summer and even at this distance of time we were and are cognizant of both the burden our absence placed on our beloved daughters and on other family members as well, and of the generosity of our family in granting us the freedom to do the fieldwork we loved. We did our best to write letters frequently to family and to friends as well, and to speak by phone with at least one family member every week.

We regret any difficulties we may have caused our daughters and hope for their forgiveness.

## Why we Wrote this Book

The decision to write this book was easy. What was much more difficult was allocating the time to start it. Each of us has always enjoyed writing, from those first early efforts in school, to the love letters of our early adult life, to letters written over the years to friends and family, to the special holiday letters we send to those same individuals each December, to the obligations of our vocational work, to the 26-page memoir of our courtship that we wrote as a gift to our daughters one Christmas, and recently to a memoir about his youth and hometown of Holstein that Gary published with Jean's editorial help in 2013. Over and over we put off starting this project under the crush of perceived obligations: family, retirement preparations, farm and home maintenance, knowing that we had an abundance of documents, journals and other materials we could refer to later. Starting a project is often the hardest part; once commitment takes root real progress can finally be made.

Robert Douglas Mead in his book, *Ultimate North: Canoeing Mackenzie's Great River*, described the difficulty we have also encountered: interested listeners can only ask questions based on their own knowledge and experiences. A listener who has not studied the Peregrine Reintroduction issue or had fieldwork experiences roughly similar to tending Peregrines in an outdoor setting for weeks at a time, usually cannot ask focused, pertinent questions. Instead, their questions tend to be generalized and we, the speakers, find it difficult to answer these valid, but general questions without presenting the context of the broader issues, and then we risk telling the listener more than they want to know. This book is intended to provide meaning and context and to leave the reader to choose when to lay down the book and when to return to the story.

As mentioned, we have many times given presentations about our Peregrine hack site jobs, but these presentations are ephemeral. The varied material we have on file from our Peregrine summers is too voluminous and not in readily accessible form. Those who write believe they have something to share. We are writing this book to preserve the memories and adventures of our Peregrine fieldwork summers in readable form and hopefully to make this story available to a wider audience. We believe in the value of environmental work as illustrated in this book. In sharing our story we also invite you the reader to participate, such participation being as fundamental as reading this book and vicariously experiencing something of those seven summers we chose to live with, and for, Peregrines. And may you be inspired to somehow do more to better the natural world we all utterly depend on for individual and collective survival, to do less harm, to study and learn more about environmental issues, even to find a way or an organization that you can help.

## Why We Spent Seven Summers with Peregrines

*From the Journals: Grave Point – Jean*
*18 July 1991 – The only thing we have is our own individual aliveness. The only way to be happy is to be happy in the living of one's own life. It is important to have work of value and to do it well. One can be moral only if one's life promotes the lives of others of all species, not only humans, and does as little damage as possible to other species or to the health of the earth itself.*

The mechanics of how we were able to spend seven summers with Peregrines have been addressed elsewhere in this book: financial considerations, job circumstances, home responsibilities, family matters, life planning, and the support of family and friends. It is more difficult to address succinctly the question of why we did it. But the thoughtful reader will have by now already deduced from the contents some driving factors in each of us that can answer the question of why. Beyond love of the outdoors, camping and birds, Jean had a substantiating, justifiable reason for this outdoor biological fieldwork, that of enhancing her teaching career in the Biology Department at the University of Wisconsin-La Crosse. As an engineer in manufacturing and industry Gary had no such justifiable reason. In our careful consideration prior to committing to the fieldwork illustrated in this book it was important to the couple (as defined by the combination of Gary and Jean as a unique third party), as well as to Jean, as well as to Gary that there were additional reasons to leave our home in Wisconsin and engage in seeking adventure while we were yet young enough to do so, and to better understand the significance of life while we could yet apply what we learned to the decades in front of us.

As mentioned in Phase Seven – Preparing the Final Reports, one requirement at each site was to prepare a brief Personal Statement of the meaning of the experience to the Hack Site Attendant. We hope these brief excerpts from several of our Personal Statements will assist the reader in understanding this issue of "Why?"

*Gary: August, 1991*

*My work last summer (in the BWCAW) and this summer with Peregrines has given me the opportunity to pursue what the heart desires. As often happens in life, the need to "earn a living" can get in the way of youthful dreams. After 25 years as a corporate engineer, it is refreshing to return to the outdoors on a 24-hour basis, day after day.*

*This summer I feel I am helping to repair abuse by humans to a species, the Peregrine Falcon. It is an opportunity to do what is right, to set an example for others, repair some environmental damage, to do what I can. The reward is seeing the falcons return to and possess their niche in a biologically diverse environment.*

*The supplementary activities of being a Hack Site Attendant have been equally rewarding: to live in the outdoors intimately enough to watch the seasons develop by observing daily changes in the plants around us, to see the shadows alter on the mountainside as the sun recedes to another winter, to watch a gopher pushing dirt out of its burrow and collect another flower stalk and to be able to share these views, observationally and philosophically, with my camping and life partner.*

*Jean: September, 1994*

*I am aware that as a human being, and especially as a citizen of a highly developed nation, my activities have a large impact on the environment. Individual choices and actions matter, so I try to simplify my lifestyle and my impact. Additionally, in serving as a Hack Site Attendant, I feel I am helping to make reparation for environmental damage by my species. This work gives me great satisfaction.*

*I also derive personal benefit from the opportunity to live outdoors for eight weeks in a remote, natural setting, this year on a private ranch in Montana. This quiet outdoor time makes my return to society, with its scheduled days, traffic congestion, crowding, materialism, and emphasis on indoor living both more terrible in contrast, and more endurable because of my summer with Peregrines.*

*Gary: September, 1992*

*I come here to alter a bit the pulse of time racing through my soul. To slow it down to the gentle courses of the seasons, to the natural rhythm of the path of the sun across the sky, the changing of the color of the grass, the movement up and down of daily temperatures, the maturation of the falcons. To escape the harsh ticking of the time clock, the maddening pace of rush hour, the blare and glare of the special sales—"for these three days only," the dreadful deadlines of reward-less responsibilities. Here our work is our life, our rewards manifest within the project, and our delights are where we instantly recognize them. Here, as a product of nature, as a result of our own efforts, as a meaningful contribution with our fellows, fly again the falcons.*

*Jean: August, 1990*

*My hack site experience will enrich the biology classes I teach at UW-La Crosse. It is one thing to lecture about environmental and ecological principles; it will be far better to speak from a specific example and direct involvement.*

*Jean: July, 1992*

*That this has been my third hack site, and that tomorrow I report to start my fourth, give evidence of how much value I place on the experience of being a Hack Site Attendant. I retain all the enthusiasm for the work, and all the respect I hold for The Peregrine Fund that I had in 1990 when I began.*

*My appreciation of Peregrine Falcons continues to grow. This year it was a great thrill to see an adult, a falcon released by The Peregrine Fund at another site two years ago. I watched this adult fly and hunt with awe, and knew more fully what the individual falcons I have helped release, can become. Somewhere some of "my" falcons are flying with that grace.*

*Jean: September, 1993*

*Already I miss the Peregrines and wonder how they are doing. I would like to be camped at the tower in early spring, waiting to see if they return. Save me a place in the open and Peregrines to watch again next season. Tomorrow would not be too soon.*

We are grateful for
Peaceful wilderness settings
Satisfactions of fieldwork, and
Lightness of minimalist living
Gained through our experiences
As Hack Site Attendants for Peregrines

# ACKNOWLEDGEMENTS

A variety of agencies and other groups funded the specific hack sites at which we worked:

Grave Point, 1990: Nez Perce National Forest

Grave Point, 1991: Nez Perce National Forest, and Idaho Department of Fish and Game

Holter Lake, 1992: Butte District Bureau of Land Management

CSKT Tower, 1992: Confederated Salish and Kootenai Tribes of the Flathead Reservation

Green River Tower, 1993: Rock Springs District Bureau of Land Management

Bar None Ranch, 1994: Turner Foundation, Inc.

Wood Lake, 1995: Lewis and Clark National Forest, Boone and Crocket Club, and Great

Falls District Bureau of Land Management

CSKT Cliff, 1996: Confederated Salish and Kootenai Tribes of the Flathead Reservation

Willow Creek Reservoir, 1996: Bureau of Reclamation

Other agencies and many individuals assisted us, including:
Wyoming Department Game and Fish allowed us to park our trailer to camp one night on our arrival in Pinedale.
Owners of three private ranches, plus their foremen and wives provided much help at three sites.

The Peregrine Fund gave us these treasured opportunities; we thank that organization and the individuals involved for their confidence in us, their willingness to keep hiring us, and for putting us in more sites in the Rockies than any other Hack Site Attendants.

We also owe a great debt of thanks to our friends and families for their support letters, phone visits and site visits, and most of all for enduring our long absences while we had some of the greatest adventures of our lives.

# REFERENCES

A variety of field guides for mammals, reptiles, amphibians, snakes, wildflowers, birds, and one about wild edible plants in the American West.

*Hacking: A Method for Releasing Peregrine Falcons and other Birds of Prey*, Steve K. Sherrod, William R. Heinrich, William A. Burnham, John H. Barclay, and Tom J. Cade, The Peregrine Fund, Inc., 1982.

*Operation Report*, The Peregrine Fund, Inc., 1989-1997.

*Peregrine Falcon Populations: Their Biology and Decline*, Edited by Joseph J. Hickey, University of Wisconsin Press, 1969.

*Peregrine Falcon Populations: Their Management and Recovery*, Edited by Tom J. Cade, James H. Enderson, Carl G. Thelander and Clayton M. White, The Peregrine Fund Inc., 1989.

*Return of the Peregrine: A North American Saga of Tenacity and Teamwork*, Edited by Tom J. Cade and William Burnham, The Peregrine Fund, 2003.

# APPENDIX ONE

<u>List of Figures</u>

Preface: Figures 1 and 2, page 12
Figure 1: Gary at World Center for Birds of Prey, Boise
Figure 2: Gary in kitchen area of Grave Point Camp

Preview: Figures 3 and 4, page 18
Figure 3: Jean with our gear and supplies at Holter Lake
Figure 4: Gear tent, kitchen, sleeping tent at Holter Lake

Introduction to the Book: Figures 5 and 6, page 26
Figure 5: Peregrine at Green River
Figure 6: Young Peregrines in early flight practice

Description of Hack Sites: Figures 7 and 8, page 30
Figure 7: Cliff hack site at Holter Lake
Figure 8: Installing Peregrines at CSKT Tower

Phase One, Installation: Figures 9 and 10, page 38
Figure 9: Jean and Specialist carrying Peregrines
Figure 10: Peregrines arrive at Wood Lake in snowstorm

Phase One, Personal Stories: Figures 11 and 12, page 74
Figure 11: Young Peregrine in transport box
Figure 12: Specialist transferring Peregrine to hack box

Phase Two, Post-installation: Figures 13 and 14, page 82
Figure 13: View into hack box through peephole
Figure 14: Jean observes Peregrines in hack box

Phase Two, Personal Stories:  Figures 15 and 16, page 98
Figure 15: Gary getting quail from freezer
Figure 16: Jean putting out quail for Peregrines

Phase Three, Release:  Figures 17 and 18, page 118
Figure 17: Young Peregrine explores cliff
Figure 18: Newly released Peregrines on hack tower

Phase Three, Personal Stories:  Figures 19 and 20, page 144
Figure 19: Our camper and the tower at Green River
Figure 20: Latrine with camouflage privacy netting

Phase Four, Intense Observation:  Figures 21 and 22, page 156
Figure 21: Gary observing falcons with spotting scope
Figure 22: Jean using scope at an O.P. with shade tarp

Phase Four, Visiting Falcons: Figures 23 and 24, page 194
Figure 23: Adult Peregrine visits Holter Lake hack box
Figure 24: Celebrating identifying visiting adult falcon

Phase Five, Relaxed Observations:  Figures 25 and 26, page 220
Figure 25: Jean on hike at Grave Point site
Figure 26: Hells Canyon scenery from Grave Point

Phase Five, Making Hay:  Figures 27 and 28, page 260
Figure 27: Gary with sickle-bar mower
Figure 28: Jean with side-delivery rake

Phase Six, Final Week: Figures 29 and 30, page 276
Figure 29: Gary in fire tower observing through peephole
Figure 30: Juvenile feeding, as seen from inside tower

Phase Six, Personal Stories: Figures 31 and 32, page 288
Figure 31: Jean prepares a meal at Holter Lake O.P.
Figure 32: Jean on trail to truck at Holter Lake

Phase Seven, Final Reports: Figures 33 and 34, page 302
Figure 33: Early reports produced via manual typewriter
Figure 34: Later reports prepared with laptop computer

Concluding Comments: Figures 35 and 36, page 318
Figure 35: Osprey above its nest at Holter Lake
Figure 36: Prairie Coneflower at Holter Lake

# APPENDIX TWO

PHASE TWO – POST INSTALLATION

PHASE THREE – RELEASE

PHASE FOUR – INTENSE OBSERVATION PERIOD

A. INTRODUCTION TO DUTIES DURING INTENSE
OBSERVATION PERIOD

B. STORIES FROM INTENSE AND SEMI-INTENSE
OBSERVATION PERIODS

C. PERSONAL STORIES

PHASE SIX – FINAL WEEK ON SITE AND CLOSING

A. INTRODUCTION TO ACTIVITIES DURING FINAL WEEK ON SITE

B. STORIES FROM THE FINAL WEEK ON SITE

C. PERSONAL STORIES

PHASE SEVEN – PREPARING THE FINAL REPORTS

B. STORIES ABOUT PREPARING REPORTS

C. PERSONAL STORIES

CONCLUDING COMMENTS

# APPENDIX THREE

Equipment Supplied by The Peregrine Fund

Spotting scope and tripod (on loan)
Large cooler (on loan)
Large water jug (on loan)
Tent
Lantern + one propane cylinder
Camp stove + one propane cylinder


Personal Equipment Recommended for Hack Site Attendants

(Modified version based on experience from the list provided us and published in RETURN OF THE PEREGRINE)

Additional spotting scope and tripod (2 of each)
Binoculars
Sleeping bag rated to 32°F.
Cot or sleeping pad
Cooking pots, pans, plates, glasses, utensils
Wash pan
Cooler
Warm clothing, including hats and gloves
Rain gear
Hiking boots
Tennis shoes
Toiletry articles
Lightweight folding chair
Extra propane fuel cylinders (16.4 oz.) for stoves
Sunscreen
Plastic tarp
Water containers
Water bottle or canteen
Reading material
Insect repellent
Large shovel
Day pack and heavy duty backpack
Flashlight and batteries

Matches
First aid kit
Cordage to secure tent, and tarps
Solar shower


Our Fieldwork Lists: clothing, miscellaneous, food
Being experienced campers, we created, and continued each
year to refine, more detailed personal lists of things to bring.

Clothing:
Boots, walking shoes
Slip-on rubber overshoes
Sandals, flip-flops
Shorts
Jeans
Underwear
Socks
Fleece pants, shirt, vest
Nylon pants, jacket
Poncho, rain pants
Long underwear
Gloves, stocking caps
T-shirts
Sweaters
Long-sleeved shirts
Hooded sweatshirt
Sweat pants

Items of clothing suitable
for town trips, & the
journey from home to hack
site

Other wearable items:
Insect head net
Sunglasses
Watch

Miscellaneous items:
Money, coins for laundry
Daypacks, large backpacks
Fanny packs
Alarm clock
Flashlights, extra batteries
Compass
Toilet tissue, toilet seat
Long 2x2 lumber (2)
Trowel, sand shovel
Saw, axe, pickaxe
Plier, duct tape
Oil for truck, winch, tools
First aid kit
Ditty kit, extra supplies
Towels, washcloths
Solar shower
Ditty kits, extra ditty items
Matches, butane lighter
Laundry & dish detergents
Camouflage blind
Binoculars (two)
Spotting scope & tripod (2 each)
Tents, ground cloths
Tiny screen tent
Tarps (2-3)
Poles, stacks, cords, ridges
Sleeping bags, liners

Sleeping pads & covers
Rug, door mat
Storage totes with lids
Blankets, pillows, cases
Camp chairs
Dry bags
Fly swatters
Sheath knives
Sewing kit
Lantern, batteries
Laundry bag
Large & small garbage bags
Whisk broom
Snakebite kits (2)

Kitchen Equipment and
Supplies:
Ice containers
Left-over containers
Canteens
Water bottles, large water
jugs
Fry pan, lid
Stir-fry pan, lid
Kettles, lids
Boiler
Coleman camp stove, spares
Propane, 11# and 1#
cylinders
Propane tank connectors
Plates, bowls, cups
Utensils for cooking and
eating
Cutting board, knives
Small and medium buckets
Coolers (hard and soft-
sided)
Thermos (2)
Seed-sprouting jar

Paper towels, plates,
napkins
Dish towels, sponges,
scrubbers
Nylon rope, clothes pins
Knee pads
Small plastic table cloth
Camp cupboards
Table board, legs
Milk crate
Spice cans, salt & pepper
Grater
Plastic jars
Large food tins
Camp-stove toaster
Bleach
Foil
Water filter
Roasting forks
Tiny campfire grill
Pie makers
Sprouting jar, screens, seeds

Food Lists:

Breakfasts:
Pancake mixes
Bannock mixes
Powdered milk
Vitamins
Canned fruit
Cranberry juice concentrate
Canned juices
Jelly
Syrup, brown sugar
Oat bran, oatmeal
Cornmeal, buckwheat flour
Flour, wheat germ, bran

Dry cereal, homemade granola
Cooking oil, cooking spray
Pecans
Tea, cocoa mix
Couscous
Baking powder, baking soda
Sugar, salt, pepper
Cake and muffin mixes
Individual-serving applesauce
Raisins

Lunches:
Peanut butter
Sardines
Crackers, several kinds
Nuts, candies, other ingredients for GORP
Cookies, several kinds
Pringles
Canned tuna, chicken, salmon, ham
Dried refried beans
Cheese spread
Jerky
Gum
Seeds for sprouting

Suppers:
Spaghetti
Noodles, several kinds
Ramen packets
Flavored rice & noodle packets
Lentils, dried soup beans

Canned meats as above plus ham & turkey
Dried tofu
BBQ sauce, ketchup, mustard
Canned vegetables
Dehydrated vegetables
Flour tortillas
Pork and beans
Tomatoes: sauce, paste, stewed
Spicy tomato soup, canned
Potato flakes
Dried diced potatoes

Home-prepared dehydrated foods:
Pears, apples, bananas
Rhubarb leather
Applesauce leather
Pineapple, strawberries
Tomato slices
Mushrooms, peppers
Carrots, celery, onions
Peas, green beans
Squash
Soup beans, refried beans
Other fruits & vegetables

Purchased dried foods:
Raisins
Dates
Apricots
Prunes
Tomato powder
Cheddar powder
Diced potatoes

## Partial List of Books Read While Doing Peregrine Work

*Arctic Dreams*, Barry Lopez

*Arrogance of Humanism*, David W. Ehrenfeld

*Birdwatching with American Women*, Deborah Strom, editor

*The Cave Bear Story*, Björn Kurtén

*The Coming Plague*, Laurie Garrett

*Darwin's Century*, Loren Eiseley

*Deep Ecology*, Bill Devall & George Sessions

*Desert Solitaire*, Edward Abbey

*Ecotopia*, Ernest Callenbach

*The End of Nature*, Bill McKibben

*Health and the Rise of Civilization*, M.N. Cohen

*It's a Matter of Survival*, Anita Gordon & David Suzuki

*Land of Little Rain*, Mary Austin

*Limits to Growth*, Meadows, Meadows, Randers, Behrens

*The Magic Animal*, Philip Wylie

*Muddling Toward Frugality*, Warren Johnson

*On Human Nature*, E. O. Wilson

*Our Stolen Future*, Theo Colburn

*Overshoot*, William Catton

*Pentagon of Power*, Louis Mumford

*Plagues and Peoples*, William H. McNeill

*The River of the Mother of God*, Aldo Leopold

*A River No More*, Philip L. Fradkin

*Run River Run*, Ann Zwinger

*The Sixth Extinction*, Richard Leakey, Roger Lewin

*The Third Chimpanzee*, Jared Diamond

*Vanishing Birds*, Tim Halliday

*What Are People For?*, Wendell Berry

*Your Money or Your Life*, Joe Dominguez & Vicki Robin

## Reptile, Mammal and Bird Lists – composites from all sites

REPTILES
Rubber boa
Western racer
Western Yellow-bellied racer
Western terrestrial garter snake
Plains garter snake
Western bullsnake
Western rattlesnake

MAMMALS

Bats, species unknown
Black bear
Raccoon
Longtail weasel
Mink
River otter
Badger
Striped skunk
Red fox
Coyote
Yellowbelly Marmot
Richardson ground squirrel
Columbian ground squirrel
Golden-mantled ground
squirrel
Red squirrel
Northern pocket gopher
Redtail chipmunk
Yellow pine chipmunk

Least Chipmunk
Beaver
Deer mouse
House mouse
Meadow vole
Muskrat
Western jumping mouse
Porcupine
Mountain cottontail
Snowshoe hare
Whitetail jackrabbit
Elk
White-tailed deer
Mule deer
Moose
Pronghorn
Mountain goat
Bighorn sheep
Domestic cattle

## BIRDS

Common Loon
Western Grebe
Eared Grebe
Red-necked Grebe
American White Pelican
Double-crested Cormorant
Great Blue Heron
Black-crowned Night-
Heron
Trumpeter Swan
Canada Goose
Mallard
Gadwall
Northern Pintail
Blue-winged Teal
Green-winged Teal
Greater Scaup
Lesser Scaup
Barrow's Goldeneye
Common Merganser
Turkey Vulture
Osprey
Bald Eagle
Golden Eagle
Northern Harrier
Sharp-shinned Hawk
Cooper's Hawk
Northern Goshawk
Red-tailed Hawk
Ferruginous Hawk
Swainson's Hawk
Prairie Falcon
Peregrine Falcon

Merlin
American Kestrel
Greater Sage-Grouse
Blue Grouse
Ruffed Grouse
Gray Partridge
Ring-necked Pheasant
Chukar
Mountain Quail
Wild Turkey
American Coot
Sora
Sandhill Crane
Killdeer
Semi-palmated Plover
Black-bellied Plover
Marbled Godwit
American Avocet
Greater Yellowlegs
Solitary Sandpiper
Lesser Yellowlegs
Long-billed Curlew
Willet
Least Sandpiper
Spotted Sandpiper
Wilson's Snipe
Wilson's Phalarope
Franklin's Gull
Ring-billed Gull
California Gull
Common Tern
Caspian Tern
Rock Dove

Mourning Dove
Northern Saw-whet Owl
Short-eared Owl
Great Horned Owl
Poorwill
Common Nighthawk
Vaux's Swift
White-throated Swift
Calliope Hummingbird
Rufous Hummingbird
Broad-tailed Hummingbird
Belted Kingfisher
Downy Woodpecker
Hairy Woodpecker
Northern Flicker
Red-naped Sapsucker
Northern Three-toed
Woodpecker
Lewis's Woodpecker
Pileated Woodpecker
Olive-sided Flycatcher
Western Wood-pewee
Willow Flycatcher
Dusky Flycatcher
Cordilleran Flycatcher
Least Flycatcher
Say's Phoebe
Eastern Kingbird
Western Kingbird
Steller's Jay
Gray Jay
Clark's Nutcracker
Black-billed Magpie
American Crow

Common Raven
Red-eyed Vireo
Warbling Vireo
Plumbeous Vireo
Cassin's Vireo
Tree Swallow
Violet-green Swallow
N. Rough-winged Swallow
Bank Swallow
Cliff Swallow
Barn Swallow
White-breasted Nuthatch
Red-breasted nuthatch
Pygmy Nuthatch
Black-capped Chickadee
Mountain Chickadee
Brown Creeper
Rock Wren
Canyon Wren
House Wren
Winter Wren
Marsh Wren
Golden-crowned Kinglet
Ruby-crowned Kinglet
American Dipper
Varied Thrush
American Robin
Mountain Bluebird
Western Bluebird
Townsend's Solitaire
Hermit Thrush
Swainson's Thrush
Veery
Gray Catbird

Cedar Waxwing
European Starling
Orange-crowned Warbler
Nashville Warbler
Yellow Warbler
Common Yellowthroat
Yellow-rumped Warbler
MacGillivray's Warbler
Townsend's Warbler
Wilson's Warbler
American Redstart
Northern Waterthrush
Yellow-breasted Chat
Western Tanager
Green-tailed Towhee
Spotted Towhee
Vesper Sparrow
Savannah Sparrow
Song Sparrow
Chipping Sparrow
Lincoln's Sparrow
Fox Sparrow
Lark Sparrow
Clay-colored Sparrow
White-crowned Sparrow
Dark-eyed Junco
Horned Lark
Chestnut-collared Longspur
McCown's Longspur
Western Meadowlark
Red-winged Blackbird
Yellow-headed Blackbird
Brewer's Blackbird
Brown-headed Cowbird

Bullock's oriole
Black-headed Grosbeak
Lazuli Bunting
American Goldfinch
Cassin's Finch
Evening Grosbeak
Red Crossbill
Pine Siskin

Hazard List

Rattlesnakes and bears
Narrow mountain roads, sometimes made slick by rain
Punctured tires
Storms of wind and lightning
Steep trails, rocks shifting underfoot
Cliff edges, and towers to climb

Murphy's Laws of Peregrine Hacking

1) The worse the weather for the attendants, the better the Peregrines seem to like it.

2) When a falcon's leg is perfectly exposed for color band identification, it will be the wrong leg.

3) The falcon you voted as most likely to stick with you the whole seven weeks will disappear on the $19^{th}$ or $20^{th}$ day of release and thus not qualify to be counted as having reached independence.

4) At least one falcon will fledge just before dark or in the rain when you cannot tell which one it was.

5) On the first feeding day after release, when dead quail bodies lie all about and stink and are crawling with flies and carrion beetles and need to be picked up, it will be your turn to go to the hack box.

6) When you have missed one or two of your Peregrines for a day or so and you suddenly excitedly count all of them flying simultaneously in the air, one of your count will turn out to be a Prairie Falcon.

7) Your capability to correctly and quickly read leg color bands will be at least 50 yards short of the closest distance from which you can safely or properly observe.

8) The greatest likelihood of falcons appearing for observation is whenever you are eating your lunch, regardless of what time that is.

9) You will miss out on seeing one of the more spectacular occurrences of your hack period because you were in the bushes answering the call of nature.

10) Your greatest need to have the personal presence of Release Specialists at your hack site will be within the next 30 minutes after they have left.

# AUTHOR PAGE

The authors are retired from their vocational fields, Jean as a biology and ornithology instructor at the University of Wisconsin-La Crosse, and Gary as a Professional Engineer. They live in a rural area of Wisconsin and actively farmed for 20 years. They have resided on their farm for nearly a half century and are restoring native prairie grasses to portions of it while utilizing the whole as a place of quiet refuge. Gary and Jean are proud of and enjoy the love and nearby companionship of two daughters and a granddaughter.

Find Jean and Gary online at:

garyandjean65@gmail.com

garyandjean65 (Facebook)

.